Jerusalem
Revealed

GW00545139

A comprehensive guide

by

Anthony King

BOXER
Publishing

Jerusalem Revealed, First edition 1997

Published by Boxer Publishing
10 Black Horse Drove
Littleport, Ely
Cambridgeshire CB6 1EG

e-mail 100547.205@compuserve.com

Cover photographs by the author:
Front: View of Al-Aksa Mosque and Mount of Olives
        from St. Mary's German Hospice
Back: Near the Damascus Gate

Maps and plans: Alan King

Layout, design and typesetting: Boxer Publishing

Printed by Redwood Books, Trowbridge, Wilts, UK

ISBN 0-9525432-2-2

ABOUT THE AUTHOR

Anthony King, a historian and photojournalist, has lived, worked and travelled throughout the Middle East for the past 30 years. Many of these were spent in Jerusalem where he frequently resided. Besides his comprehensive and intimate knowledge of the city, as a journalist he was never far from the political happenings that have shaped it since 1967. In writing this guide King clearly conveys his affection for Jerusalem and its character, one that has been fashioned over many centuries. In a place where one man's rights are another man's wrongs, he does not attempt to conceal his feelings.

Anthony King is married with three adult children and – a far cry from the parched lands of the Middle East – now lives in the fenlands of East Anglia.

Other works by the author include *Syria Revealed* and *Jordan Revealed*.

"Blessed are the peacemakers..."

This book is dedicated to all those who strive to bring peace to
this ancient city.

Contents

Maps and Plans*

Page

*Not necessarily drawn to scale

PART I
BACKGROUND

1. AN INTRODUCTION TO THE CITY
  - Situation
  - Jerusalem Today
    - Political Overview
    - Physical Jerusalem

2. HISTORY
  - Introduction
  - Earliest Period through to Ottoman Rule
  - Twentieth Century

1. An Introduction to the City

Jerusalem the golden
With milk and honey blessed
Beneath thy contemplation,
Sink heart and voice oppressed
    The Rhythm of Bernard de Morlaix, 12th C

Singing its praises

Jerusalem, Yerushalayim, al-Kuds; whichever way you look at it, fascinating – perhaps the most fascinating city in the world. *"Beautifully situated and the joy of the whole earth... Walk around her, count her towers, consider well her ramparts, enter into her citadels, that you may tell it to the next generation."* (Psalm 48)

A visit to Jerusalem will be a high point in most people's tour; and though it may not reach the ecstasies expressed above, few will be disappointed.

praying for elusive peace

This is no ordinary city. Sacred to the three great monotheistic religions, it has been fought over, wept over, died for and yearned for. It has been destroyed many times, and rebuilt many times, yet still the biblical prophecy, *"Speak kindly to Jerusalem: and call out to her that her warfare has ended..."* (Isaiah 40:2), remains to be fulfilled.

For the Jewish people it is the city of the Temple: *"If I forget you O Jerusalem, may my right hand forget her skill...If I do not exalt Jerusalem above my chief joy..."* (Ps. 137:5-6).

To Christians it is the city where Jesus was crucified, and resurrected: *"Behold, we are going up to Jerusalem; and (Jesus) will be... condemned to death...and on the third day He will be raised up."* (Math. 20:18-19)

And for Muslims it is Al-Kuds, "The Holy One", because it was to here that Muhammad was carried on his night journey by his steed Buraq, and then lifted up into heaven from the Rock: *"Glorified be He who carried His servant by night...to the far distant place of worship (that is Jerusalem) the neighbourhood whereof we have blessed..."* (The Koran, Sura: 17:1).

the compact city

Jerusalem, today, encompasses a very large area, but it is the Old City and its environs that are the focal point of its history and interest, and this covers a surprisingly small area, just 82 hectares –

"Jerusalem that is built as a city that is compacted together" (Psalm 122:3) – and even if your interests do not extend very deeply into the religious, the maze of alleys, oriental souks, and most of all the diversity of the people will enthral you like no other city can.

SITUATION

Jerusalem lies at an altitude of c782 metres, 31 degrees N and 35 degrees E, 50 kilometres from the Mediterranean Sea. It sits on a limestone ridge which separates the fertile plain to the west from the barren Judean Desert to the east.

JERUSALEM TODAY

Political overview

Jerusalem is *de facto* ruled by Israel, and is claimed by them as their capital. Very few countries recognise this and the *de jure* situation is that it is not part of Israel at all. The original UN resolution which partitioned Palestine called for Jerusalem to be an international city. However the *de facto* position is clear. Israel controls all of the city, and her will and laws prevail. Nearly all embassies are situated in Tel-Aviv, although there are consulates general in Jerusalem. The major countries even maintain separate consulates in the east and the west of the city, signifying their non-acceptance of Israel's hegemony over the whole. Most visiting dignitaries are wary of visiting East Jerusalem in their official capacities so as not to prejudice the ultimate disposition of the city which, according to the Oslo Peace Agreements, is supposed to be open.

separate living quarters

Modern Jerusalem is an ethnically divided city. The 28 years of geographical unification have not succeeded in changing this.

Most Israelis (Jews) live in the western parts of the city, with the Palestinians residing in the east. Since 1967 this east-west division has become rather blurred due to the expansion of the city and the building of exclusively Jewish neighbourhoods in the north and south. Although now not strictly correct from the compass point, the term 'West' Jerusalem still applies to the Jewish city, while 'East' Jerusalem denotes the Palestinian (Arab) city.

East Jerusalem includes the old and walled city, an area that was under Jordanian control between 1948 and 1967. Prior to that the city was more mixed, but one of the results of the conflict was separation. Palestinians still make up the majority population in the Old City and East Jerusalem, though they are easily outnumbered by Jews in the city as a whole. It all depends on what one calls Jerusalem! A city's limits can be spread almost at the will of authority, and yet still bear the name of that city.

Jerusalem is a segregated city in the sense that while Jews can live in any part of it, Palestinians can only live in their traditional neighbourhoods. The government and municipality have sequestrated much land for the building of new homes. Since 1967 tens of thousands of these have been built, mostly in areas that were only then placed inside the city boundaries. Only Jews, who can obtain large, cheap government loans, can buy these dwellings, even though many lie within the area we call East Jerusalem and are surrounded by Palestinian neighbourhoods.

crossing the boundaries

It is an odd sort of equality that allows a Jew from, say, the US or Ethiopia, who may never have even been to Jerusalem before, to buy a new home, built on Palestinian land, while a Palestinian, born and raised in the city, as were his family before him, cannot – and is therefore forced to leave the city or live, as do many, in crowded cramped conditions. Very little new housing has been constructed for the indigenous population because permits are unavailable. The fair-minded outside observer cannot but conclude that this is a deliberate policy to gently de-Arabise the city!

ancient atmosphere

What can be said is that in spite of the overwhelming Israeli presence in the city, most of the eastern part, and the Old City in particular, has retained its Palestinian/Arab appearance, and therefore its centuries-old oriental charm and character. There are many nationalist Israelis who would like to change all that, but from my years in the city I know that this will be done at the very peril of Jerusalem's tourist appeal.

fewer disturbances

Palestinians resent Israeli control of what they call their part of the city, and this is often shown in the form of demonstrations and disturbances, though these have diminished since the Oslo peace accords. While the peace agreements do not include any change in the status of Jerusalem (except that the matter will be "open for discussion" in the future), they have served to calm things down in the eastern part of the city. The events of late summer 1996, when violence erupted over the opening of an archaeological tunnel, show only too well how fragile this calm can be!

A major thorn to the Palestinians is that while the Jewish parts of the city are policed by the regular Israeli police, the Palestinian areas, including the Old City, are patrolled by a paramilitary police force usually made up of quite young men. Any Palestinian can be stopped and searched without reason, with the policeman often adopting a bullying attitude.

Israel's claim

Israel claims all of Jerusalem as its historic capital. "Jerusalem will remain undivided for all generations until the end of the world", said the then Israeli premier, Menachem Begin, in 1980. Many more such utterings have been made before and since, and all political parties state that the city is the rightful and eternal capital of Israel, although a student of her history may come to a different conclusion. Conquered by the Israelites about 3000 years ago from the original inhabitants, the city has served as the Israelite or Judean capital for only a very small proportion of those three millennia.

Palestinian claim

The Palestinians, who now make no claim to the western part of the city, insist that East Jerusalem has to be the capital of a Palestinian state, and even though they have no capability to press this claim without the support of others, it is not an assertion that they will easily withdraw. As things stand today might is right.

Physical Jerusalem

In this century alone, Jerusalem has had four rulers: Ottoman Turkish, British, Jordanian and Israeli. Each power has left its architectural mark on the city's modern building characteristics. But one feature from Turkish rule has survived which is common to all: the Ottomans always used stone for their Jerusalem buildings, and when the city began to expand rapidly during the British Mandate, a regulation was promulgated requiring all new buildings to be at least faced with stone, even if not built from it. This regulation has been preserved, and thanks to it much of inner Jerusalem has retained an aesthetic appearance.

Since 1967 there have been many improvements to the city's infrastructure, with a number that are of immense benefit to the traveller. Israel often points to this as one of the advantages of her rule. Others counter that the same applies to many cities in the world over the past thirty years; perhaps another administration would have done likewise.

fine medieval vestige

The Old City, as seen today, is mainly a medieval city, and unlike so many other once walled cities of the Middle East, retains its medieval walls in their entirety. Isolated from the rest of the city by an attractive, Israeli-built, garden border, the Old City of Jerusalem manages to carry an air of timelessness, despite the evident trappings of the modern world.

spiritual bonds

As can be expected of a city that is sacred to three faiths, the most extreme adherents of those faiths are to be found here. Surprisingly, there is little inter-faith friction between the groups, whose main gripe is against the less religious of their own creeds!

kaleidoscope of creeds

Bear in mind that besides the Israeli and Palestinian citizens of the city, there are many others in Christian religious orders from all over the world. Brightly dressed Ethiopian monks, sombrely clad Egyptian Copts, Orthodox Russians and Greeks, hooded Armenians, and many more. All these add to the colour and flavour of the city, especially when they share the same streets as the observant Jews and Muslims. If there was ever a pot-pourri of humankind, then it is here in Jerusalem. (More details of the various sects are included in Chapter 3.)

And finally...

If you can visit this city without some political partiality you are indeed fortunate; most people cannot. But whatever your feelings of the rights and wrongs of the current situation, try not to allow them to spoil your visit. The city has so much to offer in sight, sound and history – and these are what you came here to experience.

"Jerusalem is not just for living, Jerusalem is for being" – Nurit Shiloh to James McNeish, *Belonging* 1980.

2. History

INTRODUCTION

Apart from a few extra-biblical records, the very ancient history of Jerusalem remains unwritten, except in the form it is found in the Old Testament. Archaeology has shown that much of the general outline of the biblical account after David's conquest is basically factual, but some events described by the early Old Testament scribes may be more related to legend than to actual happenings.

biblical names for Jerusalem

The only mention of Jerusalem in the Pentateuch (the first five books of the Bible) is in Genesis 14:18, when it is referred to as Salem. The name Jerusalem is used in Joshua 10:1ff and the name Jebus occurs in I Chronicles 11:4.

The name Zion, which first occurs in II Sam.5:7, applied to the king's fortress and the meaning is not known. That the two appellations, Jerusalem and Zion, came to be synonymous, is mostly due to the poetry of the Psalms and the recorded utterings of the Prophets.

poetic peace

The erroneous linkage sometimes made between the name Jerusalem and peace can also be attributed to poetry and the later common belief that the ending "salem" was a corruption of the Hebrew "shalom" or the Arabic "salaam", both meaning peace.

EARLIEST PERIOD

Initial mention of the city

Unearthed artefacts show that the Jerusalem area was inhabited as early as c3000 BC, but its entry into history seems to date from the Middle Bronze Age, the 20th to 18th centuries BC.

Egyptian Execration Texts from the 19th and 18th centuries refer to Urshalimmu which probably means "Shalim (or Shalmanu) has founded". Shalim was an important western Semitic and Canaanite god. The Egyptian texts even give the names of two of its kings, Yaqir'amu and Shayzanu which are both Amorite. At that time the rulers were regarded as the earthly representatives of the deities to whom the cities were dedicated.

King of Salem honours Abraham

Parallel to the above texts we have the biblical story in Gen:14:18:
"And Melchizedek king of Salem (Shalim?) *brought out bread and*

wine [to Abraham]; now he was a priest of God Most High." The
Hebrew for the last three words is El Elyon, a popular Canaanite and
Amorite name for a deity. Could Melchizedek have been one of the
kings named above? And as Shalim's delegate on earth would he not
have been his priest?

(Of interest to some may be the fact that although Jerusalem does
not make a claim to be the oldest city in the world, as does
Damascus, both cities are first mentioned in the Bible in the same
place, i.e. Genesis, Chapter 14).

The Amorites

These very ancient Semitic people played a significant role in the early history of Mesopotamia, Syria and Palestine. They originated from the Arabian Peninsular, and were first regarded as marauding nomads.

At the beginning of the second millennium, during large tribal migrations, they occupied most of the Syria-Palestine region, setting up a myriad of statelets, including Mari, on the Euphrates, and Halab (Aleppo) in northern Syria. In Palestine they were equated with the Canaanites, who were really a variety of peoples living in that land.

vassal of the Egyptians

The next historical mention of Jerusalem is found in the Tel
Amarna Letters of the 14th C BC. In these the town is called
Urusalim; its king was Abri-Khipa (servant of Khipa), a Hurrian
female deity. Some six letters sent by Abri-Khipa to the Egyptian
Pharaoh have been found, from which it appears that Urusalim was
a vassal city-state of the Egyptians, and the town was garrisoned by
black African soldiers (Cushites). In the letters the king complained
about the conduct of these soldiers, and also about the dangers
imposed by bands of roaming 'Abiru who were causing trouble to
other local subject kings. Could these have been the Hebrews?

Although Egyptian influence over Jerusalem may have extended
through the period of the mighty pharaoh Ramses II in the 12th
century, there are no further written records.

water of worth

This early city was situated on a ridge south east of the Dung Gate,
and the ancient settlement was confined to this area until the time of
Solomon. The location was, no doubt, dictated by the only water
source in the vicinity, the Gihon Spring in the Kidron Valley.

sun stands still

The next biblical reference to Jerusalem is in the Book of Joshua,
10:1-3. Here it is related how Jerusalem's king, Adoni-Zedek, allied
himself with other Amorite kings and attempted to take the town of
Gibeon because it had made a peace with Joshua. The people of
Gibeon appealed to Joshua for help and, in a battle at Gibeon, Joshua
"slew them with a great slaughter". The remnant of the Amorite
army was pursued to the valley of Ayalon where, after Joshua sought

help from the Lord, *"the sun stood still, and the moon stopped..."*.

Later after capturing them, Joshua had the kings hanged. However Jerusalem was not taken.

stubborn Jebusites

According to Joshua 15:8, Jerusalem was to be included in the territory allotted to the tribes of Judah and Benjamin. However the Bible relates that *"... as for the Jebusites, the inhabitants of Jerusalem, the sons of Judah could not drive them out"*. When and how these Jebusites replaced the Amorites, the Bible fails to tell us!

DAVID AND SOLOMON

Epic story

For the next few centuries the only real source of information we have on Jerusalem is taken from the Bible, with its mixture of fact and fable. Some of the writings have been verified by archaeology, others have not, but in general the Bible gives us a fairly accurate picture of those times.

David takes Jerusalem

David became king of Judah around 1000 BC. His first capital was at Hebron, but after unifying all the Israelite tribes decided to make Jerusalem his capital. *"Then David and all Israel went up to Jerusalem and the Jebusites...were there. And the [Jebusites] said to David 'You shall not enter here'. Nevertheless David captured the stronghold of Zion..."* (I Chron.11:4-7). (Zion was clearly the name of the Jebusite citadel.)

David did not kill the Jebusite inhabitants, and in all probability they were absorbed into the Israelite population which may have been a reason for the constant backsliding into Canaanite practices in the future.

sumptuous city of David

David rebuilt the city: *"So David lived in the stronghold, and called it the city of David. And David built all around from the Millo and inward."* (II Sam.5:9). (The Millo, meaning "filling" was an area that had been raised by filling in.)

David, by all accounts a great fighter and dedicated expansionist, increased his realm to include most of the inhabited regions east of the River Jordan, much of southern Syria, as well as nearly all Palestine. Such a large empire brought in a lot of

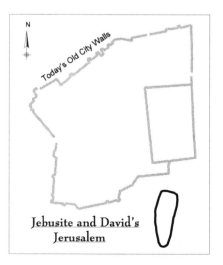

Jebusite and David's Jerusalem

9

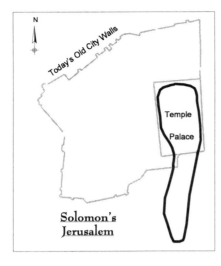

N

Today's Old City Walls

Temple

Palace

Solomon's
Jerusalem

treasure which enabled him to extend the city and build for himself a fine palace and harem. It is recorded that Hiram, king of Tyre, sent cedar wood, carpenters and stonemasons for this purpose (II Samuel 5:11).

plateau purchased

Wanting to build a religious altar David approached Araunah, probably a royal Jebusite, with an offer to buy a "threshing floor" situated on the plateau north of the ancient city. Though offered it without charge David insisted on paying, and erected an altar there (II Samuel 24:18ff). (Later, Solomon and Herod would build their temples there.)

David had the Ark of the Lord (the Israelite religious symbol) brought to Jerusalem, so by his conquest the city became the political and spiritual capital of the Israelite tribes.

David's city never expanded much beyond the confines of the Jebusite one, covering at the most about four hectares.

Solomon's splendour

When Solomon became king, around 965 BC, the city was really prospering. The Bible pointedly records that Solomon indeed inherited a very rich kingdom (I Kings 4:20-28 and II Chron.1:14ff).

transcendent Temple

By deciding to construct a fine palace for himself and a temple for the Lord (II Chron.2:1), Solomon put Jerusalem on the map for all time. These were built on the flat plateau with the temple towards its centre and the royal palace, the largest building in the city, to the south and stretching across to the valley of David's City. Whether Solomon's palace was more sumptuous than the temple we will never know. From what we know of Solomon's character, it probably was.

The two buildings took at least 20 years to construct, and no trace of either of them has been found, various destructions and layer upon layer of other buildings having obliterated them.

popular paganism

During the latter part of Solomon's reign, many dormant Canaanite practices re-emerged and this may have been one of the causes of the subsequent partition of the kingdom after his death, in c930 BC.

KINGDOM OF JUDAH
Divided domain

Rehoboam, one of Solomon's sons, succeeded to the throne, but was immediately confronted by a rebellion from the northern part of his kingdom which led to its division into Israel in the north and Judah, with Jerusalem as its capital, in the south. According to II Chron. 11:14ff the northern kingdom had degenerated into Canaanite pagan practices: *"For the Levites left their pasture lands and their property and came to Judah and Jerusalem, for Jeroboam and his sons had excluded them from serving as priests to the Lord."* (II Chron 11:14).

Rehoboam's ransom

The break-up of the empire built up by David, coupled with the loss of the northern – and richer – part of the kingdom caused the weakening of Jerusalem's position both in the political and economic spheres. This was sensed by the Egyptian ruler, Shishak, who invaded Judah. Rehoboam was compelled to pay a large ransom to avoid having Jerusalem captured (II Chron.12:1-9).

Israel invades

Jerusalem continued as the capital of Judah under the various kings, sometimes at peace, sometimes at war. During the reign of Amaziah c780 BC, the city was invaded and taken by Joash, the son of the King of Israel, Jehu. He destroyed part of the walls, and made off with a lot of treasure (II Chron 25:17-24).

In 727 Hezekiah became king of Judah. Around 721 the Assyrians under Sargon II invaded and destroyed the northern kingdom. Although most of the population was taken away as captives, many must have been able to seek refuge in Judah and Jerusalem. This enabled Hezekiah to expand the city – this appears to have been in a mainly westerly direction – and to strengthen its walls. To prepare the city for a siege Hezekiah dug his famous tunnel under the city so that the waters of the Gihon Spring could flow into the walled city.

siege of Sennacherib

This proved a wise move as the Assyrian King, Sennacherib, laid siege to the city in 701, but later withdrew without taking it (II Chron. 32: 1ff).

Manasseh taken prisoner

Hezekiah was succeeded by his son, Manasseh, who became king at the tender age of twelve. According to II Chron 33:2-8, during the early part of his long reign Judah and Jerusalem reverted to their old pagan customs which in reality were never far from the surface. The Chronicler further adds that at some time during his long reign Manasseh was captured by the Assyrians and taken to Babylon, but was returned

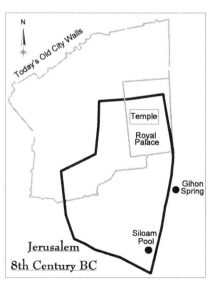

Jerusalem
8th Century BC

to his throne later (II Chron. 33:11-13). On his return he improved Jerusalem's walls, apparently on the west side of the Gihon Valley (ibid 33:14).

During the reign of Josiah, c640-609, the city seemed to have returned to Israelite Temple worship, and Jerusalem again became the focus of the nation's religious life (II Chron. 34 & 35:1-20).

In 609 Josiah was killed in the Battle of Megiddo by King Neco of Egypt, and was succeeded by his son, Joahaz who was quickly deposed by the Egyptians who made his brother, Jehoiakim, king in his stead (II Kings: 23:29-34). Jehoiakim was followed by his son, Jehoiachin in 597.

Babylonian banishment

In 597 the Chaldean-Babylonian ruler Nebuchadnezzar advanced on Jerusalem, and in order to save the city Jehoiachin and his family surrendered to him. They were taken as captives to Babylon, and in 596 Nebuchadnezzar made Zedekiah the king. Zedekiah was to be the last king of the original Judah and, with the exception of a period during Hasmonean rule, the last independent Jewish ruler of Jerusalem.

Ten years later, in 586, Nebuchadnezzar came against Jerusalem again, and after a siege that lasted some months took the city: *"And he burned the house of the Lord, the king's house, and all the houses of Jerusalem... So all the army of the Chaldeans... broke down the walls around Jerusalem. Then the rest of the people who were left in the city ... Nebuzaradan the captain of the guard carried away into exile."* (II Kings 25:9-11).

The total period that Jerusalem was under the sovereignty of the House of David lasted a little over 400 years.

POST EXILIC AND PERSIAN PERIOD

Very few Jews (the name Jew is derived from the Hebrew *Yehudi*, i.e. a person of Judah) were left in Jerusalem after the destruction, and the centre of religious life moved with the population to Babylon, where many became settled. In spite of some of the poetry that supposedly emanated from Babylon, many of the exiles became reconciled to their new homeland.

Persians permit return

In 539 Babylon fell to the Achaemenid Persians under Cyrus, who in 538 issued a decree allowing those Jews who wished, to return to Jerusalem and rebuild the Temple. Some chose not to, having long made their homes in the east. According to Ezra 2:64, the number that returned was 42,360.

Temple restored

Conditions in Jerusalem were wretched; those Jews who had remained were very poor, and other peoples from the surrounding nations had moved into the area. Security was difficult, the walls of the city having been destroyed. Rebuilding and resettlement proceeded very slowly, and the new Temple, no match for Solomon's splendid edifice, was only completed during the reign of Darius, c510.

ramparts rebuilt

The impoverished state of affairs persisted until c445 when Nehemiah, a dignitary at the court of the Achaemenid ruler Xerxes, became governor of the province. In the book of Nehemiah he describes how he found the city with its walls *"broken down and its gates consumed by fire"* (Neh. 2:13). He continues to tell how the walls were rebuilt in the face of hostility from the other peoples: *"As for the builders, each wore his sword girded at his side as he built..."* (Neh. 4:18). In spite of the difficulties the walls were re-erected in the space of 52 days (Neh.6:15). After the reconstruction the city was considerably smaller than it had been prior to its destruction, covering not much more than the Temple area and David's city.

The city – and Judah in general – was governed by Persian-appointed governors and by the high priests.

HELLENISTIC ERA

The defeat of the Persians by Alexander in 333 BC led to Jerusalem becoming part of his empire. Although Josephus records that the great warrior visited the city, it is unlikely that he actually did.

Ptolemy comes to power

After Alexander's death in 323 and the division of his lands between the Ptolemies and the Seleucids, Jerusalem became part of the domains of the former. Ptolemy I Softer, the first ruler, allowed Judah and Jerusalem a measure of self rule, but this was far from popular. In Jerusalem power was exercised by the high priests and a council of elders. The city remained the centre of Jewish religious worship, but many of the citizens began to adopt a Hellenistic way of life.

Seleucids seize the city

In 198 the city was conquered by the Seleucids, and this was welcomed by the citizens of Jerusalem. The Seleucid ruler, Antiochus III, guaranteed to the Jews the right to live and worship in their own way.

Temple tarnished

This all changed in 175 when Antiochus IV Epiphanes became Seleucid ruler. In a determined attempt to bring Hellene culture to all, in 169 or 168 he issued laws prohibiting, on pain of death, the rite of circumcision and the religious observance of the Jewish Sabbath. At the end of 168 an altar to Zeus was erected in the Temple and a pig was sacrificed.

Hellenised Jews

All this intolerance was not greeted with distaste by everybody. The city, which had been under Hellenistic rule for well over 100 years, had developed numerous Greek institutions. Many of the upper and ruling classes had adopted a Greek way of life, with a diluted form of Judaism.

revolt of the Maccabees

However the actions of Antiochus led to the revolt in 167 by Judah Maccabee and his brothers. Unable to enter Jerusalem, they mounted a blockade around it. After fighting off successive attempts

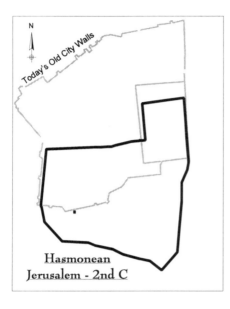

Hasmonean
Jerusalem - 2nd C

by the Seleucids to lift it, in 165 Judah occupied the Temple and other parts of the city.

Temple re-consecrated

In December of that year the Temple was cleansed of all pagan objects, and re-dedicated. (This is, of course, commemorated by the Feast of Dedication or Hanukkah, the Festival of Lights.) In spite of this, the Seleucids were not defeated and were able to hold on to their citadel, the Akra.

liberator killed

Antiochus died in 164, and the next couple of years saw a succession of claimants to the Seleucid throne. This enabled Judah to found the Hasmonean dynasty and launch an all-out war to free the country of Seleucid rule. Judah was killed in 160, but further internal disputes in the Seleucid empire enabled Jonathan, Judah's brother, to almost free Jerusalem and Judea from Seleucid domination. The garrison at the Akra held out, though, until 141.

HASMONEAN RULE

In spite of the continued Seleucid presence in Jerusalem, Jonathan became the first Hasmonean ruler, in 152, with the title of High Priest. Hasmonean is the name usually applied to the Maccabean dynasty (Josephus, Antiquities 12:263). In 141 the Seleucid king, Demetrius II bowed to reality and withdrew his garrison from Jerusalem, thus making Judea independent.

city enlarged

Jerusalem expanded in a westerly direction almost as far as the line of the present west wall, but its growth north was minimal. When the first Aristobulus succeeded to the title of High Priest in 104 he also called himself King. This dual title continued until the end of the dynasty. As with David almost 850 years earlier, the Hasmoneans expanded their realms, enlarging the kingdom and increasing the importance of the city. At times the Hasmonean domains included most of northern Palestine and much territory east of the River Jordan, where Alexander Yannai, besides conquering the Decapolis cities, forced many of the people to convert to Judaism.

struggle for succession

Alexander Yannai died in 76 and was succeeded by his widow, Salome Alexandra. After her death in 67, a conflict for the throne broke out between her sons Aristobulus and Hyrcanus. Aristobulus took the throne as Aristobulus II, and Hyrcanus with help from the Nabateans, unsuccessfully tried to dislodge him.

Romans resolve dissension

In the meantime Pompey, who had taken control of the Seleucid empire in 64 BC, decided to intervene, effectively ending any independence the Hasmoneans enjoyed. He declared Hyrcanus to be the ruler, and Aristobulus and his supporters took refuge in the Temple.

In 63 Pompey entered the Temple, killing Aristobulus. Hyrcanus was left as high priest but the real ruler was Antipater of Idumea who broke the kingdom up into provinces; one of his sons, Phasael, became governor of Jerusalem, and another, Herod – who attached himself to the Hasmonean dynasty by marrying Mariamne, the granddaughter of Hyrcanus – became governor of Galilee. Antipater was killed in 43 BC and with Roman help the two sons became the rulers of Judea.

Antony and Antigonus

In 40 BC Antigonus Mathathias, a son of Aristobulus II, with the help of the Parthians seized Jerusalem. Hyrcanus and Phasael were killed, but Herod was able to escape, and went to Alexandria to enlist the support of his friend Mark Antony.

After being declared King of Judea by the Roman senate he returned to Palestine and invaded Jerusalem, but was unable to defeat Antigonus. He again sought and received the assistance of Antony who sent a considerable army which laid siege to the city in late 38 BC.

In spite of holding out for five months, the city fell in the spring of 37, and Antigonus was killed.

Thus ended the Hasmonean rule of Jerusalem. It had lasted in total 115 years, less as an independent kingdom.

HERODIAN/ROMAN PERIOD

Ruthless ruler

Known as "the Great", Herod was not a Jew by birth, but an Idumean. (Idumea, from Edom, was the area of southern Palestine.) One of his first acts after becoming King was to kill all 45 members of the Jerusalem Sanhedrin, the Jewish religious elders. As a cruel authoritarian he set about the destruction of the traditional Jewish way of life in favour of the Roman. He appointed and dismissed high priests at will and strengthened his position by ingratiating himself with the real masters, the Romans.

great builder

In spite of the fact that he was much disliked by the Jewish population, he transformed Jerusalem with his lavish building. The Temple Mount was enlarged and the Temple rebuilt and magnificently decorated. The city walls were expanded northwards (the second north wall) to approximately where the first part of the Via Dolorosa is today, and the city covered roughly two thirds of its final area.

Antonia fortress constructed

Where the Hasmonean tower called Baris was located, northwest of the Temple area, Herod built a fortress, which he named after Mark Antony, the Antonia, and, according to Josephus, a hippodrome somewhere south of the temple plateau. He also built a huge palace just south of today's Jaffa Gate. Three towers stood guard over the edifice; Phasael, Hippicus, and Mariamne. Part of the Phasael tower still survives in the Citadel.

Pontius Pilate, provincial procurator

Herod died in 4 BC, and the Romans turned Judea into a Roman province. Although Herod's son Antipas continued as king the real ruler was the Roman Procurator who had his seat at Caesarea on the coast. It was during the tenure of one of these procurators, Pontius Pilate (AD 26-36), that the crucifixion of Jesus took place.

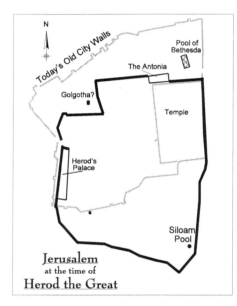

Jerusalem
at the time of
Herod the Great

Under succeeding Herodian kings Jerusalem's walls expanded northwards, and during the reign of the first Agrippa it continued to expand, and eventually (the third north wall) reached the line of the present northern wall.

religious strife

During the first century AD Jerusalem was plagued by religious dissension between different streams of Jewish thought. In particular, the disagreements between the Pharisees and the more traditional Sadducees (from Zadok, the High Priest in David's time), were particularly bitter.

Romans defile Temple

At the same time Roman rule became much more brutal, and there were many acts of desecration in the Temple that inflamed Jewish passions, and further exacerbated the situation.

In AD 64 the First Jewish Revolt broke out, and by August 66 they had gained a very temporary control of the city. Much buoyed by their victory, they set up the trappings of government including the minting of silver coins. Victory, though, did not halt the internecine conflict, and this was to be a factor in their eventual defeat. Josephus records (in Wars of the Jews, V:188) that the insurgents burned the Antonia fortress, Herod's palace, and parts of the upper city. At this time, the small Christian community of the city left to live in Pella east of the Jordan.

Romans put to flight

An initial attempt was made to put down the rebellion in November that year. Cestius Gallus, the governor of Syria, launched an unprepared attack to crush the insurrection. Although he nearly took the Temple, his forces were compelled to retreat, followed by the Jewish insurgents: *"They* (the Jews) *pursued the Romans all the way to Antipatris* (east of modern Tel-Aviv) *but failed to catch them; so turning back they carried off the machines and despoiled the dead, collected the booty that had been left behind, and with hymns of victory marched back to the capital. Their own casualties were negligible but the Romans and their allies had lost 5,300 infantrymen and 480 cavalrymen killed."* (Josephus, Wars II:528.)

the ravages of hunger

In 67 Vespasian prepared to march on the city, and by 68 it was besieged by Titus. A siege wall was built around the city preventing any supplies from reaching it. Famine became very severe, and hunger became rampant. Josephus records:

"Corn was nowhere to be seen, men broke into houses and ransacked them. If they found any, they maltreated the occupants for saying there was none; if they did not, they suspected them of having it hidden more carefully and tortured them. ...if they still had flesh on their bones, they were deemed to have plenty of stores... All human feelings, alas yield to hunger... for when hunger reigns, restraint is abandoned. Thus wives would snatch the food from husbands, children from their fathers, and – most horrible of all – mothers from the very mouths of their infants..." (Josephus, Wars of the Jews, V:428).

Other accounts by Josephus of the situation in the besieged city and the atrocities enacted there illustrate how dreadful was the situation – factional violence only adding to the other miseries.

more death and destruction

Unable to withstand the tight Roman stranglehold, the city fell to Titus in AD 70. Josephus records very graphically the harrowing results of this fall: *"While the Temple blazed, the victors plundered everything that fell in their way and slaughtered wholesale all those who were caught. No pity was shown for age, no reverence for rank. Children and greybeards, laity and priests alike were massacred... the ground was nowhere visible through the corpses, but the soldiers had to clamber over heaps of bodies in pursuit of the fugitives."* (Wars of the Jews, 8:V:1)

escape to slavery

With the destruction of the Temple, the city was levelled to the ground. Only the towers around Herod's Palace were left standing as protection for the Tenth Legion who pitched camp there. Those who had not been killed were taken as captives and became slaves.

ROMAN ERA

Jewish centre moved

A Roman decree was issued banning Jews from living in the ruins of Jerusalem. If Jerusalem remained to many Jews the spiritual centre of their faith, the practical centre was moved to Yavne, near the Mediterranean coast, where a rabbinical school was founded. Slowly some Jews did return to the ruins of Jerusalem and it appears that some building work must have taken place, as sources record that later there were a number of synagogues.

the second revolt

In 130 Hadrian visited the city and decided to establish a colonia, Aelia Capitolina, on the site. In 132, provoked by the building of Aelia and by other Roman decrees, especially the prohibiting of the rite of circumcision, the Jews, led by Shimon Bar-Kokhba a messianic zealot, rebelled for a second time. Those who had resettled in the city were joined by others from the area and, by using guerilla tactics and their knowledge of the Judean desert, its caves and wadis they were able to force the Roman Garrison to withdraw.

Jews expelled again

In the summer of 135, in a ruthless counter attack, Septimius Severus retook the city, killing or expelling all who lived there. Jews were again forbidden to live in the city under pain of death.

Aelia Capitolina

The Roman city of Aelia Capitolina had a totally different layout to the destroyed city of Jerusalem. The shape is the one that determined the plan of the old city as it is today. In common with most provincial Roman cities, two main thoroughfares crossed the city: the north/south cardo which began at the present Damascus Gate, and the west/east decumanus, which started at the present Jaffa Gate and reached what is now the Bab al-Silsileh of the Haram. As was usual in Roman cities where the two thoroughfares crossed, a tall, columned tetrapylon was built. There was a large forum, and part of the triple entrance arch can still be seen in the Russian Alexandrovsky Hospice near the Church of the Holy Sepulchre (see page 80).

temples built

The cardo was colonnaded and at its northern end stood a column in honour of Hadrian (the Arabic name for the Damascus Gate is "Bab al-Amud", the Gate of the Column). A temple to Jupiter was constructed on a site called the "Quadrata". This may have been the level platform of the Haram, but no remains of this have been found. On the site where the Church of the Holy Sepulchre was to be built later, a Roman temple to Venus was erected. The entire south west corner of the city was occupied by the Legio X Frentensis (Tenth Legion). To repopulate Aelia, Hellenised Syrians and others were brought in.

imperial visit

Aelia Capitolina was not an important city, and few events of significance took place there. Perhaps the most notable one was the visit there by the new Emperor Septimius Severus in 201.

the first pilgrims

From the end of the second century and into the third more Christians, many of whom were converted Jews, began to establish themselves in the city, and many others came as pilgrims. In fact it was around this time that these faithful began to seek "Holy Places". This encouraged Jews also to visit, and gradually the ban weakened. Jerusalem soon had a bishop, Alexander Flavian, who in 212 established a library. A native of Cappadocia, he travelled to the city as a pilgrim but was entreated by the community to stay as their bishop. Scholars of the day such as Origen from Alexandria and Julius Africanus, a native of Jerusalem, began researches into Christianity and Africanus' work *Chronography*, started in 215, attempted to explain the origins of the faith.

torture and martyrdom

In 250 the Emperor Decius decreed that all in his realm should attend a pagan ceremony. Alexander, the bishop of Jerusalem refused, and he was tortured and put to death. During the simultaneous reigns of the emperors Diocletian and Maximianus Herculius, 284 to 305, persecution of the Christians increased, but all this came to an abrupt end in 313 when the new emperor, Constantine, issued the Edict of Milan making Christianity legal throughout the Empire.

THE BYZANTINE CITY

Jerusalem becomes Christian

The conversion of Constantine to Christianity in the early 4th century and the incorporation of Palestine into the Eastern Empire in 324 changed the face of Aelia, now reverting to the name Jerusalem. In the same year the bishop of the city, Makarios, sought and received permission to destroy the Roman Temple of Venus, long held to be the site of Jesus' tomb, which, according to tradition, was discovered underneath it.

Byzantine Jerusalem

Helena's amazing "discovery"

In 326, urged by Bishop Makarios, the emperor's mother, Helena, visited the city to see for herself the bad state of Christian sites. Legend holds that whilst visiting the spot of the destroyed temple she discovered the "True Cross" in a nearby cave thus "confirming" that the site was that of the Tomb and Golgotha.

The 6th C mosaic map of Jerusalem found in Madaba, Jordan

The Church of the Holy Sepulchre was consequently built on this location, and dedicated in 335.

For the next century and a half Jerusalem expanded as a Christian city, the walls being extended to include Mount Zion, and later the Tyropoeon Valley. More churches were built; these included the Chapel of the Ascension on the Mount of Olives in 378 and the church at Gethsemane in 390. In 431 the city was made a Patriarchate. Around the year 440 Jews were again allowed to dwell there.

Madaba mosaic map

The mosaic map found (in the 1880s) on the floor of the Church of St. George in Madaba, Jordan, shows the extent of development in Jerusalem during the time of Justinian (527-565). A new basilica, the Nea, had been erected at the southern end of the cardo and this part of the thoroughfare was colonnaded. There was a palace for the bishops adjoining the Church of the Holy Sepulchre, and numerous other churches both within the city and without. Although there is no record of any buildings on the Temple Mount, the map does show some structures.

Chosroes bloody conquest

Much effort was expended by Justinian and later rulers to secure the eastern frontiers of the Empire against the growing strength of the Sasanian Persians. This was to no avail, and in 613 Chosroes II took Damascus, and the following year, with the help of Jews, Jerusalem.

The slaughter and devastation was immense. The Church of the Holy Sepulchre was burned, and the remnants of the "True Cross" were taken to Ctesiphon, the Sasanian capital. The city was then handed over, mainly, to the Jews, who according to some accounts acquitted themselves no less brutally than the Persians. These accounts relate that thousands of Christian prisoners were put to death at the Mamilla Pool (now Independence Park).

"Cross" returned

The city was soon returned to the Christians, and some of the ravaged buildings, including the Church of the Holy Sepulchre, were restored by Modestus, Abbot of a nearby monastery. The victories of the emperor, Heraclius (r.610-641), enabled the Byzantines to re-enter Jerusalem in 629, and in 631 the "True Cross" was rescued, and returned to Jerusalem with all pomp and ceremony.

FIRST MUSLIM ERA

The return of Byzantine rule was not to last long. Weakened by the Sasanian war Palestine quickly fell to the advancing Arab armies. In 636 Heraclius was decisively beaten at the Battle of the Yarmuk, and in the spring of 638 the Patriarch, Sophronius, surrendered the city to 'Umar, the Muslim Caliph.

Mu'awiya becomes Caliph

Initial Muslim rule under 'Umar was very benevolent, with the Christian holy place being protected (see history of Church of the Holy Sepulchre), and this was extended into the Omayyad period.

Mu'awiya, the first Omayyad ruler, had himself proclaimed Caliph in Jerusalem in 661, and by 672 the first, not-so-large mosque had been built at the southern end of the former Temple area (described by the Christian traveller Arculf around that time).

Arabs choose a name

After the conquest the city was known as Beit al-Maqdis or Holy House (similar to the Hebrew name for the Temple – *Beit Hamikdash*), although the Roman name of Aelia and Urishalim, a corruption of Jerusalem (Hebrew *Yerushalayim*), were also applied.

advent of the golden dome

In 692, the third Omayyad Caliph, Abd al-Malik, built the Qubbat al-Sakhra, the Dome of the Rock, over the rock on which Muslims believed Muhammad had stood before ascending to heaven. It is said that one of al-Malik's intentions in building the edifice was to rival the importance of the Church of the Holy Sepulchre. Whether or not that was so the mosque, in spite of numerous repairs, refurbishments, rejuvenations and rebuildings, remains even today the most outstanding visual structure in Jerusalem.

home to three faiths

Although in the first decades after the Muslim conquest the majority of people living in the city were Christians, by the first years of the 8th C the Muslim population had grown significantly. Whether or not a sizeable community of Jews had dwelt in the city throughout the Byzantine era is a matter of conjecture, but certainly after the Muslim occupation the Jewish presence was firm.

Around 710 Halid Ibn al-Walid (the architect of the Great Mosque of Damascus) rebuilt and enlarged the al-Aksa Mosque making it the principle congregational Muslim prayer house of Jerusalem (as it is today). In spite of this Jerusalem was not considered a very important city; indeed the capital of the province was Ramleh, a newly founded and totally Islamic city some 30 kilometres to the west.

protection from Aix-la-Chapelle

With the advent of Abbasid rule in 750 Jerusalem became neglected. The Omayyads had been based in Damascus, not far away, but with the new seat of power in Baghdad, Jerusalem was very distant. Some of the rulers did visit the city, but these visits were few and brief. In the early 9th century Charlemagne was able to pose as the Protector of the Christians in Jerusalem, and due to his help and dealings with the Abbasid rulers, Christian enterprise expanded.

rule from Egypt

In the latter half of the 9th century the Abbasids began to weaken and fractionalise, with different dynasties springing up in various areas, particularly Egypt. In 878 the Tulunids from Egypt annexed the province and though Abbasid rule was restored in 905, thirty years later the Ikhshidids, also from Egypt, became the masters. Few records are available of the city during these times, although it is known that a custom of interring the Tulunid and later rulers in the holy city prevailed.

inter-faith strife

It also seems that communal relations began to break down; so much so that in 932 the Christians of the city wrote to Henry I, the Holy Roman Emperor, protesting about the behaviour of the Jewish population.

In 938 rampaging Muslims caused devastation to many Christian buildings, including the Church of the Holy Sepulchre. In 966 further unrest occurred and this time the Patriarch was killed.

Shi'ite carnage

In 969 the Fatimids (a Shi'ite clan with mystical leanings) established themselves as rulers in Egypt and soon after all of Palestine and Syria was annexed. Although the regime was at first tolerant of non Muslims, the second Fatimid Caliph, al-Hakim, by all accounts a demented man, let loose in 1009 a wave of persecution, pillage and destruction on the Christians. The Church of the Holy Sepulchre was destroyed, as were many other Christian shrines. Further destruction occurred in 1034 when an earthquake struck the city.

renovation of the ramparts

From 1033 to 1063 the walls were restored and replanned. Some areas which were previously inside, such as Mount Zion, were placed outside.

Seljuk severity

In 1071 Jerusalem was captured by the Seljuk Turks, who were already in control of Syria and Iraq. In 1076 a revolt against the Seljuks was put down with great cruelty and loss of life. After a siege that lasted forty days the Fatimids retook the city in 1098.

first Crusader conquest

Then, on 15th July 1099, Jerusalem succumbed to the First Crusade. In the space of 30 years, Jerusalem had had three different rulers.

CRUSADER JERUSALEM

Terrible Christian carnage

The Crusaders reached Jerusalem on June 6th 1099. After trying to take the city by direct assault they set about building siege towers. Dividing the main forces into three, one led by Godfrey of Bouillon, one by Raymond of Toulouse and the third by Tancred they attacked on the night of 14th June. Raymond managed to set his tower against the wall by Mount Zion. Godfrey de Bouillon set his tower against the NE, and Tancred was able to scale the walls in the NW. Unable to withstand the onslaught, the Fatimid garrison retreated to the Citadel where they eventually surrendered. In a repeat of a scene of carnage that they had played only a few months earlier in the town of Maarat-al-Numan in Syria, the Crusaders systematically massacred the Jewish and Muslim population. The few who escaped were captured and sold into slavery. The slaughter was dreadful; Muslims were burned alive in their mosques and Jews in their synagogues. In order to fill the emptiness left by the killing of so many, the Crusaders encouraged Christians from east of the Jordan and other locations to settle in the city.

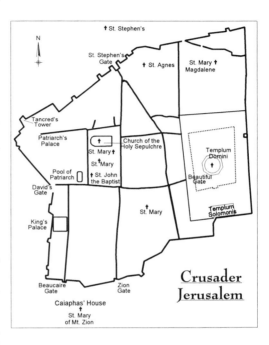

Crusader Jerusalem

Crusader king

In 1100 the Crusader Kingdom of Jerusalem, or Regnum Hierusalem was established with Baldwin I as the first king. That Jerusalem flourished during this time is of no surprise. For here were all the offices of administration and church institutions. Everything was heavily supported by a constant flow of pilgrims from Christian Europe.

pilgrims stay

The extent of the city remained as in Muslim times, but after the initial period the population began to rise. This was partly due to the many pilgrims who remained. The Crusader period was also a term of much construction. A palace for the Patriarch was built, and the area now called Muristan turned over to the Hospitaliers. The

Knights Templar were given the al-Aksa Mosque which they called Templum Solomonis. The citadel near the Jaffa Gate was restored, and the king's palace was built nearby.

a time to build churches

This is the time that many Christian traditions began to firm up. In particular the route and rite of the Via Dolorosa (see box page 83). Muslim holy places were changed into Christian ones. The Dome of the Rock was renamed Templum Domini. The greatest construction work of all was the complete rebuilding of the Church of the Holy Sepulchre with everything contained under a single roof. Other constructions included the churches on Mount Zion, and that of St. Anne.

forgotten French

During the Crusader duration, Jerusalem was an entirely different city from the one before or the one afterwards. Only Christians were permitted to live within the walls, and most of these were Latins, there being only very few from the Eastern Rites, and these were mainly Syrian Orthodox. Medieval French was the vernacular, although most documents were written in Latin. The majority of the people were from France or French lands, with a scattering of Germans, Poles and Spaniards.

Jewish and Muslim merchants

Though they were not allowed to take up residence in the city, both Jews and Muslims were permitted to trade there. How strictly the rule on residence was kept is not known. The medieval Jewish traveller, Benjamin of Tudela, who visited in the late 12th C, mentions some Jewish dyers near the citadel. During the Crusader occupation the final shape of the (old) city was settled.

magnanimous Muslim

Crusader rule in Jerusalem lasted nearly 100 years. In July 1187 a combined Crusader army was heavily defeated by Salah al-Din at the Battle of the Horns of Hittin, west of Lake Tiberias (the Sea of Galilee). By November the great Ayyubid warrior was at the gates of Jerusalem. The city soon surrendered, and in contrast to the Christian victory of 1099 there was no bloodletting. Of those taken captive, many were to be freed after ransoms were paid.

holy Haram

Salah al-Din banned Latin Christians from the city, and all the major holy places including the Church of the Holy Sepulchre were taken over by Christians from the Eastern Rites. The Muslims regained their mosques, especially the Dome of the Rock and al-Aksa, and the Haram al-Sharif would henceforth be an exclusively Muslim holy area. Many other Christian buildings were converted for Muslim use; the hospital of the Hospitaliers Knights Templar (the Muristan), was converted into a Muslim hospital (although much of the practice here was already in the hands of Arab physicians).

Jewish joy

Much to their satisfaction, Jews were again allowed to dwell within the walls, and Salah al-Din even encouraged this. Many of them came from as far afield as the western Maghreb, Yemen, and

later on (1209-1211) from England and France (Encycl. Judaica).
The Ayyubids were great builders of Muslim structures. In Damascus and Aleppo their building legacy remains among the finest. They also left their mark on Jerusalem, particularly on the Haram.

walls weakened

The Crusades were again threatening, and in 1220 the Ayyubid ruler, al-Malik al-Mu'azzam, decided to destroy parts of city walls as he reckoned that if the city should fall it would be easier to retake if the fortifications had been reduced. This action proved superfluous as in the event the Crusaders managed to get control of the city by diplomacy rather than war.

diplomatic deal

With the splitting of the Ayyubid dynasty Jerusalem came under the jurisdiction of the Ayyubid ruler in Cairo, al-Malik al-Kamil. He, not wanting a confrontation with the Holy Roman Emperor, Frederick II, leader of the Crusade, entered into a treaty with him which handed Jerusalem back to the Christians. Muslims were allowed to keep their shrines, specifically those on the Haram. Frederick crowned himself king in the Church of the Holy Sepulchre.

Khwarizmian conquest

This second occupation of the city by the Europeans was brief, lasting 15 years until 1244. In that year Khwarizmian Turks attacked and sacked the city. The Holy Sepulchre was despoiled and many Christians and Jews killed. The Khwarizmian conquest came to an end three years later when the Ayyubid Sultan al-Malik al-Salih Ayyub regained control. He died in 1249 and the city passed to the Ayyubid ruler of Syria, al-Malik al-Nasir Yusuf Salah al-Din.

Mamelukes thwart Mongols

In 1250 Mamelukes, the slave guards of the Ayyubid rulers in Egypt, rebelled and took power, and were immediately in conflict with the Ayyubid rulers in Damascus.

In 1259 the Mongols under Hulaga invaded Syria and Palestine. The Mameluke sultan, Baibars, seizing the opportunity, set out to crush them. At the Battle of Ain Jalut, Goliath's Spring (now Ein Harod, south of Haifa), the Mongols were overcome, and all of Syria and Palestine became part of the Mameluke domains. Jerusalem remained under Mameluke rule until 1516.

MAMELUKE RULE

At the start of Mameluke rule Jerusalem was in a very depressed condition. The threat of the Mongol invasion had led much of the population to flee the city, taking with them as much as they could. The Jewish scholar Moses ben Nahman (Nahmanides) who came to sojourn in 1267, reported that only about 2000 people were living in the city, 300 of them Christian, and two Jews! By establishing a synagogue he was able to persuade some of the Jews who had fled to return and re-establish the community. (Encycl. Judaica.)

impoverished province

At first Jerusalem was attached to the province of Damascus, but towards the end of his life in 1376, the sultan, al-Malik al-Ashraf Sha'ban II made the city and its environs into a separate province, under the direct concern of the sultan. The walls of the city remained in their ruinous state and repopulation did not seem to be of great concern to the Mameluke sultans, their main interest seeming to be the religious importance of Jerusalem to Muslims, and a place of theological study. Many madrassas and other pious foundations were established, most of them housing the tombs of the founders. Some of the finest Muslim buildings in the city date from these times and, though neglected, can still be seen today.

funding for holy places

The Qubbat al-Sakhra, the Dome of the Rock, and al-Aksa were both repaired and much attention was paid to the Haram; its walls and water system were among the beneficiaries of the improvements.

The Christian Jerusalem of the Crusades vanished, and was replaced by an environment that was thoroughly Muslim. Inhabitants who were not fully engaged in religious matters made their living mainly as merchants, and the great souks in the centre continued as the primary sources of commerce, although the small population made this none too lucrative.

city of Islamic scholarship

So many madrassas were established that Jerusalem became a veritable centre of Islamic scholarship. Many of the theologians who taught were among the most famous of the period.

religious intolerance

As so often in times past (and present), theology and fanaticism

Occupation of Jerusalem through the centuries

c1900-c1000 BC	Canaanites, Jebusites
c1000-c930 BC	Kingdom of Israel
c930-586 BC	Kingdom of Judah
586-538 BC	Babylonians/Chaldeans
538-c332 BC	Achaemenid Persians
332-198 BC	Ptolemies
198-164 BC	Seleucids
164-63 BC	Hasmoneans (first under the Seleucids then independently.
63 BC-AD 638	Roman/Byzantine
638-1099	Arab Muslim
1099-1187	Crusader
1187-1229	Arab Muslim
1229-1244	Crusader
1244-1516	Mameluke Muslim
1516-1918	Ottoman Muslim
1918-1948	British Mandate
1948-1967	East Jerusalem and Old City under Jordanian rule, new city under Israeli rule.
1967-	de facto Israeli rule.

went side by side. Christians were regularly harassed by Muslims, and this was especially true for the Franciscans who, after having left the city when Acre fell in 1291, began to return around 1330 when they settled on Mount Zion. At least twice in the 15th century they attempted to construct a church to Mary on Mount Zion, only to have it pulled down.

Harassment also extended to the Jews. A tax imposed on them in 1440 forced some to leave, finding it impossible to pay. The ravages of the Black Death in Europe, coupled with a Papal suggestion that Venetian ships should avoid transporting Jews, also affected a community that relied on a regular influx of pilgrims and aid. Rabbi Ovadiah of Bertinoro who travelled to the city in 1488 criticized the poverty and repression. In 1495 another traveller reported that about 200 Jewish families dwelt in the city. (Encycl. Judaica).

OTTOMAN RULE

In 1453 Constantinople fell to the Ottoman Turks. Soon they were advancing through Syria and by 1516 Jerusalem had succumbed, initiating a rule that would last 402 years.

Suleiman's golden era

In 1520 Suleiman al-Qanuni, the lawgiver who we in the west call "the Magnificent" became sultan, ushering in a period of splendour for the Ottoman world. For Jerusalem this meant the rebuilding of the city walls, still largely in the state they had been in since the first half of the 13th C.

It took from 1537 to 1541 for the ramparts to be reconstructed, and with the exception of the New Gate, the walls and gates we see today are from that reconstruction. Suleiman also refurbished the exterior of the Dome of the Rock by replacing the old mosaics which then covered the walls, with fine marble slabs and surfacings. These endured until 1950 when they were partly replaced by the Jordanians with financial support from others.

the sultan builds a pool

The water supply to the city was also improved by repairing the channels that brought water from Solomon's Pools, south of Bethlehem. The Sultan's Pool, below Mount Zion, was excavated in 1536, and by damming the Hinnom Valley it became a reservoir. A *sabil* or public fountain can be seen on the road that crosses it.

decline in significance

In spite of these and other architectural achievements, the city soon fell into decline. To the Ottoman sultans, Jerusalem held little political significance; the Crusades were dead and buried, and expanding and holding territories in Europe assumed greater importance. Though it had its own governor, the city's status fluctuated, sometimes being part of the *villayet*, province, of Damascus and sometimes of Sidon. Few Turks actually settled in the city yet, while Arabic remained the vernacular, many Turkish words became part of everyday speech – and persist until today.

poll tax burden

Heavy taxation was placed upon Christians and Jews alike, so much so that by the end of the 17th century the Georgian Christians, who in any case had been dwindling in numbers, left the city altogether. However, the Jewish population increased slightly, mainly with scholars settling in the city. Because they were engaged in study rather than gainful employment, it was only the contributions of outside communities that enabled them to exist and pay the required *kharaj* or poll tax.

Throughout the 17th century the Jewish population numbered between 1000 and 1500 souls. From a record of the poll tax at the end of the 17th C it appears that of the c1000 Jews in the city, one quarter were scholars, the remainder being merchants or craftsmen (Encycl. Judaica).

Christians in conflict

During the 16th C the population of Christians slowly increased and composed many denominations. Conflicts between these were often quite bitter, especially as regards "rights" in the Church of the Holy Sepulchre.

The authorities continued to oppress them with a variety of taxes, including a heavy one on marriage and a pilgrimage tax. The intervention of the European powers, and in particular France, helped to alleviate their position somewhat.

tardy treaty

A capitulation treaty between the "most Christian of Christians", the French king Francis I and Suleiman was reached in 1535. It was expected that this agreement would control the activities of France vis-à-vis the holy places and protection of pilgrims in Jerusalem. But it was nine years (1544) before a consul was appointed in Tripoli (Syria), and it took until 1624 for France to appoint one in Jerusalem, so the agreement had only a marginal effect.

The consul, M Jean Lempereur, although bringing some relief to the Catholic Christian community, was hampered from fulfilling all his tasks, and it was recorded in 1631 that *"the Turks do not refrain from perpetrating their tyrannical deeds on monks and the Catholic Christians who are not monks. These deeds would have been a thousand times more difficult to bear were they not curtailed by the French consul..."* (La Terre Sainte 1664). The French were able to maintain a consul in the city until 1713, when disputes with the local governor forced a withdrawal.

The Franciscan Friars, "Custodia Terra Sancta", had the responsibility of looking after all western Christian pilgrims no matter from what denomination. Pilgrims from the Orthodox churches, as subjects of the sultan were in a different category.

Ottomans in decline

The 18th century was marked by a further decline in the fortunes of the city, parallelling ebbing fortunes in the Ottoman Empire generally.

By the century's end the European powers had increased their awareness not only of the Christian holy places, but of the region's economic value, and this was manifested by further capitulation treaties.

European influence increases

In 1838 the British were allowed to open a consulate in the city. At first headed by a vice-consul, a full consul, W. T. Young was appointed in 1841. In 1843 the French reopened their long-since closed consulate.

The establishment by Pope Pius IX of a Latin Patriarchate in 1847 was disturbing to the non Latin Christians of Jerusalem as one of its aims was to arrest the growing influence of Protestants.

commerce expands

When Mohammad Ali, the viceroy in Egypt challenged the Ottoman authorities and took control of the city from 1831 to 1840, the European powers eventually intervened to restore Turkish rule. This resulted in an even deeper involvement of the Europeans in the affairs of the Empire and of Jerusalem particularly. More consulates opened, and the new shipping routes between Italy and Jaffa increased the flow of visitors and pilgrims, and this was to transform the city over the next two or three decades.

plethora of post offices

An unusual feature of these years was the operation of postal services by different European countries. In 1848 the Austrians opened their post office on the site of today's Christian Information Centre, just inside the Jaffa Gate. This was soon followed by those of Italy, France and Prussia.

The intervention of the Europeans coupled with improvements in the Ottoman administration led to an increase in population, especially of Jews, whose enterprise was heavily aided by their co-religionists in Europe and North America. By 1845 it was estimated that the city's population was around 15,000, about half of them being Jews. Life for many remained squalid inside the confines of the city walls, especially among the Jews as the Jewish Quarter could not cope with the influx.

extra-mural development

The 1860s saw the development of the areas outside the walls that came to be the "new city". Moses Montefiore, a rich philanthropic British Jew, built Mishkenot Sha'ananim, on the south side of the Hinnom Valley, the first residential area outside the walls, and soon other neighbourhoods, mostly Jewish, were established slightly further afield. Mahaneh Yisrael, along the road to Jaffa, was established in 1868 by Sephardi (eastern) Jews, and a year later Nahlat Shivah, closer to the walls, came into being.

On the road to Bethlehem Arabs established the area of Abu Tor, followed by other districts such as Ba'aqa and Qatamon. Outside the northern walls Arab quarters were established near what is today the Rockefeller Museum and Musrarah, opposite the Damascus Gate.

Prior to these extra-mural developments, the city gates had been closed at night. Now they were left open 24 hours a day, helping to create a sense of cohesion between the old and new cities.

carriageways and telegraphs

From 1865 on, development of the new city proceeded apace. Many buildings went up, including Talitha Kumi, a school for Arab girls near where the Hamashbir department store is today. In 1865 Jerusalem was linked by telegraph with Jaffa; by 1868 a road passable by carriages was in use on the same route.

The influx of Jews into the city made them the majority, and the constant flow of funds from outside ensured that Jewish development in the new areas was the most widespread, new quarters being continually added. In 1874 the ultra-religious Jews from Eastern Europe built the Mea She'arim district, just north of the old city.

The Arab Muslims remained largely confined to the old city, and though from the 1870s onwards Jews outnumbered Muslims, the latter continued to be (and still are) the most populous group inside the walled area.

spread of modernity

In the 1880s further developments gave the city a more "modern" character. Shops were opened along the streets of the new city; better roads linking the city to the coast and other towns of Palestine were constructed and in 1887 the city became a separate *sanjak* with its own governor. By 1890 the population was estimated to be 43,000.

Towards the end of the century, when Turkish nationalism began to take hold in Istanbul, the Arabs of the region became conscious of their own (Arab) national identity and thoughts of an independent Arab Kingdom in Syria (then comprising Syria, Jordan and Palestine) began to emerge. In 1897 the World Zionist Movement was founded with a declared aim of a Jewish state in Palestine. It was these two seemingly irreconcilable ambitions that paved the way for the conflicts that were to engulf the region in the 20th C.

visit of Kaiser Wilhelm

The 19th C closed with a visit by the German Kaiser Wilhelm II, who came to open the Erlöserkirchen, the Church of the Redeemer.

THE TWENTIETH CENTURY

The history of Jerusalem – and indeed all of Palestine in the 20th C – has been the subject of many contemporary books, and it would be beyond the scope of this volume to go into it in detail. If you are interested in getting an in-depth knowledge of recent history, I refer you to the bibliography. A summary is as follows:

1900-1914 Further Jewish immigration to Jerusalem and the establishment of many new neighbourhoods.

1914-1917 Turkey enters First World War on the side of Germany. In 1915 Britain gives undertaking to the Emir Husayn, in exchange for his assistance against the Turks, that any Arab territory liberated would become part of an Arab Kingdom (McMahon Correspondence). In 1916 Britain and France conclude an agreement to carve up the area between them (Sykes-Picot Treaty).

1917 British Government promises a Jewish National Home in Palestine (Balfour Declaration). In December, General Allenby enters Jerusalem and 30 years of British rule begins.

1920 League of Nations gives mandate for southern Syria

	(Palestine and Jordan) to Britain, and Northern Syria (Syria and Lebanon) to France.
1922	Britain sets up municipal council in Jerusalem comprising six Jews and six Arabs, two of them Christian; the mayor is an Arab. Jewish immigration continues almost unrestricted.
1925	Hebrew University opened on Mount Scopus.
1925-1930	Increase in the Jewish population causes great concern among the Arabs who riot in protest. Many deaths.
1932-1937	Many more Jews immigrate due to persecution in Germany. British Government commission, the Peel Commission, recommends partition of Palestine between Jews and Arabs, Jerusalem and environs remaining under a mandate.
1939	Jewish immigration into Palestine severely restricted, and later halted altogether.
1942	Irgun Zvai Leumi, a Jewish terrorist group, vows to fight the British until a Jewish state is established.
1947	United Nations decides to partition Palestine into Arab and Jewish states with Jerusalem and its environs to be internationalised.
1948-1949	In May 1948 the British Mandate ends and war breaks out between the Israelis, who have proclaimed their own state, and the Arabs who oppose it. In April 1949 an armistice is agreed and Jerusalem is divided. The entire Old City and the eastern part become part of Jordan while the western, and new part are incorporated into Israel. No major country recognised this disposition of the city.
1949-1966	Frequent skirmishes between Israelis and Jordanians on the line that divides the city.
1967	In June war breaks out between Syria, Egypt, and Jordan (Six Day War). Jerusalem, and all the territory west as far as the Jordan River falls to the Israelis. Israel annexes the eastern part of the city.
1967--	Arab Jerusalem becomes an occupied city.

PART II

TOURING JERUSALEM AND ENVIRONS

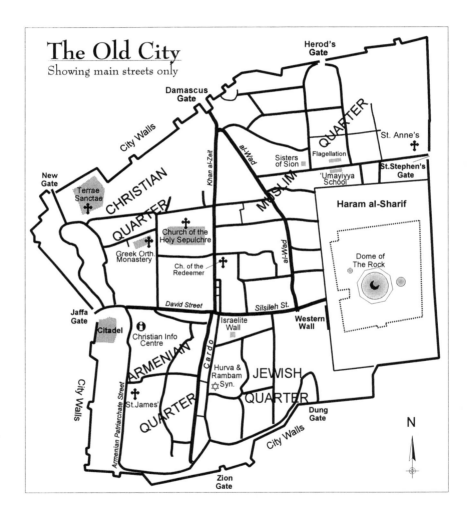

The Old City
Showing main streets only

Herod's Gate

Damascus Gate

City Walls

New Gate

Terrae Sanctae

CHRISTIAN QUARTER

MUSLIM QUARTER

St. Anne's

Sisters of Sion

Flagellation

'Umayiyya School

St.Stephen's Gate

Haram al-Sharif

Khan al-Zeit

al-Wad

al-Wad

Church of the Holy Sepulchre

Greek Orth. Monastery

Ch. of the Redeemer

Dome of The Rock

David Street

Silsileh St.

Jaffa Gate

Citadel

Christian Info Centre

Israelite Wall

Western Wall

Cardo

ARMENIAN QUARTER

Hurva & Rambam Syn.

JEWISH QUARTER

St.James'

City Walls

Armenian Patriarchate Street

Dung Gate

City Walls

N

Zion Gate

3. An Introduction to the Old City Quarters

The Four "Quarters"

Today the walled city is divided into four quarters, though of course they are not of equal size. They are the Muslim, Jewish, Christian and Armenian quarters. This division is certainly not historic, and while there is some early mention of Muslim and Jewish areas, the term "quarter" is a 19th C European designation. Communities have always tended to live close to sites they hold most sacred, and Jerusalem, with its varied religious and cultural mix, is no exception. Christians chose to live near to the Church of the Holy Sepulchre, Muslims in the vicinity of the Haram al-Sharif, Armenians around St. James' Cathedral and Jews as close as possible to the Western Wall.

non-exclusive divisions

In spite of this, and the fact that most people preferred to live among their like, each area was never totally homogeneous. Some Muslims lived in the Christian and Jewish quarters, and certainly by the last decades of the 19th C, there were Jews living in the southern Muslim and Armenian quarters. Although they may have had business interests there, I can find no evidence of Jews having lived in the Christian Quarter, a circumstance that (perhaps for political sensitivities) prevails today.

abundance of sub-divisions

A feature of these quarters, except perhaps for the Armenian, is that they became further divided according to denominations and background.

Take, for example, the area in front of the Western Wall which, until 1967, was a built up area and part of the Muslim Quarter. It was inhabited by Muslims from the Maghreb and known as the Magharibi. These were the descendants of Moors expelled from Spain after the re-conquest by Ferdinand and Isabella. Black African Muslims lived in the area around Bab al-Hitta, where they had their own hospices and madrassas.

Syrians join the Armenians

Among the Christians, Greek Orthodox and Latins tended to live separately, and other denominations had their own, often small, localities. The Syrian Orthodox did not live in the quarter at all, gravitating around their Monastery of St. Mark in the Armenian

Quarter. Since there was virtually no Protestant presence in the city till the mid 19th C, when this did arrive, it was mainly extra-mural.

together but separate

In the Jewish Quarter a similar situation developed, with Sephardim (Jews of Spanish and Maghreb origin) living together adjacent to their synagogues, while the Ashkenazi Jews (those of Eastern European background) did likewise. Even smaller Jewish groups such as Karaites and Yemenites congregated in their own little clusters.

A distinct Christian presence in the Muslim Quarter was established during the 19th C with the building (or rebuilding) of the churches and shrines along the Via Dolorosa.

In post 1967 Jerusalem the only quarter that remains virtually exclusive to a particular group is the Jewish Quarter.

RELIGIONS

The following explanations will hopefully help you find your way through the religious maze which is Jerusalem. While the descriptions below refer to people who dwell both within and without the walled city, you will encounter a potent concentration of them all during your wanderings around the quarters.

Christianity

Jerusalem exhibits a diversity of Christianity unmatched by any other city in the world. Many Westerners assume Arabs are Muslims, but since the inception of the faith many Arabs (as well as Jews) became followers. Though many converted to Islam in later centuries, a minority resisted.

Nearly all the indigenous population belong to the Greek Orthodox, Latin and Greek Catholic churches, but almost every other denomination is represented in the city by followers in holy orders. Most significant among them are the Eastern persuasions, many of which we in the west never encounter or thought were consigned to history!

The major church for Arabs living in or around Jerusalem is the **Greek Orthodox**, which should really be called the Eastern Orthodox in this part of the world. While the Greek clergy in the city use Greek for their liturgy, the Arabs, while following the traditional rite of the Greek and Byzantine Church, pray in Arabic – *Allah* is God for Christians as well as Muslims.

Next come the **Latins**, but they are considerably fewer in number. Although **Greek Catholics** (Melkites) make up the largest Christian denomination in Israel proper, they have few adherents in Jerusalem in spite of there being a patriarchate there.

Almost all Palestinian Christians are churchgoers and even if they do not attend on a regular basis *belong* to their church.

Other Churches

Armenian: The Armenian community in Jerusalem are not, of course, ethnic Arabs. Most identify with the Palestinians. Their numbers are estimated to be around 3000 persons. Their clergy's presence is very noticeable – you cannot miss the priests who wear black cassocks with pointed hoods.

Syrian Orthodox: The Syrian Orthodox Church is one of the oldest in Christendom. They claim to be *the* oldest. The language of the liturgy is Syriac (Aramaic), the language of Palestine at the time of Jesus. Most of their faithful are spread around the world. They are ethnic Arabs (though the largest community is in Southern India). They number about 500 in Jerusalem, with another 1,000 in Bethlehem.

Ethiopian Orthodox: Almost all the fewer than one hundred devotees are clergy. They can be recognised by their black cassocks with bright colourful linings and turbans. Their prayer language is ancient Ethiopian, Ge'ez.

Coptic Orthodox: The word Copt come from *Aiguptos,* the Greek name for the pre-Arab peoples of Egypt. In Egypt, where practically all of this denomination live, Copt is just another word for Christian. Although roughly ten percent of Egyptians are Copts they are not really ethnic Arabs. Most of those who live in Jerusalem can be called Palestinians. The clergy wear black cassocks and turbans.

Assyrian Church of the East: Also known as Nestorians, Chaldeans and the Church of Persia, the origins of this little-known denomination can be traced to the first century. Most of the faithful in the ME live in Iraq and Iran. Some 800 souls live in Jerusalem and the West Bank. Strangely enough, their leader in Jerusalem is British! And you may see him in the Old City streets wearing a grey cassock.

Smaller communities are the **Maronites** and the offshoots of some Orthodox Churches who have attached themselves to Rome. All mainstream – and quite a few not-so-mainstream – **Protestant** churches have followers and/or clergy in the city, but their overall number in relation to all the Christians is small. Many, if not all, of these are heavily engaged in missionary activity.

Judaism

There are two main Jewish groups, **Sephardim** and **Ashkenazim**. Sephardim are from Iberia (Sephard is Hebrew for Spain) from where they were expelled in 1492, settling all over North Africa, the Balkans and the Levant, some eventually finding their way to Jerusalem. With the establishment of the State of Israel and the consequential animosity towards Jews in the Arab world, most of those who had remained in North Africa immigrated to the new state. Many speak Arabic and it is often difficult to distinguish them from the Arab population.

Ashkenazim (from the word Ashkenaz, an old Hebrew word for Germany, come from Eastern Europe. Most Jews in Britain and the US are Ashkenazim.

In most areas of belief there is no difference between the two communities, although they adhere to separate customs.

As is well known, Saturday is the Jewish Sabbath. This starts at dusk on Friday and ends at dusk on Saturday. Friday is either a non-working day or more often a half day. Jewish festivals are also non-working days, starting the evening before. You can find a partial list of these on page 249.

constraints

The Jewish dietary code prohibits the consumption of pork, crustaceans and certain kinds of fish. Meat and milk may not be consumed within four hours of each other. Among the very orthodox a man will not sit next to a woman he does not know as she may be in her menstrual cycle which makes her ritually "unclean". Religious men do not cut their sideburns, hence the long curls around the ears so often seen.

The Jews who live in the Old City are almost all strictly observant, following every letter of the Law. However, the majority of Israelis are not religious, and they adhere to few, if any, of the ritual practices. In fact, surprising as it may seem, the majority of Israeli Jews are among the most secular people anywhere!

Islam

Of the two forms of Islam, Sunni and Shi'ite, all Muslims in Jerusalem are the former. They comprise the majority in the walled city and in the eastern city.

Like Jews, Muslims do not eat pork, but they have no restrictions on mixing milk and meat or on the consumption of shellfish. Alcohol is of course prohibited in Muslim law.

busy day of rest

Friday is the Muslim Sabbath, but it is not as strict an affair as is the Jewish one. After late morning prayers, shops etc open up, making it the most busy shopping day. In spite of what you may read, Palestinian Muslims as a whole are not extremists, those who are being a very small minority – and few of these live in Jerusalem. To most people Arabs are Muslims, in spite of the fact that a small minority are Christian (as mentioned above). Even Muslim Arabs themselves consider their ethnicity to be a part of their faith. I have met many non-observant Muslim Arabs, but none who admit to being totally secular.

4. The Muslim Quarter

INTRODUCTION

I have divided this quarter into two tours. The main one is from St Stephen's Gate along the Via Dolorosa, Tariq al-Wad and Tariq Bab al-Silsileh. The second tour – really intended for those with extra interest and time – is around Herod's Gate.

largest quarter

Occupying the northwestern part of the walled city, the Muslim Quarter is not only the largest of walled Jerusalem's quarters but it is also the most populous. Bounded on the north and east by the city ramparts, to the south by Tariq al-Silsileh and in the west by Souk Khan al-Zeit, its total area covers about 30 hectares.

Although now well built up, until the second half of the 19th C the very NW part of the quarter comprised mainly empty tracts of land. Only the increase in population throughout the late 19th C eliminated most of these empty areas.

For the visitor most of the interest in this quarter lies along the Via Dolorosa and the area west of and adjacent to the Haram al-Sharif.

mainly Muslim

The Muslim Quarter, apart from the churches and shrines along the Via Dolorosa, is mainly exactly what its name implies. Being in close proximity to the mosques of the Haram it has for centuries been the heart of the Muslim city.

In the last 20 years or so some properties in the al-Wad street vicinity have been purchased by, taken over or "returned" to Jewish religious groups and individuals, eager to establish their presence in this part of the city. The fact that Israelis can gain property in the Muslim Quarter, whereas Palestinians are not permitted to do the same in the Jewish Quarter can bring an outside observer to draw his own conclusions. An added irritant to the indigenous Palestinians is that the Israeli occupied buildings are frequently draped in the Israeli flag.

Muslims least well off

Of all the inhabitants of this city it is the Muslims who are generally the least well off. This is reflected in the quarter by overcrowding and the use of old, ramshackle buildings as dwelling places. A result is the general dirtiness of the area, with many corners being used to dump infrequently collected rubbish. Despite

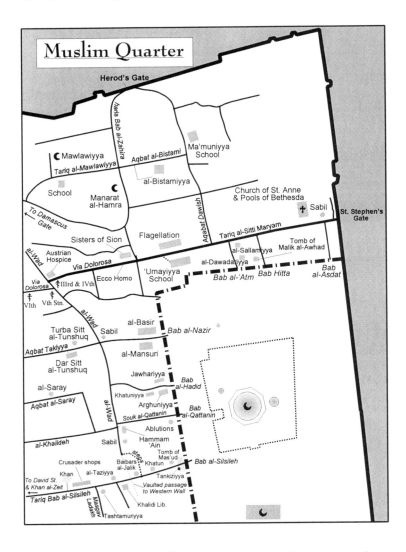

the fact that Muslim families are large, there are few play areas for the children who are forced to use the streets and alleys for recreation. As far as the Old City is concerned, the Muslim sector certainly seems to be the least invested in.

best accesses

Three gates give direct access to the quarter, two from the north which are the Damascus Gate (Bab al-Amud) and Herod's Gate, and St. Stephen's Gate from the east. My main walk starts from the latter, but you could also join it from the Damascus Gate by walking along Tariq al-Wad (the left fork at the bottom of the steps) for c225 metres to the corner of Via Dolorosa and the Austrian Hospice. You can then turn left and explore the route from St. Stephen's Gate (500 metres away) either in reverse or as written.

beware of street names!

A word on street names. Since the city came under Israeli control in 1967, in their zeal to Hebraise the city, many street names have been changed or Hebrew ones added to the Arabic. Naturally this has not pleased the local Palestinian population, and as a result many of these signs have been defaced.

Throughout this book I have tried to give the traditional and current street names, but some of the smaller ones may be known differently or not known at all! I have given alternatives where this might help. So please follow the directions and the plans. Different maps, depending on whether Israeli or Palestinian published, will give different names.

> ▸ **Walk No. 1 –   From St. Stephen's Gate along the Via Dolorosa to the Crusader Market**

MAIN FEATURES: **St. Stephen's Gate – Church of St. Anne – Pools of Bethesda – The Antonia – 'Umariyya School (Ist Station) – Monastery of the Flagellation (IInd Stn) – Ecce Homo Arch – Sisters of Sion Convent – Lithostraton – Polish Chapel (IIIrd Stn) – Armenian Catholic Patriarchate (IVth Stn) – Dar al-Sitt Tunshuq – Souk al-Qattanin – Gate of the Chain – The Tankiziyya – Crusader Market.** TIME: **1-2 hours.**

▸ St. Stephen's Gate

Gate of many names!

Directly opposite the Mount of Olives is the gate where, according to tradition, Jesus entered the city at the beginning of that decisive final week. It is known as **St. Stephen's Gate** to Christians because it was thought to be one of the possible locations where Stephen was stoned to death (Acts 7:54-60). (The other is outside the North or Damascus Gate – see page 134.) Muslims know it as Bab Sitti Maryam, Lady Mary's Gate, because it leads out to the Virgin Mary's tomb at the foot of the Mount of Olives. In Hebrew it is called Sha'ar ha-Arayot, the Lion's Gate, because of the carved lions at the sides of the arch. In Old and New Testament times it might have been the Sheep Gate mentioned in Nehemiah 3:1 and John 5:2.

Yet another name was bestowed by the Crusaders, whose choice was the Jehoshaphat Gate as it led into the valley of the same name (Wadi Kidron), while the early Ottomans knew it as Bab al-Ghor, or The Valley Gate, as it was the way to the Jordan Valley, al-Ghor in Arabic.

making way for cars

As seen today, it was built by Suleiman the Magnificent in 1538. A faded inscription on the inside of the gate records this fact for

41

posterity. The original design incorporated a right angled turn which exited to the south, but during the British Mandate the west wall was removed, eliminating this and permitting cars to enter. Outside the gate to the north there was once a pool, Birket Sitti Maryam, but this has now been filled in.

large pool

Just inside the gate and to the left is an entrance to al-Haram al-Sharif (no entry for tourists!), called **Bab al-Asbat**, the Gate of the Tribes. The Crusaders named it Paradise Gate. In the area outside it there once stood the largest of Jerusalem's pools, Birket Isra'il, which supplied water for use on the Haram. This pool had been dug in Second Temple times, and was fed by water from a small tributary of the Kidron, possibly via the pools of Bethesda just to the north.

Many 19th C visitors and researchers referred to this pool, which by then had completely dried up and was used for dumping refuse. There were two arches along the western side, and the southern edge abutted the northern wall of the Haram.

There are differing measurements as to its size, but E. Robinson, the noted archaeologist gave it as c120 metres long and c45 metres wide (E. Robinson, *Biblical Researches*, 1841). He even thought that the original pool may have continued further west and been part of the Antonia complex. By the time of British rule the pool was so full of rubbish that it was impossible to consider it as a pool and because it was an eyesore and health hazard, it was filled in.

much of Mary

The street inside the gate is Tariq Bab Sitti Maryam, the Gate of Lady Mary Street (the Israelis have renamed it in Hebrew Rehov Sha'ar Ha'Arayot, the Lion's Gate Street), and Jesus' mother is much remembered here. Immediately through the gate an ascending lane leads off to the right. On the far corner, facing the main street, is a fountain built by Suleiman and named for Mary, **Sabil Sitti Maryam**. Although uncared for now, the beautiful Kufic inscription is still prominent.

birthplace of Mary?

A few metres further on is a Greek Orthodox building that announces itself in large letters to be the **"Birthplace of the Virgin Mary"**. Step inside and down some stairs and the guardian will show you a rock-hewn room which, he will tell you, is where the mother of Jesus was born. Venture down a further flight of spiral stairs and through a narrow rock corridor to a partly hewn rock cave where, again he will inform you, Mary fell into eternal sleep. Next door is the more traditional

Inside St. Stephen's Gate

birthplace of Mary, while the equally more traditional site of her death is on Mount Zion.

▸ The Church of St. Anne

The traditional one

Out in the street turn west and another few metres along is the entrance to the Greek Catholic Monastery and Church of St. Anne, with the **Pools of Bethesda**, which pre-date the church, behind. This spot has been associated with the birthplace of Mary since the 2nd C.

History

The Church of St. Anne, named for the mother of Mary, was built by the Crusaders in the 12th C. It was constructed over the traditional birthplace, following the typical Crusader plan. After the reconquest of Jerusalem by Salah al-Din in 1187, the building was turned into a madrassa for Shafi'ite Muslims, and an inscription over the main entrance records this event. In spite of this, Christians continued to venerate the site as the home of Joachim and Anne, and from time to time were allowed to pray there. During early Ottoman times the church became unoccupied and fell into ruin.

Sultan's gratitude

In 1856 the Sultan Abdul al-Majid presented the place to Napoleon III in gratitude for France's help during the Crimean war. In the succeeding years it was completely restored, and given into the care of the White Fathers.

Crusader classic

The 12th C church, built in the classic Romanesque style, has been restored just as the original. It is a modest building devoid of embellishments. A cruciform basilica, it is divided into the main nave and two side aisles, each ending in an apse. The ceiling of the nave is higher than those of the side aisles, giving the impression that the structure inclines to one side.

Note the splendid entranceway, with a pointed arch, and hood mouldings. Look to your left to see the inscription mentioned above.

The Church of St. Anne 19th C

In the southern aisle, you will find the steps which lead down to the crypt that was once a rock hewn cave. Straight ahead is an altar to Mary, while to the left is her icon.

▸ The Pools of Bethesda

Jesus heals

The Pools of Bethesda are to the north and have been heavily excavated since 1870. There are two pools, both rock cut. That on the north, about 50 by 40 metres, is supposed to date from the 8th C BC, while the southerly one, some 60 by 70 metres in size, dates from the 3rd C BC. Around the beginning of the 1st C BC, grottos were dug out at the eastern end of the pools and used as healing pools or baths, as the waters were accredited with healing properties.

The older, north pool supplied water to the Temple area and was filled by run-off rainwater. In Herod's time it was known as the Sheep's Pool or Piscina Probatica, a favourite bathing place for the sick and disabled. It was this pool that was the scene of one of Jesus' healing miracles:

"Now there is in Jerusalem... a pool which is called in Hebrew Bethesda, having five porticoes. In these lay a multitude of those who were sick, blind and lame, waiting for movement of the waters; for an angel of the Lord went down at certain seasons into the pool, and stirred up the water; whoever... stepped in was made well... And a certain man was there, who had been thirty eight years in his sickness. When Jesus saw him... He said to him 'Do you wish to get well?' The sick man answered Him, 'Sir I have no man to put me into the pool when the water is stirred up'. Jesus said to him, 'Arise take up your pallet and walk.' And immediately the man became well..." John 5:1-9

After the rebuilding of the city by the Romans in AD 135, a temple to Seraphis Aesculapius was erected across the pools, and temples to this deity were always associated with healing sick people.

Byzantine building

In the 5th C a church was constructed over the pagan temple, and this was dedicated to Mary due to the 2nd C tradition that she was born near here. This church is depicted on the Madaba mosaic map in Jordan.

The church was a basilica, with the western half built over the pools, and the eastern on the site of the Roman temple. In order to build across the deep pool, arches were constructed that raised the church 15 metres above the pool bottom. You can still see one arch standing in the southern pool. The basilica was destroyed by the Sasanians in 614, but rebuilt afterwards. It was most likely destroyed again in 1016 by the fanatical Fatimid caliph, al-Hakim.

When the Crusaders took over the city they erected the new church dedicated to the birth of Mary, while building a small chapel on the site of the Byzantine edifice.

This is a complicated area to understand, and of great help is the explanatory diagram at the eastern end of the pool, as well as the historical notes inside the entranceway from the street. You are urged to read these.

spoiled by graffiti

After visiting the pools, continue walking along Tariq Bab Sitti Maryam, through the vaulting to the cross streets, about 80 metres. The short street to the left leads to **Bab Hitta**, a gate to the Haram. Just before the gate, on the right side, you will see the **Tomb of al-Malik al-Awhad**, a distant relative of Salah al-Din, dating from the end of the 13th C. Unfortunately, the quite fine facade of this former madrassa has been disfigured by Palestinian nationalist graffiti. On either side of the entranceway are recycled Crusader marble pillars. The window, just beyond, is decorated with elaborate Mameluke carving. Bab al-Hitta, or Remission Gate, at the end of the street has a wooden gate and vaulted antechamber dating from Ayyubid times. However as you may not enter the Haram from here, you will get but a peek of it.

Faisal of Iraq

Less than 50 metres further along Tariq Sitti Maryam, an arch spans the street and a side road, Tariq al-Malak Faisal, leads to **Bab al-'Atm**, another entrance to the Haram which is not for visitors. The name of this road was changed to al-Malak Faisal, as just inside the Haram is the tomb of Faisal II, the last king of Iraq, and cousin of King Hussein of Jordan, who was slain in the 1958 revolution. The gate itself is also sometimes referred to as Bab al-Faisal.

gloomy road

A short detour along Tariq Bab al-'Atm (or Faisal) is worthwhile, although being vaulted it is rather dim. To the left are some interesting Mameluke windows which look out onto the hall of the **al-Sallamiyya Madrassa**, a theological school built around 1340 by a certain al-Majd al-Sallami. Entrance to this is slightly further on.

The doorway is always ajar so a glance inside is in order. The portal, which is Mameluke, has a deep alcove with inset benches. Inside is a vaulted entrance hall, also with inset benches. This leads into a courtyard with what was a large hall to the north. As is quite common with many of these old institutions, parts have now been converted into homes as the area is overcrowded, and quite poor.

Further down is another madrassa, the **al-Dawadariyya** which was also a Sufi (Muslim mystic) monastery. This was built in 1295 by 'Alam al-Din Sanjar al-Dawadari, an army commander who served under both Baibars and Qala'un. The building has a fine entranceway and facade, which may be difficult to appreciate because of the dim light. It now serves as a kindergarten. At the end is the Bab al-'Atm or Gate of Darkness.

high spot

Return to the main street, which now is vaulted for c25 metres. The street name in Arabic changes here to Tariq al-Mujahaddin. Just past the vaulting, Aqabat Dawish turns off to the north (right) and eventually reaches Herod's Gate (see Walk 1B below). The beginning of this initially stepped street, with its buttresses and vaulting is very picturesque and photogenic. I find it one of the most

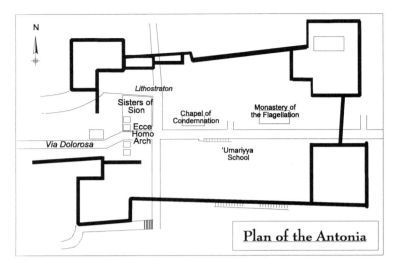

N

Lithostraton

Sisters of Sion

Chapel of Condemnation

Monastery of the Flagellation

Ecce Homo Arch

Via Dolorosa

'Umariyya School

Plan of the Antonia

attractive street views in the Old City.

The route now begins to climb towards what was an acropolis and site of the Antonia, a tower and fortress of considerable importance in Roman Jerusalem. Its elevated position may not be immediately clear today, but it can be better appreciated from the 'Umariyya school (see below) or during your visit to the Haram al-Sharif.

▶ The Antonia

The Antonia fortress was built over the area that includes today the 'Umariyya school, the Monastery of the Flagellation, and the Sisters of Sion convent. As the Antonia Tower has been accepted by Christians since the 13th C to be the site of the Roman Praetorium where Pontius Pilate had Jesus condemned and scourged, the first and second stations on the Via Dolorosa are marked here. In spite of this tradition, the situation of this office was in all probability the site of the Citadel by the Jaffa Gate. Such a prognosis throws the entire route of the Via Dolorosa into doubt – but there you have it!

tower of Hananel?

Some sort of tower existed on the rock incline here in the reign of the Seleucid Antiochus IV, who had it demolished. (Could this have been the Tower of Hananel mentioned along with the Sheep Gate in Nehemiah 3:1?). In the second century BC the Hasmoneans built a new tower on the site, the Baris, which served as a stronghold until Pompey's occupation in 63 BC.

named for Antony

Around 36 BC Herod rebuilt the structure and named it after his friend Mark Antony. Josephus describes it thus:

"Antonia, situated at the junction of two colonnades...was built on a rock... It was the work of King Herod and revealed in the highest degree the grandeur of his conceptions. In the first place from the very bottom the rock

was faced with polished stone slabs both for ornament and to ensure that anyone who tried to climb...would slip off; next before the actual tower was a one metre wall, and inside this the whole elevation of Antonia rose 20 metres into the air. The interior was like a palace in spaciousness and completeness; for it was divided into rooms of every kind to serve every need, colonnades, bathroom, and wide courtyards where troops could encamp... In general design it was a tower with four other towers attached, one at each corner; of these three were 25 metres high, and the one at the SE corner 38 metres, so that the whole Temple could be viewed..."   Josephus, Wars, V:237

destroyed

In AD 66 during the First Jewish Revolt the fort was captured by the Jews. After Titus retook the city in AD 70 the stronghold was totally rased.

► 'Umariyya School

Although the entrance to the 'Umariyya school is situated a few metres past the Monastery of the Flagellation, for the sake of good order, especially if you are following the Way of the Cross, it should be visited first. It is there that the **First Station** of the Via Dolorosa is marked, and where the processions begin. It is approached up a flight of steps on the left and is officially only open to visitors out of school hours. Once up the stairs entry is into a courtyard.

iwan with a view

Most of the construction is mid 19th C when it was used as a Turkish barracks. Go up some steps to the south where you'll come to the oldest part of this site, consisting of the remains of a 14th C Mameluke madrassa, perhaps built on part of a pre-existing structure.

The huge arch is an *iwan* and has two windows that furnish a magnificent view of the Haram al-Sharif and the Dome of the Rock. From here you will be able to appreciate the Antonia's commanding position over this significantly strategic area.

► Monastery of the Flagellation

Palm trees and flowers

From the school, retrace your steps and just through the arch at the top of the incline you come back to the **Monastery of the Flagellation**, the site of the **Second Station** of the Via Dolorosa. You enter through an arched gate into a very attractive courtyard, with palm trees and colourful flowers.

The Crusaders built two churches here in the 12th C, the Church of the Flagellation on the right (E), and the Church of the Condemnation on the left (W). After the Muslim reconquest the site was abandoned and lost to them, and the buildings were later used for many other purposes, including a rubbish dump, a stable and a weavers' workshop.

crown of thorns

In the early 19th C the place was just a ruin, but in 1838 Ibrahim Pasha, the Egyptian ruler of Jerusalem, gave the site to the

Franciscans, and the Chapel of the Flagellation was re-fabricated in its medieval style by Maximilian, King of Bavaria, a few years later. You will see the stone plaque to the left of the entrance which records this. In·1927 it was further restored and this is the edifice standing today.

The chapel is a single aisle affair, with a dome over the altar. Note the crown of thorns which embellishes the dome·(Matthew 27:29). In the sanctuary are three stained glass windows. The centre one portrays the scourging of Jesus, the one on the right the release of Barabas and, to the left, Pilate washing his hands after having condemned Jesus to the cross.

ancient pavement

In the early 20th century excavations to the west revealed the remains of a medieval chapel, probably dating from the mid 13th C, but its history is rather obscure. This was rebuilt in 1903 into the present **Chapel of the Condemnation**. Outside the entrance are large Roman flagstones that continue into the **Convent of the Sisters of Sion** next door. This pavement is taken to be the **lithostraton** (see below), but in reality it dates back to the Roman city of Aelia Capitolina.

Hadrian's Arch

Back in the street, which can now be called the **Via Dolorosa** (though 19th C maps do not call it so), continue west till the next crossroads, and on the north side (left) is the Convent of the Sisters of Sion. Immediately past the convent is the **Ecce Homo Arch** which spans the Via Dolorosa, so-called because tradition has it that this was where *"Jesus... came out wearing the crown of thorns and a purple robe. And Pilate said 'Behold the Man!'"* (John 19:5). However, the arch was in fact built much later by the Emperor Hadrian in AD 135. It was part of a triple-arched triumphal gate. The part that spans the Via Dolorosa is the central span, while the remains of the northern one can be seen inside the Sisters of Sion Convent. The southern span has long since gone. On the west face of the central arch was an inscription that read TOLLE TOLLE CRUCIFIGE EUM. Today you can only see the first TOLLE, and this very faintly, on the left side.

► Sisters of Sion Convent

The convent is built on land purchased by Fr. Marie-Alphonse Ratisbonne in 1857. (Fr. Ratisbonne was a convert from Judaism.) The architect designed the convent's church, the Church of Ecce Homo, to incorporate the northern remains of the Hadrianic gateway, and it forms part of the church's choir. The wall of rock at the rear of the church is a section of counter-scarpment of the northern protective moat of the Antonia.

the actual pavement?

The convent is best known for the pavement or Lithostraton (Greek) or Gabbatha (Aramaic) referred to in John 19:13, large pieces of which are preserved within the convent. However, like so much else in this city, tradition does not equate with the facts, since the paving dates from the Roman rebuilding of the city as Aelia

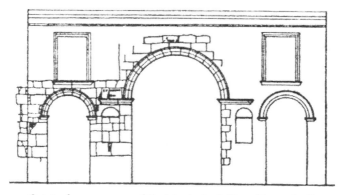

Original appearance of Hadrian's Arch (Ecce Homo Arch)

Capitolina in 135. This notwithstanding, some believe (wishfully) that although it may be from a later date, John's Gabbatha was still on this location. The pavement lies about two metres below the surface of the road today.

games with the condemned

Grooves were chiselled in the smooth paving to prevent chariots from slipping. In an area where the Game of the King, played with the unfortunates about to be executed, is thought to have been enacted, playing boards incised in the paving stones by the Roman soldiers are noticeable.

hewn pool

The pavement stands above an ancient cistern or pool equated by researchers with the Struthion (Ostrich) Pool mentioned by Josephus (Wars V:11:4). This was a double pool hewn out of solid rock. The reservoir had a row of arches and a barrel-vaulted roof. All you can see of this today is a very small section.

The convent is open to visitors every day except Sundays between 8.30-12.30 and from 14.00-17.00. The sisters will show you around. Entry is limited, and often because of the many groups, the doors are locked. If so, you will just have to wait. As the convent incorporates a pilgrims' hospice you may also stay there (see section on accommodation).

Greek grotto

Just west of the Sisters of Sion Convent is a Greek Orthodox building with a sign "The Prison of Christ". This is built upon part of the Antonia acropolis counterscarp, and incorporates some grottos, one of which the Greeks say was the prison where Jesus was held before his trial. The Orthodox begin their procession from here on the Orthodox Good Friday.

downhill walk

The road continues west and downhill to where it ends in a T-junction with Tariq al-Wad, or the Valley Road, so named because it follows the Tyropoeon Valley which cuts the city in two. It is so built over that it is not readily recognisable as a valley. A turn to the north (right) will lead you to the Damascus Gate and south (left) to Tariq Bab al-Silsileh and the Western Wall area.

did Jesus tread here?

On the right corner is the **Austrian Hospice** which was used as a municipal hospital until the late 1980s. It was built in 1863. On the left, in the Tariq al-Wad, some stone slabs belonging to the road of the Roman city have been excavated. Long hidden 2-3 metres under the surface they were discovered in the early 1980s during the placing of a new sewer system. They were then relaid on the modern road. Tariq al-Wad was an important and perhaps porticoed artery of Roman/Byzantine Jerusalem.

▸ Third and Fourth Stations of the Cross

At the end of "Via Dolorosa Street" and directly to the left is a chapel, now closed. In 1947-8 the chapel was renovated with help from Polish soldiers, and is sometimes known as the Polish Catholic Chapel. (It is now part of the adjacent Armenian Catholic building.) The chapel's entrance is on al-Wad Street with the gate flanked by two pillars, which are essentially pieces of the same one. The pillar was found partially buried in the nearby ground. The column when erected marked the "actual" spot where Jesus stumbled carrying his cross and, as such, indicates the **Third Station of the Cross**. Above the closed door is a carving of Jesus stumbling.

Byzantine bath?

The **Armenian Catholic Patriarchate** and the Church of Our Lady of the Spasm is right next door and marks the **Fourth Station of the Cross**. This was the site of the Hammam al-Sultan, the ruins of which still stood in the 19th C. Some archaeologists believe that Byzantine thermae could have existed here long before. Excavations in the 1870s exposed mosaics as deep as six metres below the surface and these could have been from a three apsed 13th C Crusader Church. In one of the apses was a Byzantine mosaic depicting two sandals. Thirteenth century tradition believed that these were the footprints of Mary, and later the spot where Jesus met his mother. The present structure dates from 1880, but some of the older remains have been preserved.

The IVth Station of the Cross

two routes

From here you can either continue along the route of the Via Dolorosa, or explore more of the Muslim Quarter. My main route is the latter, but I first continue with a sub-route that encompasses the former. If you wish to skip this or walk it later, turn to page 52.

▸ **Walk No. 1B –**   **Sub-route continuing along the Via Dolorosa**

MAIN FEATURES: **Franciscan Oratory (Vth Station) – Church of St. Veronica (VIth Stn.) – Chapel of VIIth Stn.**
Some 40 metres past the Armenian Catholic Church the Via Dolorosa turns right into Tariq al-Alam, or just "Via Dolorosa".

sacred stone
The **Fifth Station of the Cross** is on the left corner. Tradition has it that on this spot stood the house of Simon the Pharisee who helped carry Jesus' cross. This small oratory was erected by the Franciscans in 1850 who built into the west wall the stone that originally marked this station. The depression in the stone is said to have been caused by a knock from the Cross, or by Jesus' hand when he leaned against it. It has been made deeper by the hands of countless pilgrims touching this revered indentation.

pretty pottery
This stepped street with its overhead buttresses is the most attractive section of the Way of the Cross, and almost every shop is aimed at the tourist. There are a few places selling fine Armenian decorated pottery, and if you are interested in these, you will want to pause and look.

The **Sixth Station of the Cross** is located half way up on the left, just where a buttress spans the alley. This is said to be the place where Veronica wiped the sweat from Jesus' face. In the words of Mark Twain:

> *"The strangest thing about the incident that has made her* [Veronica's] *name so famous, is, that when she wiped the perspiration away, the print of the Saviour's face remained upon the handkerchief, a perfect portrait, and remains so unto this day. We knew this because we saw this handkerchief in a cathedral in Paris, in another in Spain and two others in Italy!"*   Innocents Abroad, 1869

The Station is marked by the **Church of the Holy Face and St. Veronica**. There seems to have once been a Byzantine church and later a Crusader monastery here. The building, which was acquired by the Greek Catholics towards the end of the 19th C, includes a church dedicated to St. Veronica and a renovated crypt. It is now a convent of the Little Sisters of Jesus.

judgment posted
The street comes to an end at a T-junction with the Souk Khan al-Zeit. When the Romans built Aelia Capitolina, the market street formed an intersection (decumanus) with the cardo, and as such was marked by a tetrapylon. Opposite is the **Seventh Station of the Cross**. This spot has been, since Crusader times, associated with the Porta Judicaria or **Judgment Gate** where the Romans posted notices of execution for the condemned, but as part of the Way of the Cross it marks the Seventh Station where Jesus fell again. This is a highly

significant stop on the route, for it was to show pilgrims that the site of the Church of the Holy Sepulchre indeed lay outside the walls in the first century AD. In medieval times, as now, it was very difficult for the faithful to visualise the city as it once was. So here, it was pointed out, was the gate that led out to the site of execution. The second north wall ran very close to this spot.

The site was purchased by the Franciscans in 1875, and in 1894 they erected a chapel. A red granite pillar from the original Roman tetrapylon marks the Seventh Station.

All the other Stations of the Cross are in the Christian Quarter and are dealt with in that chapter. For a detailed list of the 14 Stations of the Cross see box on page ?.

> **Continuation of Walk No. 1 from page 50**

▸ Dar (or Saray) al-Sitt Tunshuq

Fit for a lady!

Continue south on al-Wad Street, which here is mostly vaulted, for about 100 metres past the Fifth Station of the Cross, till you reach a crossroads. The street to the right is 'Aqbat Takiyya. Walk up about 120 metres and on the south (left) is the **Dar (or Saray) al-Sitt Tunshuq,** dating from 1388. Built as a dwelling for a lady of uncertain origins, this fine Mameluke monument was converted into a charitable institute by one of Suleiman's wives. Towards the end of the 19th C it became the palace or saray of the Ottoman governor. Later it was turned into an orphanage. There is also a large carpentry workshop.

Mameluke magnificence

The Mameluke facade, if restored, could be one of the finest in Jerusalem, with four entranceways. Walk up the street to the last entrance and then make your way back to al-Wad St. as you view the building. The last entrance, the furthest up the street, is the highest, and is elaborately decorated. It has a moulded frame with very faded and dirty-looking orange and white masonry, with a black notched course. Above the window is an inscription taken from the Koran, Sura 15:46-55. To the east (lower down the road) is a large round window that opens to the main chamber.

Just past this is the next entrance (the third up the street). The widest of the four, it is closed with a steel and mesh gate. Inside, beneath all the vaulting, is the busy carpentry. This entrance is the least impressive, consisting mainly of orange and black stone. Lower down the street the next entrance is also blocked up. This is the most ornate. At the top is a half dome with stone *muqarnas* inside. Below is the grubby orange and white masonry so common in these Jerusalem monuments from the Mameluke period. The final doorway (the lowest down the street) leads into the school and has been replaced.

Tunshuq's tomb

Facing the third entrance is the **Turba Sitt al-Tunshuq**, the tomb of the lady who built the palace. The tomb chamber is on the right side. This edifice with its 12 metre high dome was later converted into a private dwelling. Return to al-Wad street.

wasted fountain

Cross over al-Wad and enter Tariq Ala al-Din (or Tariq Bab al-Nazir) which leads to the Bab al-Nazir of the Haram. On the corner is a finely carved fountain, the **Sabil al-Nazir** built by Suleiman in 1537. This, like so much else, has fallen into a state of near ruin, and nobody seems to care. Such a monument in most European cities would have been restored long ago, whoever had to foot the bill!

blind inspector

Some 50m down on the left is the **hospice** built by Ala al-Din Aydughdi al-Basir dating from 1270. When he became blind Sultan Baibars made him an al-Nazir, inspector, of the Haram. Above the entrance is an inscription recording the founder's name. He was so notable that his judgments were respected by almost everyone, and he gained the name al-Basir, the knowledgeable. The entranceway leads into a courtyard surrounded by rooms. On the east side of the portal is a window with its original grille. Inside is al-Basir's tomb.

black guards

In Ottoman times the hospice was a billet for Sudanese who served as guards on the Haram. It is now used by African Muslims who have a mosque there.

On the opposite side of the street is the **Ribat al-Mansuri**, a hospice for Muslim pilgrims built in the 1280s by the Sultan Qala'un. The very inset entrance, with inset benches and an arch above, leads via a passage into a large open courtyard and the hospice's rooms are around this.

During later Ottoman times it also housed the Sudanese guards of the Haram. Part was converted into a prison.

At the end of the street is the **Bab al-Nazir**, or the Gate of the Inspector or Watchman.

winding street

Back on al-Wad St. continue south under the vaulting to the next turning on the east (left). This is Tariq Bab al-Hadid and, after curving a bit, reaches the gate of like name to the Haram. Most of the buildings in this street are Mameluke, and although the once glorious facades could do with a good scrub and restoration, their original character can still be appreciated.

Walk along and through the winding tunnel. On the north side of the street, just before the gate is the **Jawhariyya Madrassa** and **Ribat Jawhariyya**, a pilgrim hospice. These were built in 1440 by a Jawhar al-Qunuqbayi, an Ethiopian.

chevron pattern

The entrance portal has the orange and white stonework with two windows opening to the hall on the right. On the upper part of the facade – to the east – are three windows. One is plain, but the other two have chiselled chevron decoration around them, and the centre one also has three levels of *muqarnas* at the top.

The building now houses the Department of Islamic Archaeology,

and is built on two levels. Damaged in the early 1970s by archaeological tunnelling, it was restored in the 1980s.

Governor of Damascus

At the end of the street you now reach Bab al-Hadid, the Iron
Gate, which dates in its present form from the 1350s. On the south
side of the road, just before the gate, is the **Arghuniyya**, the tomb
and madrassa of Arghun al-Kamili who once served as a governor of
Damascus. This madrassa was built in 1358. The facade, like many
other monuments from the Mameluke period, has the familiar faded
orange and white stonework and a high entrance portal with
windows on each side and the builder's inscription all around the
recess. The east window looks into the tomb chamber and has the
original grille, while the west window has been made into a "cubby
hole" shop.

To the west of this is the **Khatuniyya Madrassa**. A vaulted
passage leads into a courtyard enclosed by rooms that were once
used for prayer or study. Now they are residential.

▸ Souk al Qattanin

Aleppo-like souk

Back on Tariq al-Wad, a walk of just over 50 metres south will bring
you to a crossroads with the **Souk al-Qattanin** or Cotton Merchants'
Market, to the left. This was once one of the finest souks in the city,
and reminds me of the outstanding souks of Aleppo. Now, to the
detriment of the city, it is dark, dreary and deserted. Constructed in
1337 by Tankiz al-Nasira for the Sultan al-Nasir al-Din Muhammad
it had become a junk yard by the 19th C. It was cleared and repaired
in the latter part if the 19th C on instructions of the Sultan Abdul
Hamid, and restored further during the British Mandate.

This completely covered souk, with gates at both ends, reaches the
Bab al-Qattanin of the Haram (no entry for visitors). Sadly, this
souk is off the main market area of the city, and has been virtually
abandoned. From my experience in other cities of the Middle East,
I am sure it could be converted into a local and tourist shopping area
of very great attraction. Unfortunately, the finance for such projects
usually goes to other areas of the city.

khan and baths

Because it is scarcely frequented, the place is very dimly lit. The
95 metre long souk is covered by a vaulted roof. There are 30 pairs
of recesses, some shops and some workshops with living quarters
above. Nearly all these recesses appear to be permanently locked.

On the left by the 8th recess (from al-Wad St) there was once a
khan, the Khan al-Qattanin, dating from the middle of the 15th C.
Facing was the Khan Tankiz, and south (right) of recesses 17-20 is
the closed up porch of the Hammam al-Shifa' baths, built in the mid
14th C. At the 21st recess an opening leads to the ablutions of the
Haram.

public conveniences

The covered souk ends with steps that lead up to the Bab al-
Qattanin. This fine gate, with carved wood panels, was built in 1336,
and appears to have then been a new entrance to the Haram. Just

south of the gate is the **Bab al-Mathara** or Ablution Gate which leads to the ablutions mentioned above (you may use them).

Right at the beginning on the south side is the **Hammam al-'Ain.** The entrance to this is just around the corner in Tariq al-Wad. Once in a very ruined condition, the Department of Islamic Archaeology restored it in 1984, but it is now closed. Just past the Hammam on the left is another of Suleiman's now dilapidated fountains. Most passers-by will not even notice it!

supporting vaults

Tariq al-Wad ends with a tunnel that emerges near the Western Wall plaza (see page 125). Just before, an ascending flight of steps leads off to the left, reaching Tariq al-Silsileh, the Street of the Chain (in Hebrew, Rehov Ha'Shilshelet). The tunnel is made up of the vaults that support the street above, as it crosses the Tyropoeon Valley (see below). The vaults were buried under centuries of rubble, and cleared in the late 1970s to enable direct access from Tariq al-Wad (and the Damascus Gate) to the Western Wall. This route is used by the ultra-orthodox Jews from the Mea She'arim Quarter, north of the gate. It makes al-Wad one of the few streets in the Old City where these curiously clad men rub shoulders with traditionally robed Arab inhabitants of the Muslim Quarter.

Roman decumanus

At the top of the steps is Tariq Bab al-Silsileh, which could easily be called "Mameluke Turba Street" as it has so many tombs from that era. Almost facing and just around a corner are steps which lead down to the Western Wall plaza. It is one of the main arteries of the Old City, linking up with David Street and Souk Khan al-Zeit. It dates from Hasmonean and Herodian times. The eastern end is above the Western Wall plaza. In the Roman city it formed part of the E/W decumanus that ran from the (now) Jaffa Gate.

Turn east (left) into the Tariq, and continue towards the **Bab al-Silsileh** or Chain Gate. About 50 metres down, on your left, just through a vaulted section is the Turba Khatun, a mid 14th C tomb of an unknown woman.

A further c40 metres will bring you almost to the gate,

The Street of the Chain, 19th C

55

but just before it is the **Tomb of Sa'ad al-Din Mas'ud** an official of the Sultan al-Nasir Muhammad (c1294-1309). The entranceway with *muqarna* decoration is beneath the vaulting. The room to the east is the tomb chamber and has two windows, both with grilles.

▸ Bab al-Silsileh (Gate of the Chain)

This, the main gate to the Haram al-Sharif, is preceded by a small square. It lies in an almost straight line from the Jaffa Gate, the route which formed the major E/W decumanus of the Roman and Byzantine city.

subterranean aqueduct

On the south side of the square is the **Tankiziyya** (see below). To the west, facing the gate, is the **Sabil Bab al-Silsileh** erected by, guess who? This lovely fountain's upper arch is decorated with Arab geometric designs. In the centre is a rosette, a Crusader emblem, placed here by the fountain's builder. Below is a sarcophagus which was used as a receptacle for the water that was channelled here through a subterranean aqueduct. To the east are twin gates: the **Bab al-Sakina** or Gate of Divine Presence and permanently closed, and south of it the actual **Bab al-Silsileh**, the Gate of the Chain.

the still Beautiful Gate

The gates originally formed an entrance to the Crusader temple area when they were called the Beautiful Gate. Much of the Crusader work survives in spite of Ayyubid rebuilding in the late 12th C.

The capitals of the gate's pillars are of carved floral, animal and human motifs, although the last two have been so defaced as to render them almost unrecognisable. Muslim law does not allow representations of living creatures. Above the gates are cupolas.

▸ The Tankiziyya

Mufti's residence

The building on the south (right) side, is a significant Islamic building, known as the **Tankiziyya,** a madrassa named for Tankiz al-Nasiri.

From 1329 al-Nasiri was governor of Damascus. Besides building the Souk al-Qattanin (see above page 54) he was responsible for other buildings in both Jerusalem and Damascus. He was buried in Damascus in 1343. During the reign of Sultan Qait Bey the building was the seat of the head *qadi*, and was known as the *Mahkama* or tribunal. In late Ottoman times it served as a court of justice. In the 1920s the structure was completely restored, and became the home of the not-so-pleasant Mufti of Jerusalem, Amin al-Husseini. After 1948 the Jordanians turned it into a religious seminary.

modern appendages

The building has now been requisitioned by the Israel Police so you cannot go inside. However it does have a very fine facade, even though it may be marred by a modern security door and CCTV camera. The Tankiziyya is built above **Wilson's Arch** (see page 127). It is thought that the council chamber where the Sanhedrin (Jewish religious court) met in late second temple times was situated in the general vicinity; some think it was on this spot.

The high and inset entrance which adjoins the outer arch of the Chain Gate incorporates three rows of *muqarnas* above which is a half-dome. The builder's inscription runs around the course above, and at both ends is his blazon, a chalice, with another above the actual door.

About turn and make your way back west on Tariq Bab al-Silsileh.

tombs of Muslim warriors

Just by the steps, on the right, where you ascended from al-Wad Street, you will see on the west corner the **Tomb of Baibars al-Jalik** who fought alongside the Sultan Qala'un when he defeated the Mongols at the Battle of Homs in 1281. The tomb chamber is the one closest to the steps.

About 45 metres further along on the left is the **Tomb of Baraka Khan**, now completely rebuilt inside and with a restored Mameluke facade. Baraka Khan was one of the leaders of the Turkomen who invaded Syria in the late 1230s and 1240s. They restored Muslim rule to Jerusalem after al-Kamil had handed the city back to Frederick II (see History page 25). In the last part of the 19th C the building was rebuilt by the Khalidi family, and became the Khalidi library with over 12,000 books and manuscripts.

more tombs and many trinkets

Opposite on the north side of Tariq Bab al-Silsileh is **al-Taziyya**, a madrassa named for Sayf al-Din Taz, and built c1361. Taz was an official of Sultan al-Nasir Muhammad. The facade has a lintel with a dedication inscription and insignia. There were two tomb chambers at street level which are now shops, and the upper level, typically 18th C Ottoman, is used for dwellings.

Around here are many souvenir and trinket shops. The shopkeepers know that at the top of the street you will be entering a very touristy area and are bent on taking some money off you before you get there. The touting is, therefore, very pronounced!

fancy facade

Another short distance on the south side of the now vaulted street, and on the corner of Harat Maydan or – as it is called in Hebrew – Misgav Ladakh Street (not a translation) that leads into the Jewish Quarter, is the **Tashtamuriyya** endowed by Sayf al-Din Tashtamur around 1382. He was an important adviser to the Sultan al-Ashraf Nasir al-Din Sha'ban (1363 to 1376). He retired to Jerusalem and built this madrassa where he lived and was interred. The entranceway on the Tariq was almost in the centre of the facade, and is elaborately decorated. The tomb chamber to the west of this is domed, and has two windows with iron grilles and marble mosaic on the sills. In the chamber are two tombs, the further one of Tashtamur's son. On the south wall is a mihrab. Although not generally open to visitors you may be allowed to look around. Ask someone.

▸ Crusader Market (Khan al-Sultan)

Facing are small shops that have been built into the outside of the **Crusader Market**. Twenty metres before the end of the street you come to the entrance to the market, later the **Khan al-Sultan**. This was rebuilt by Sultan al-Zahir Sayf al-Din Barquq around 1387. Khans were important places in cities as they provided lodging, storage, stables and trading areas for out-of-town merchants. This well-preserved khan is today, as are so many like places in the souks of Damascus and Aleppo, occupied by small workshops and the like.

quite deserted

Turn right into the now almost deserted area. On each side of this entrance passage are shops with living and storage areas in the galleries above. At the end is a large courtyard with rooms all around the sides. Like the Souk al-Qattanin this market is now mainly unused, except for those parts which have been turned into dwellings.

important junction

Back on the main street it soon meets a point where many streets and alleyways come together, the main ones being David Street, Souk Khan al-Zeit and Jewish Quarter Street.

From here you can either walk to the Damascus Gate along Souk Khan al-Zeit (500 metres) or begin exploring the Jewish or Armenian Quarters.

▸ Walk No. 2 – From Herod's Gate to Damascus Gate

MAIN FEATURES: **This short tour starts from Herod's Gate, located about half a kilometre east of the Damascus Gate, takes you through the northern part of the Muslim Quarter to the Damascus Gate.** TIME: **30-50 minutes.**

▸ Herod's Gate

The appellation "Herod's", was given to this gate by medieval Christian pilgrims because it led to Deir Abu Adas, the Monastery of the Father of Lentils situated near the bottom end of Shari'a Dawish and thought to have been the site of the Palace of Herod Antipater. The Muslims call it Bab al-Zahra, roughly meaning the Gate where they Stay Awake. Al-Zahra was the name of a Muslim cemetery (now gone) opposite, where those who had undertaken the *haj*, pilgrimage to Mecca, were buried. According to the Koran these will be the first to be resurrected. In Hebrew it is known as Sha'ar Ha-Prakhim, the Gate of Flowers, due to its floral decoration.

easier entry

The present gate provides direct entrance into the Old City. Formerly, though, it was a tower that was entered via a wicket on its eastern side, and opened into the inner side of the wall that faced the city. The present arrangement dates from the late 1870s, when the increase in population in this area required speedier and unimpeded access. You can still see the remains of the eastern entrance, with its pointed arch.

Jewish inhabitants

This NE part of the city was where the Jews lived until the Crusader conquest. It was in this area that Godfrey de Bouillon

managed to break into the city, at a point just east of the present
Herod's Gate on 15th July 1099. A huge cross was erected on the
spot which remained as long as the Crusaders ruled the city.

After massacring all the Jews and most of the Muslims, the
Crusaders settled Arab Christians from the north in the area and it
became known as the "Syrian Quarter". Many churches were built,
but none survive as such.

differing names

Pass through the gate and turn left, following the road around to
the right. There can be some real confusion with the street name
here. The municipality (Israeli) call it Derekh Sha'ar Ha'Prakhim
(Flower Gate Way), whereas most non Israeli maps show it as
Shari'a Muhammad Dawish. It eventually leads to Tariq Bab Sitti
Maryam, not far from the Monastery of the Flagellation (see page
47).

About 150 metres down on the east (left) side is the **Ma'muniyya
Girls School,** on the site of the 12 C Church of St. Mary Magdalene.
The first church built here was used by Syrian Orthodox, and the
Syrian Patriarch of Antioch visited it in 1166. In the late 12th C an
official of Salah al-Din, Faris al-Din Ma'mun, turned it into a
madrassa. Some time later it fell into disuse but as late as the mid
19th C ruins of the church could still be seen. Now there is nothing.

mystic's madrassa

Continuing south for c30 metres turn west (right) into 'Aqbat al-
Bistami, and 60 metres along on the south (left) side you will come
to the **al-Bistamiyya,** a madrassa dedicated to Sheikh Abdullah, a
Shafi'i mystic. Although there are no inscriptions this building is
generally accepted as being his madrassa. The inside is inhabited by
the caretaker and comprises of rooms around a court. An entrance at
the SE corner of this court, set in a semicircular vaulted niche, opens
onto two vaulted rooms with mihrabs. The room to the east contains
a tomb, but not of the founder as he is buried in the Mamilla
Cemetery (see page 207). Not normally open to visitors you may ask
to be allowed in.

old tower

Continue west on 'Aqbat al-Bistami for the 70 or so metres to the
crossroads and you reach Shari'a al-Zahra (or Ha'Tsari Ha'Adom),
which to the right leads back to Herod's Gate. Turn south (left) and
c40 metres down on the right is the 16th C **Manarat al-Hamra,** the
red minaret. Although the tower is 16th C, the mosque by it has been
virtually rebuilt.

dancing Dervishes

About face and return to the crossroads, turning west (left) into
Tariq al-Mawlawiyya. Carry on till you come to a school, the
Mawlawiyya School on the left. Just past it, on the right is a narrow
alley that is entered through a tunnel. In the middle of this vault you
will see a door on the right with a red arrow pointing down. In here
is the **Mawlawiyya Mosque.** Formerly a modest Crusader church it
became a mosque in the early 13th C. Unfortunately this building is
not open to visitors, but it is still worth a glance.

59

The original 12th C church, measuring about 14 by 7 metres, was explored by E. Pierotti. In his *Jerusalem Explored* (1864) he found that the church had three aisles all of which ended in apses. Four central pillars supported the groin vaulted roof. After the Crusader withdrawal it became a mosque, and later a Dervish convent. The Mawlawis were known as the Dancing Dervishes.

traditional appearance

This whole area is quite densely populated and, though renovated over the past years, retains a very traditional appearance. I just like to wander about poking into the side alleys which are often vaulted and buttressed. This area of the Old City has remained totally Palestinian.

From here a picturesque winding street leads you to the **Damascus Gate** and the new **Lu'lu Mosque**. The modern structure includes the **tomb of Badr al-Din Lu'lu Ghazi** who endowed the place in 1374.

5. The Christian Quarter

INTRODUCTION

The Christian Quarter covers the NW part of the Old City, encompassing an area of c18 hectares. It is the second largest of the Old City's quarters. As you will easily see, it is situated at a higher elevation than the rest of the city. The entrances to it are either from the Jaffa or New Gates. (Walk No. 1 below starts from the former.)

The quarter is delineated on the east side by the Souk Khan al-Zeit and by David Street to the east. This area was only incorporated into the city with the building of Aelia Capitolina (see History, page 18).

following the faith

As explained in the Introduction to the Old City Quarters (Chapter 3), while the different faiths tended to live close to their most holy shrines, the neighbourhoods were never totally segregated. This notwithstanding, the area we now call the Christian Quarter was primarily populated by Christians, mainly Greek Orthodox and Latin. Until the 19th C nearly all the utilised churches were located in this quarter, as were two mosques.

Today the quarter is all built up, but at the beginning of the 19th C there was quite a lot of undeveloped land, the Muristan for example, was farmland.

palatial patriarchates

The buildings of the quarter vary a great deal. The area between the Jaffa and New Gates, the very NW is comprised, in the main, of large buildings, most constructed in the last c120 years. Both the Latin and Greek Catholic Patriarchates are located here, as well as official offices.

This area has seen at least two redevelopments since the end of the 19th C when a section of the wall east of the Jaffa Gate was demolished to allow the German Kaiser to enter by carriage. A new opening was made in the north wall and given the name of the New Gate. Street names have changed and the ones in use today are often named after the chief building in that street.

ordinary folk

The northern part of the quarter, between Tariq al-Khanqah and the Damascus Gate is very residential, and populated by the ordinary people. The dwellings are built in an almost continuous line, many with courtyards. The standard of living also varies greatly. Some places are clean and tidy, while others give quite a run down

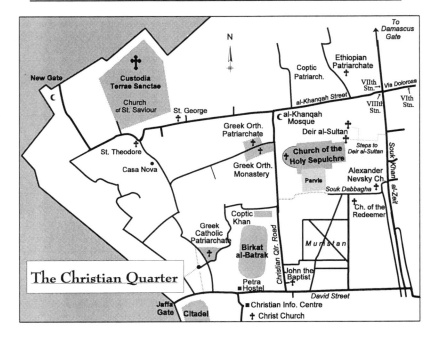

The Christian Quarter

impression. The winding lanes are often stepped and quite picturesque. Cars cannot be used in this area.

There are a few churches and convents in this sector which are not of particular interest, but you can enjoy strolling around, just sampling the ambience of the local life. During the Orthodox Easter season hundreds of pilgrims, mainly from Greece and Cyprus (for some reason mostly tiny elderly widows clad in black) find rooms to stay here as the price of regular hotels is too high. On a pleasant spring day they can be seen squatting on stools in the yards, filling the air with a chattering of Greek.

leather look

The main shopping streets are David or Bazaar Street, and Christian Quarter Road, known in the last century as Tariq al-Batrak, the Street of the Patriarchs. Both these streets are now full of "tourist" shops. (If you are after a leather jacket or coat look along the latter, but as elsewhere your bargaining skills had better be good. On a recent visit I halved the first quoted price, and still felt I paid too much!)

speaking the lingo

One of the remarkable attributes of the shopkeepers here is their ability to change from one language to another as groups of tourists and pilgrims pass by. When they detect a Spanish group the pitch is all in Spanish, and the prices are in pesetas. Immediately they are gone, a Greek group arrives and Greek is now the language of the street and the drachma the bargaining currency. It's quite remarkable how they converse in so many languages and switch between them at will. Of course all can handle English with no trouble, but whether it's French, German or Italian, it's all in a day's work for these oriental entrepreneurs.

More general shops are found in St. Francis Street which later becomes Tariq al-Khanqah, which in turn leads into Souk Khan al-Zeit, the main souk of the Old City.

THE VISIT

There are many monuments to see, the main point of interest here being, of course, the Church of the Holy Sepulchre, the *raison d'être* and focal point for the entire quarter.

> ► **Walk No. 1 –** **Through Old City to Church of the Holy Sepulchre and Deir al-Sultan Monastery**

START: **Jaffa Gate**; MAIN FEATURES: **Christian Information Centre – Pool of the Patriarchs – Church of John the Baptist – the Muristan – Church of the Redeemer – Church of the Holy Sepulchre – Alexander Nevsky Church – Deir al-Sultan** TIME: **Anywhere between 1.5 and 3.5 hours, depending on how long you linger in various places and stop to look in shops. A rush job can be done in 1.5 hours, but you will miss much. Try to allow at least 2.5 hours.**

► Christian Information Centre

Enter the city via the Jaffa Gate. On the right is the Citadel (see Chapter 11) and to the left a Government information office. We are now in a sort of plaza, with the Christian Quarter on our left (north). Straight ahead is David St. which was part of the E/W decumanus of the Roman/Byzantine city. Facing the Citadel (to the right of David Street) is the Christian Information Centre, where there is a good selection of books on the Christian holy places and details of most Christian activities in the city. This building stands on the site of the 19th C Austrian Post Office (see History, page 29).

endless antique supply

David Street, a narrow stepped alley, was, until just a few years ago a souk not dissimilar to the others of the city, with grocery, vegetable and spice shops mixed among the tourist souvenir and antique sellers. Now the food shops have all gone and pricey tourist shops line the whole street. Many may sell "antiques" of rather dubious age, the products of local present day workshops. As one shop resembles another, each proprietor will verbally accost you trying to make sure that if you are buying he will catch you before the next one does! "No charge for looking" is the common pitch. You are warned that this location may be the most expensive to purchase your souvenirs!

► Pool of the Patriarch (Birkat al-Batrak)

Just a few metres down, on the left but totally hidden by the shops, is a pool known variously as the Birkat al-Batrak, the Pool of the

63

Patriarch, or Birkat al-Hammam, the Pool of the Bath, and Hezekiah's Pool. Countless tourists, (who decide to visit the city without a good guide book!) must have walked down this street never knowing that this large pool existed.

It obtained the first name because it belonged to the (Latin) Patriarch in Crusader times, the second due to the fact it once supplied water to the local – now defunct – bathhouse and the third because some thought it was built by that Judean king.

view from hostel lounge

The only way you can get a view of this pool is from the lounge of the Petra Hostel right at the beginning of David Street. Just go in, past the money changer's booth, and up the stairs into the very shabby hostel. Then go up a second flight of stairs into the "lounge", and from the window you get a very good view.

Although sometimes named after Hezekiah, there is nothing to denote a connection with him. It is more likely to be from the Hasmonean period and started life as a quarry before becoming a reservoir. In Roman times the Tenth Legion was camped to the south of this area, and a pool of that size would have been required for their water needs.

Pool of the Patriarch, 19th C   *De Saulcy (Jerusalem)*

not a pretty sight

It is completely surrounded by buildings, the most prominent being the Coptic Khan (see page 86), to the north. Until the 19th C the pool was still used and besides being supplied by rain water during the season, was fed by an aqueduct from the Mamilla Pool, west of the Jaffa Gate (see page 207). Mid 19th C visitors reported it to be never more than half full even after a rainy winter. Sadly the pool is now a mess, being used as a convenient rubbish dump for the surrounding dwellings. The only water now is from the winter rains and because of the rubbish, is filthy. A 19th C picture shows it looking completely different.

Continue east down David Street for c50 metres to the first turning on the left, Christian Quarter Road, formerly Tariq al-Batrak, the Street of the Patriarch. Turn here, and c30 metres along on the right

is the access to the (now) Greek Orthodox Church of St. John the
Baptist.

▸ Church of St. John the Baptist

History

Head(s) of the Baptist

After John was decapitated by Herod Antipas to please his wife's
daughter, Salome, at Mukawir in Jordan (Matthew 14:3-11), his
body was turned over to his followers for burial. Where it was
actually interred is anyone's guess. According to one story the head
was buried on the site of the cathedral bearing his name in
Damascus, which later became that city's Great Mosque; there is still
a Muslim shrine to this effect inside the building. Another version
places his head in the courtyard of the Russian Orthodox Church of
the Ascension on the Mount of Olives.

roving relics

Other stories claim parts were buried in Alexandria, Constantinople and Jerusalem. Perhaps this was the reason why this church
and monastery, as it once was, was built. The earliest parts, the crypt
and substructure, date from the 5th C. During the Sasanian pillage of
Jerusalem in the early 7th C the building was destroyed, but was
partially restored after the Byzantines re-took the city.

Amalfi connection

In the 11th C it was completely rebuilt by the pious Merchants of
Amalfi, who, after installing themselves in Jerusalem, then became
important benefactors to the Christians there. The church was then
served by the Benedictine Order. After the Crusader withdrawal in
1187, it seems to have been left unoccupied, and later there were
reports that it had been turned into a mosque, although there is no
physical evidence to substantiate this.

By the beginning of the 17th C it was Greek Orthodox property,
and there was an adjoining hospice for pilgrims. In the 1840s, while
the 5th C church was being excavated, a reliquary of considerable
worth was discovered. It was removed to the Church of the Holy
Sepulchre.

The Visit

Entry is directly into a quiet, shady courtyard, well shielded from the
bustle of the outside souks. The church is kept locked, but the
keyholder is usually somewhere around, so if you want to view the
inside take the trouble to find him. Ask the residents who live up the
stairs just inside the entrance. The church is essentially the 11th C
building with later improvements. It is *trefoil* shaped with apses in
the north, south and east. The domed roof is supported by four
pillars. The iron grille over the altar is 12th C. Remains of the
Byzantine building can be seen in the vaulted crypt, some six metres
below the present level.

You can see the exterior of the apse from the Souk Aftimos in
Muristan (see below).

Crusader precinct

Return to David Street and continue down c30 metres and turn left at the next street (there is no name on it). This area, now called Souk Aftimos (Eftymios), is part of the Muristan, a precinct once occupied by the Crusader Order of the Hospitaliers, Knights of St. John.

▸ The Muristan

History

The Muristan, is a square area that borders David Street on the south, Christian Quarter Road on the west, Souk al-Lahamin (Souk of the Butchers) on the east and the Church of the Holy Sepulchre on the north. Although an important area in Crusader Jerusalem, there are few tell-tale signs of the past, any ancient ruins lying deep below today's street level and well covered by late 19th C redevelopments.

Charlemagne's church

In the Roman and Byzantine periods the Forum is thought to have been located here. In the 9th C Charlemagne, who was guardian of the Christians in Jerusalem, built a church which was cared for by the Benedictines. Like most other Christian sites in the city it was destroyed by the Fatimid caliph, al-Hakim in the early 11th C.

Mary Major and Mary Minor

When some of the Merchants of Amalfi settled in the city (mid 11th C) they acquired the land here and built a monastery and church, St. Marie la Latine, partly over the ruins of the previous structure. The Lutheran Church of the Redeemer now stands over the ruins. By the end of the century the Merchants had also established a convent, dedicated to Mary Magdalene. One of these became known as St. Mary Major, and the other St. Mary Minor,

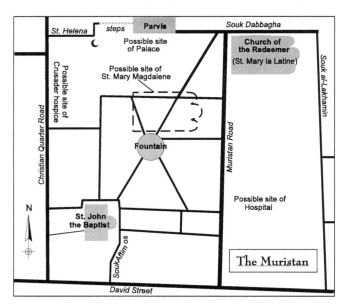

but it is not completely certain which was which.

In the Crusader era the area was taken over by the Knights of St. John, who established a hospice and hospital on the site, hence their name "Hospitaliers".

hospital of note

They ensconced themselves in an HQ and palace on the north side of the precinct, most likely on the site of the Greek Orthodox Monastery of Gethsemane, facing the Church of the Holy Sepulchre. The subterranean remains of a market have also been uncovered on the south side, adjacent to David Street. By the mid 12th C the hospital had grown, and was superior to any in Europe, no doubt aided by the very advanced Arab medical practices.

Muslims take over

After Salah al-Din's retaking of the city in 1187, and the subsequent expulsion of the Christians, the Church of St. Mary la Latine became a mosque, that of St. Mary Magdalene became a Shafi'ite madrassa and the hospital was used for Muslims. Thus the name Muristan, which is derived from the Kurdish for hospital (Salah al-Din was a Kurd). In 1216 Salah al-Din's son built a mosque in the northwest on what is now St. Helena Street, an alley which leads from Christian Quarter Road to the Church of the Holy Sepulchre. That mosque, the **Omariyya Mosque**, named for the Muslim conqueror of Jerusalem, still stands today, although it had to be restored by Sultan Abdul Hamid when the minaret collapsed after an earthquake.

grass among the ruins

After the second, and shorter, Crusader occupation a hospice still functioned in the area, probably under the jurisdiction of the Franciscans. In the late 15th C a traveller described it as large, but dirty and ruinous. Not long afterwards it was abandoned. By the late 17th C the Greek Orthodox Church had taken control of the SW part (see Church of John the Baptist, above), but most of the area was covered in ruins and grass. This is how it was found in the mid 19th C by visitors from Europe.

In 1869 the Crown Prince of Prussia, Frederick Wilhelm, visited Jerusalem, and the sultan, Abdul al-Aziz, made him a gift of the eastern part of the Muristan, the western part already being the property of the Greek Orthodox Patriarchate. The Lutheran Church of the Redeemer, and the Martin Luther School now occupy the "German" half (see below).

modern fountain

In the wake of the German development in the eastern part of the Muristan, the Greek Orthodox Patriarchate decided to redevelop their portion. At the turn of the century they rebuilt it as a modern market area. In the centre they erected a fountain in honour of the silver jubilee of Sultan Abdul Hamid. This section is called **Souk Aftimos**, a corruption of the name of the then Patriarch Eftymios. This is now an agreeable shopping area, if rather on the quiet side. Many of the shops here specialise in luggage and leather bags, and if these are something you wish to buy try here.

In the SW, just at the end of the short lane you entered by, is the apse of the Church of John the Baptist (see above). Just north of the central fountain is where the Church of St. Mary Magdalene was located, but no ruins are visible today.

Turning east (right) leads to Muristan Street which when built by the Germans was called Prince Frederick Wilhelm Street.

▸ Church of the Redeemer

Gift of the Kaiser

At the northern end of Muristan Street is the Lutheran **Church of the Redeemer** or Die Erlöserkirchen, built on the land given to Prussia in 1869. This gift was very fortuitous, for until that time the Lutherans had shared the Anglican Christ Church at the Jaffa Gate, and they were anxious to terminate this affiliation.

The church was constructed with funds raised by the Evangelische Jerusalems-Stiftung and building started in 1893. Often during the course of the work, the operation had to be suspended because of archaeological discoveries.

In 1898 Kaiser Wilhelm II and his wife Augustus Victoria travelled to Jerusalem for its consecration, and it was for this visit that part of the city wall at the Jaffa Gate was demolished.

belvoir from the belfry

The church is built on the site of the medieval Church of St. Marie la Latine (see above). The building is best known for its belfry, the highest vantage point in the Old City. This tower can be climbed (for a small fee) and from the top there is a magnificent view over the entire city. Well worth the effort unless you're claustrophobic or have difficulty climbing stairs – there are hundreds of them!

On the north side, the original entrance to the medieval building has been restored, but it's now sealed. Its arch is decorated with figures representing the months, which though named, are not now legible. The church, a Gothic style cruciform, while thoroughly modern, stands on the foundations of the 11th C ruins which now lie deep below the surface.

Lutheran Church of the Redeemer, c1910

moment for contemplation

After the hustle and bustle of the city's souks and the rigours of sightseeing, the Church of the Redeemer, with its contemplative organ music, is a truly peaceful place to rest a while.

South of the church is the area where it is thought the Knights of St. John of Jerusalem had their hospital. Although excavations have revealed remains of a large structure they are not conclusive. The site is now occupied by the Lutheran School, the **Martin Luther Schule.** (In 1882 the British Order of the Knights of St. John, a modern extension of the Crusader Order, established an ophthalmic hospital in the city and a plaque records this.)

My tour route now takes you into the **Church of the Holy Sepulchre,** perhaps the most intriguing building in this ancient city. Outside the Lutheran church turn north (right) and continue the few metres to **Souk Dabbagha.** Turn left, and the entrance to the church's forecourt lies ahead through the arched doorway.

▸ The Church of the Holy Sepulchre

"One naturally goes to the Holy Sepulchre...it and the place of the Crucifixtion, and, in fact, every other place intimately connected with that tremendous event are ingeniously massed together and covered by one roof – the dome of the Church of the Holy Sepulchre".

Mark Twain, The Innocents Abroad, 1869.

Most hallowed place

For many Christians, the Church of the Holy Sepulchre is the holiest shrine of their faith. Yet it is a strange building with a strange atmosphere, and one which most western Christians will find hard to feel spiritual about. Its gloomy, cold interior is about as far from the dreamy concept of a "green hill, without the city's walls" as anyone could concoct, and it will require all your faith if you have it – or all your imagination if you don't – to equate it with the hill of Calvary and the garden tomb prepared by Joseph of Arimathea.

austere welcome

At Easter the church takes on a livelier aspect, with colourful ceremonies and processions. But most of the year you will not find any warm Christian greetings, or even a smiling face on the many priests and monks, who go about their daily rituals in an almost automated fashion. They never deviate from the manner or time of day they perform them or – most important! – the route they take, lest they trespass on another denomination's "rights".

fighting factions

For this ancient building is not owned by any one denomination or even by a united Church, but instead it is carved up into jealously – even fanatically – guarded areas. Thus instead of being a unifying factor for Christians, the site of the Crucifixion has become one of the most divisive!

Yet of all the holy buildings in Jerusalem, no matter from what religion, the Church of the Holy Sepulchre has stood and functioned in one shape or another, the longest.

History

Site of Crucifixion and Tomb?

The site of this church lay outside the city walls until the building of the Roman city, and archaeological research has shown that there had been quarrying of tombs in the area. It was also on a slight incline which rose towards the west. Whether this can be equated with a hill is a matter of conjecture. Suffice it to say that there are notable archaeologists who support the site as a possible, even likely, Golgotha and others, equally notable, who do not.

where was the rock-hewn tomb?

There is also the fact that the tomb is no more than 75 metres away from the supposed site of the crucifixion. Only the Gospel of John states that these places were close to one another: *"Now in the place where He was crucified there was a garden; and in the garden a new tomb in which no one had yet been laid."* (John 19:41). Matthew's Gospel simply states, *"...and laid it in his own new tomb which he had hewn out of the rock..."* (Math. 27:60). The accounts in the gospels of Mark and Luke are similar to Matthew. Therefore the tradition that both places were very close rests solely on the Gospel of John. There is also another problem! According to Matthew 27:57, Joseph was rich man; would he have prepared a tomb for himself so close to a place of public execution?

All this notwithstanding, for nigh on 1600 years Christendom has declared this site as that of both the Hill of Golgotha (or Calvary) and the Tomb of Jesus, and all subsequent activity here has been based upon that premise.

early tradition

Tradition has it that as early as AD 45 followers of Jesus accepted this site as that of Jesus' tomb. However, because of the facts narrated below, this cannot be substantiated.

Around AD 66 most Christians from Jerusalem fled to Pella, on the east side of the river Jordan. In AD 70 Jerusalem was totally levelled and destroyed. In AD 135 a new Roman city, Aelia Capitolina rose in its stead and was entirely different from the destroyed city. Confusingly, the site of the Crucifixion was now inside the walls. As Christians did not resettle in the city until the end of the second century, even if devout believers had prayed at a particular spot prior to AD 66, is it likely that the same spot could be located 130 years later in an entirely new and enlarged city? Some scholars and archaeologists find evidence for this, while others do not.

turned into temple of Venus

When Hadrian rebuilt Jerusalem as Aelia Capitolina (after the AD 70 destruction), a temple to Venus was erected on this site, on a high terrace. By the time Constantine incorporated the city into the Eastern Christian Empire in 324, the tradition that the temple stood over the site of Jesus' tomb was firmly established. Certainly a tomb or tombs were discovered underneath, but as it had been a rocky area outside the walls, this came as no surprise. As in so many matters of this nature, faith is the deciding factor, and the faith of countless

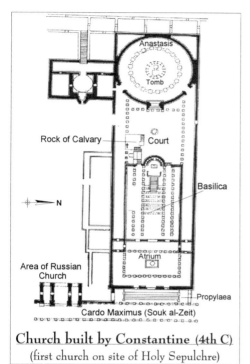

Church built by Constantine (4th C)
(first church on site of Holy Sepulchre)

Christians has declared this to be the authentic location.

Cross discovered

In the year 326, Constantine's mother, Helena, visited Jerusalem and legend has it that she discovered the "True Cross" in a cave nearby.

split building

The first Church of the Holy Sepulchre was not as we see it today – one huge edifice – but essentially two buildings, a basilica and a rotunda.

The propylaea, or entrance, was from the east along the cardo maximus. A triple gateway with an elegant facade was approached up a broad flight of steps. At the top three entrances led into an open colonnaded atrium. From this courtyard three doors led into the basilica, or martyrium.

beautiful decoration

Four rows of columns divided this into five aisles, the centre one being the broadest. The church was c45 metres long by c26 metres wide and its most distinguishing part was the beautifully decorated half circular apse at the western end.

West of the basilica was a second court, where to the southwest was the rock of Golgotha open to the sky, and standing some 4.75 metres high. At the west end of the courtyard was the facade and entrance to the Rotunda or the Anastasis (Resurrection) which enclosed the Holy Sepulchre. The Rotunda was c63 metres in diameter and with its double level of galleries, was capped by a wooden cupola.

Thus the Constantinian edifice stretched from the Souk Khan al-Zeit to the west end of the present church, making it significantly longer than the structure standing today.

Construction of this first Church of the Holy Sepulchre began in 326 and the Martyrium was consecrated in 335. The Anastasis took much longer as the rock face into which the tomb had been cut had to be excavated away. This was not completed until after 345.

Sasanian sacking

The Sasanian invasion of 614 led to the church being burned and the fragment of the "True Cross" taken. It was later restored by Modestus, abbot of the monastery of Theodosius east of Bethlehem.

'Umar protects the edifice

After the Arab conquest of the city in 638, a later historian, Eutychius, an Egyptian Christian, records how " *'Umar refused to perform his salaat (prayers) in the basilica of the Church of the Resurrection and instead said his prayers on the steps at the entrance in order, as he explained, to prevent the Muslims from using the authority of his example to turn the church into a mosque.*" 'Umar also guaranteed the safety of all the Christian sites in the city.

wanton destruction

This happy situation did not last, and according to Eutychius, early in the tenth century the shrines within the church were destroyed by aggressive Muslims. The entrance was turned into a mosque, ironically because 'Umar prayed there!

The worst devastation occurred in the early 11th century, when the Fatimid Caliph, al-Hakim in an outbreak of crazed fanaticism had most of the church, including the tomb, destroyed. So thorough was the destruction that, according to the Arab historian, Yahya, the demolishers cut through the tomb to the bedrock to utterly wreck it. To complete the blight, an earthquake struck the city in 1034, compounding the earlier havoc.

Byzantine rebuilding

Some 20 years later the Byzantine Emperor, Constantine Monomachos, was given permission to rebuild, but sufficient money was only provided to restore the Anastasis. Thus the 11th century Church of the Holy Sepulchre was a far smaller affair than Constantine's. It comprised mainly of the rotunda, with side chapels and the preceding court. Entry from this court into the rotunda was through a huge arch, the Arch of Monomachos. As the tomb had been completely obliterated, a rectangular construction topped with a cupola replaced it.

Crusader Jerusalem

Then in 1099 the Crusaders made their bloody entry into Jerusalem.

Over the next half century they rebuilt and restructured most of the church, and when finished the site of the Crucifixion and the Tomb were under the same roof for the first time. The new church was dedicated on 15th July 1149, half a century after the Crusader conquest. The edifice you can visit today is basically the result of this labour.

the new church

The fact that the building contained constructions of differing architectural designs meant that it lacked harmony. The Rotunda was preserved virtually in the reconstructed form of the preceding century, a Byzantine conception, while the new Crusader church was of a definite Romanesque style. Between the two stood the Great Arch of Monomachos, also a Byzantine affair.

Some of the Crusader kings were interred in the Church.

An Easter Mosaic

Not many people know it, but a Muslim holds the key to Christendom's most sacred shrine. Every morning he ceremoniously unlocks the massive wooden entrance to Jerusalem's Church of the Holy Sepulchre – traditional site of Jesus' crucifixion, burial and resurrection. At 7pm he securely locks it – and then takes the key home. His family has guarded the key for generations, not as a symbol of any Muslim claim to the spot, but to satisfy the jealousies between the numerous Christian sects whose rival interests in the historic building have often erupted into less than brotherly love!

Though frequently violent in their vehemence to control one corner or other of the cavernous basilica, these factions nevertheless bring into the sepulchre's gloomy interior a colour and diversity perhaps unmatched by any other place of worship. Latins, Greek and Armenian Orthodox, Ethiopians, Syrian Jacobites and Copts – each group with its own distinct ritual, dress and language – together portray a fascinating mosaic of Christianity.

This is especially true during Orthodox Easter week when the church comes into its own, drawing thousands of local worshippers as well as pilgrims from around the world. The armed Israeli patrols keep a discreet distance from the Via Dolorosa, where cross-carrying pilgrims ply the route to Calvary (inside the church); from the Palm Sunday processions at the start of Holy Week to the exuberant "holy fire" ceremonies after midnight on Easter Saturday, Christian Jerusalem puts on its liveliest performance.

The outdoor processions were toned down on occasion in recent years to identify with the *intifada* uprising (95 per cent of Jerusalem's Christians are Palestinian), but inside the church the festivities always proceed. Nothing stifles the drums of the dancing Ethiopians on the church roof or the medley of chants and psalms reverberating from the simultaneous services of each denomination throughout the week. Smoky white incense flows thick from waving censers and the atmosphere is heady.

At 7pm on Easter Saturday the keeper of the key locks up and goes home as usual, sealing hundreds of worshippers into the sepulchre. Tradition has decreed that the church must be closed at that time, and the congregants must remain in the locked tomb till morning. When midnight tolls, the church becomes ablaze with the light of a thousand candles and resounds with joyous shouts of *"Christos Aneste"*, "Christ is risen". In the sanctuary on the site where 2000 years ago the history of the world changed forever, the gathering of men, women and children praise God through the night while waiting for the Muslim to release them.

They see no irony in this, nor in the fact that next week it will be guns as usual along the Via Dolorosa: their hope is in their faith.

Muslim reconquest

In 1187 Salah al-Din reconquered Jerusalem; in contrast to the Crusader conquest his was notable by the lack of slaughter. But the Latin Christians were expelled from the city, and only the Orthodox rites had access to the church. In later years the Latins were permitted to return and resume their duties in the church.

brief Crusader return

In 1229 under a deal between al-Malik al-Kamil Nasir al-Din, the Ayyubid ruler, and Frederick II of Germany the city was returned to Crusader rule, a period that lasted but 15 years. Frederick crowned himself king in the church.

turn of the Turkomen

His rule ended perfunctorily in 1244 when an army of Turkomen, driven out of their homeland by the Mongols, raided Jerusalem and despoiled the church, slaying all the Christians inside. The Turkomen remained in Jerusalem for two years before they were forced out and the city returned to Ayyubid rule.

sale of "rights" in the church

By 1350 the church was controlled by the Greeks, Armenians, Syrians, Copts, Ethiopians as well as Latins, but the difficulties in paying the Ottoman taxes forced some denominations to sell their "rights" to others. By the end of the 17th century most of the areas inside the building were owned by the Latins, Armenians and Greeks.

bad blaze

Much damage was caused in 1804 when a fire broke out in a chapel off the Rotunda. Seven of the supporting columns dating from the 11th century collapsed, causing much of the structure to fall. The fire provoked a great controversy. Some blamed the Armenians, believing they had deliberately set the fire because, being the only denomination with enough money to restore it, their "rights" would be enhanced. However, one traveller who visited in 1808 blamed it on a Greek monk who accidentally set fire to some wood (A. Curzon, Visits to the Monasteries of the Levant, 1849).

Crusader kings removed

In the event, the rebuilding was carried out mainly by the Greek Orthodox who succeeded in obtaining the finance from Russia, then the protector of the Greek Orthodox Church. This action enabled them to increase their already dominant position in the building. During the reconstruction nearly all vestiges of the Crusaders, especially the tombs of Godfrey of Bouillon and Baldwin I, were removed.

Throughout the century, and into the next, rivalry between the denominations continued and, on occasion, intensified. A British traveller wrote:

> *"Among the crowds who gather in this porch and worship under this dome, there are twenty rivals, and not two brothers. A pilgrim of one country believes the pilgrim from another country to be a heretic and a scoundrel, a deserter from the true church, a denier of the true God... Every monk in Jerusalem imagines that his Christian neighbour is already damned... A Muslim has no better light...but what excuse can a Christian imagine for his brother who has had his choice, and has wickedly selected an impure creed!?"*
>
> W.H.Dixon, The Holy Land, London, 1865

The courtyard, nowadays so orderly and usually full of groups receiving an explanation from their guide, was vastly different in the 19th C. In the wake of swelling crowds of pilgrims, the yard often resembled a souk, with souvenirs, holy items, even food being sold. Money changers and lodging touts also frequented the area, hoping to service this increased traffic.

Six Day War

An earthquake in 1927 shook the building so badly that scaffolding had to be erected as support. In the early 1960s a programme of restoration work was agreed between the various denominations, but the 1967 war and the subsequent *de facto* change in ruler interrupted this. In recent years the work has been implemented by the Israelis.

It is a curiosity that this holy site of Christianity has such turbulent owners that quite often it is the Israeli police that have the task of keeping order!

The Visit

"In its history...it is the most illustrious edifice in Christendom. With all its clap-trap side-shows and unseemly postures of every kind it is still grand, reverend, venerable...for fifteen hundred years its shrines have been wet with the tears of pilgrims from the earth's remotest confines;"

Mark Twain, The Innocents Abroad, 1869

The Church of the Holy Sepulchre is open every day between 4.30 and 17.00. Visitors must be suitably dressed. Shorts are not allowed, and women should have their arms and backs covered. There are many ceremonies during the day, and details of these and of special ones can be obtained from the Christian Information Centre near the Jaffa Gate, opposite the Citadel.

enclosed forecourt

Whether you approach from the Muristan, as this tour does, or from Christian Quarter Road, you enter the forecourt or **Parvis**, which is enclosed by church offices on the east and west sides and the Greek Orthodox **Monastery of Gethsemane**, on the south side. Part of the forecourt is the roof of an ancient cistern that dates back to before the building of the church. Remains of the colonnade on the south side can still be seen (and sat upon!). The paving is that laid during the Crusader rebuilding.

three chapels

On the west side are three chapels, entered from a passage in the centre, originally built in the 11th century on the site of the baptistery of Constantine's building. The first one (southernmost) is the Greek Orthodox **Chapel of St. James,** (Jesus' brother and the first Bishop of Jerusalem); the middle one, also Greek, is the **Chapel of Mary Magdalene** and nearest the entrance is the Armenian **Chapel of the Forty Martyrs.** This is dedicated to forty Roman soldiers in Lesser Armenia who converted to Christianity. When they refused to renounce their new faith they were frozen to death on a lake of icy water. The bell tower above this chapel was built by the

Crusaders around 1170. Note that in the normal course of events visitors are not allowed in these chapels.

weighing the souls of the dead

On the opposite side are three other offices: The first (on the corner) is the **Monastery of Abraham**, owned by the Greek Orthodox. It was originally built in the 12th C, later destroyed and then rebuilt by the Greeks in 1690. According to Byzantine tradition it is the site where Abraham was prepared to offer Isaac as a sacrifice. Massive vaults support the chapel's roof. The Armenian Orthodox **Chapel of St. James** is in the centre, with next to it the **Chapel of St. Michael**, owned by the Copts. Inside is a painting of

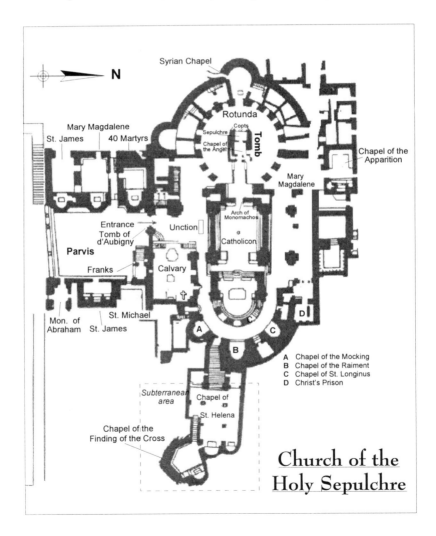

the saint weighing souls of the dead. From here a stairway leads up to the Ethiopian Chapel, then out on to the roof and the Coptic Patriarchate, both of which we'll come to later. Usually only the last of these chapels can be visited.

broken steps

Above the east wall of the Parvis, and adjoining the church is a small domed enclosure with incomplete steps. This was the Crusader entrance to the church on Golgotha (Calvary). Later it became the **Chapel of the Franks**. The lower part is the **Chapel of Mary the Egyptian**, a 5th century convert to Christianity who was denied access to the church.

lone ladder

Almost above the church entrance is a solitary ladder. The story of this is that many years ago one of the denominations tried to do some repairs, but the others objected as this may have led to a claim by the repairers for jurisdiction over that area! The work was abandoned and the ladder left!

The entrance facade with its double-storeyed arcade, is the original one built during the reconstruction in the first half of the 12th C. Part of this recycles Roman material from the 2nd C. There are two adjoining entranceways, the eastern one bricked up since the Crusaders' departure. Each entranceway is flanked by a trio of marble pillars mounted on high bases. Their capitals are adorned with acanthus leaves. These support a carved lintel, but they are not original, those having been taken away to the Rockefeller Museum after the 1927 earthquake.

Englishman's tomb

Between the doors, under the wooden boards, is the tomb of Philippe d'Aubigny, a crusading English knight, who died in 1236.

Entering the church is a decidedly sombre experience. For much of the year the gloomy interior is accentuated by the brilliance of the light outside, and it takes a few moments for your eyes to adjust.

kissing stone

To the immediate right is a flight of steep stairs that reaches up (supposedly) to **Golgotha** or Calvary. Beyond, just before the be-pictured wall is the **Stone of the Unction**, where according to tradition Nicodemus anointed Jesus' body after it was removed from the cross (recorded only in John's Gospel, 19:39-40). The slab of stone, with jars of perfumed oil suspended above it, dates from the early 19th C, having replaced the 12th C slab destroyed in the fire. Ownership rights to this particular piece are not too clear, so the icons of all the denominations hang above. Many of the pious prostrate themselves at this spot, kissing the slab.

the hill of Golgotha

Ascend the steep stairs to the traditional site of the Crucifixion. This area is also the location of the **10th, 11th, 12th, and 13th Stations of the Cross** along the Via Dolorosa (see box, page 83). There are two chapels although they appear almost as one. The one on the south is Latin, and that to the north Greek Orthodox. Each denomination guards its rights very zealously, and a Latin nun sweeping will not dare let her broom stray into the Greek half!

The Latin Chapel, the **Chapel of the Nailing to the Cross** is adorned, on the ceiling, with a 12th C mosaic depicting the Ascension, although the very dim light will make it almost impossible to see! This chapel marks the 10th and 11th Stations of the Via Dolorosa. Just to the south, and visible through a window is the **Chapel of the Agony of Mary**, or Stabat Mater.

The adjacent Greek Orthodox chapel is the **Chapel of the Raising of the Cross**, and is the 12th Station of the Via Dolorosa. On the east side the monks will show you the rock in which the Cross was placed. Between the two chapels is the 13th Station of the Cross where, after removal from the Cross, Jesus' body was received by Mary. This is portrayed above the altar in the Latin chapel. The glass showcase houses a wooden bust of the Lady of Sorrows, and dates from the 16th or 17th C. It was given by Portugal in 1778.

cave of Adam

You can descend via the second staircase at the rear of the Greek chapel. Directly underneath the Calvary site is the **Chapel of Adam.** There is a myth (or legend) that the skull of Adam was discovered here. More of the rock of Calvary can be seen from here.

the Tomb

Continue past the Stone of Unction, through two massive pillars into the Rotunda or Anastasis. The Holy Sepulchre or edicule stands in the centre. Inside this rather strange marble structure, built after the 1808 fire, is the traditional **Tomb of Jesus**, and it has been venerated as that for at least 1700 years. Inside are two very small chambers; the first an anteroom, the **Room of the Angels** has a small altar which is supposedly made from the boulder that sealed the mouth of the tomb *"...and he (Joseph) rolled a large stone against the entrance of the tomb..."* (Matthew 27:60). From here a low doorway leads to the actual tomb, the **14th and final Station of the Cross**. It is illuminated by the flickering glow of wax candles, and on the right side is the niche covered by a marble slab which is where Jesus body was laid. However, bear in mind that other considerations aside, this tomb was completely wrecked by the Fatimids in the early 11th century (see page 22). The site is officiated by Latin, Armenian and Greek Orthodox priests.

queues

Depending on the time of day and season of the year, there is often a long waiting queue to visit this spot. Sometimes, when religious ceremonies take place around this area, the tomb is closed to visitors.

Coptic corner

Outside and at the western end of the sepulchre is a tiny **Coptic Chapel** where a solitary monk is crouched underneath the tomb. Here, if you also crouch, you will be shown what purports to be a fragment of the original tomb which resisted the Fatimid destruction. This is the only "right" the Copts still have inside the actual church.

the Jacobite presence

The Syrian Orthodox Chapel of St. Nicodemus is located behind the tomb structure in the west exedra. According to late tradition the tombs of Joseph of Arimathea and Nicodemus are located here.

the Latin presence

North of the Anastasis is the Latin **Altar of Mary Magdalene**. It has a 12th C marble floor of round and square tiles, and was only discovered during repairs in the late 1950s. Beyond it is the newly restored, and modern looking, Franciscan **Chapel of the Apparition** where legend states that Jesus appeared after his resurrection. By the altar is a column, the **Column of the Flagellation** to which Jesus is supposed to have been tied when he was whipped by the Roman soldiers. The original chapel dates from the 11th and 12th centuries. Here Latin rite masses are held.

Opposite the front of the tomb structure is the **Great Arch of Momomachos** built in the 11th C by the Byzantine emperor.

centre of the world

Through the arch is the **Greek Orthodox Catholicon**, or cathedral. This is situated in the main part of the Crusader church and has now been embellished with the decoration associated with Orthodox churches. There is a tradition that the centre of the world was located here and the spot is indicated by an omphalos. This Catholicon is situated where the courtyard that separated the basilica from the Anastasis, in the Constantine Church, was located. Numerous ceremonies are conducted here, and there are seats for two of the important Greek Orthodox Patriarchs, those of Jerusalem and Antioch.

mixed design

The original Crusader church with its Romanesque and Gothic design is still discernable from within and without this Greek cathedral. Yet parts of the more oriental character of the Emperor Monomachos' structure of the 11th C still remain, and have been incorporated into the 12th C Crusader design. Outside and on the north side are huge columns and supporting blocks and arches of recycled bits and pieces, called the **Arches of the Virgin**.

from legends to chapels

At the very eastern end of this area is the **Prison of Christ**. It was here, according to a Crusader legend, that Jesus and the two thieves who were executed alongside him were held prior to the Crucifixion.

Just south of this are a trio of small chapels situated in the apses of the 12th C church. The first (nearest the Prison of Christ) is the **Chapel of St. Longinius** belonging to the Greek Orthodox. An ancient fable relates that Longinius was the Roman soldier who *"pierced His side with a spear, and immediately there came out blood and water."* (John 19:34). The fable recounts that Longinius was blind in one eye but on being touched by the blood and water was cured. He thus atoned and believed.

South of this is the Armenian **Chapel of the Division of the Raiment**: *"And when they had crucified Him they divided up His garments among themselves..."* (Matthew 27:35).

The southernmost of these chapels is the Greek Orthodox **Chapel of the Mocking** or Crowning with Thorns: *"And after weaving a crown of thorns, they put it on His head...and mocked Him saying*

'Hail King of the Jews!'" (Matthew 27:29).

Helena's find

Behind these chapels is a flight of steps leading to the **Chapel of St. Helena**. On the walls of the stairs are many crosses carved through the centuries by pilgrims. This large, c20 x 13 metres, hall is divided into three aisles with two apses. It dates from the Crusader rebuilding, and the north and south walls could be part of the foundations of Constantine's basilica. In the SE corner another, shorter, flight of steps leads down to the **Chapel of the Finding of the Cross**. It was here (then a cave), according to tradition, that Helena found the "True Cross". The Greek Orthodox own the right hand side and the Latins the left. The statue is of Queen Helena holding her discovery.

up on the roof

The other parts of the Church of the Holy Sepulchre to be visited are on the roof. These are the Ethiopian monastery of **Deir al-Sultan** and the **Coptic Patriarchate**. They are accessible either through the Chapel of St. Michael (which is sometimes closed) or from Souk Khan al-Zeit around the corner. As the round-the-corner route is always available and there are a couple of associated places on the way, my tour will continue that way.

▸ Church of St. Alexander Nevsky

White Russians

Exit the parvis east through the arched gateway (the one you entered) and walk straight ahead along Souk Dabbagha passing the Church of the Redeemer. On the left are a few very expensive carpet and antique shops. After c75 metres on the left corner is the Russian **Church of St. Alexander Nevsky**, once the Jerusalem HQ of the "White Russian Church in Exile".

Russian revelations

Constructed in 1882 following the visit to Palestine by the Grand Duke Sergei Alexandrovitch, it first had the appellation of the Alexandrovsky Hospice. Not often visited this building has yielded some interesting discoveries. **To visit, between 09.00 and 15.00, ring the door bell and a guardian will let you in, and show you around.**

former forum

The guardian will lead you to the top of a wide flight of steps. From here you can see the remains of the northern arch of Hadrian's triple-arched entrance to the forum of Aelia Capitolina, which stood just east of the present Church of the Holy Sepulchre. At the bottom of the steps turn left. A few metres along, you will see a door on the right wall which once led out to the Roman cardo (today Souk Khan al-Zeit). Facing and to the left (now partly covered by pictures) are the remains of the walls of the Temple of Venus and the walls of Constantine's basilica, an entrance to which probably lay just beyond. The uncovered wall continues further north beyond this building and a section is visible from inside a bakery (see below). The floor was part of the very wide and colonnaded Roman cardo.

site of the Judgment Gate

According the Russian Orthodox tradition this is the site of the Judgment Gate where Jesus was led out of the city to Golgotha, and all other things being correct, this is very possible.

Outside the church turn left and follow the zigzag until it reaches **Souk Khan al-Zeit**, c30 metres. This very busy street follows the line of the cardo maximus of Aelia Capitolina and the Byzantine Jerusalem. We will have to pass along here again so a description will wait until then (see Chapter 10).

inside the sweet shop

Turn left and after about 50 metres you reach a flight of steps on the left. Just inside the recess by these steps is Zalatimos Sweet Shop, an establishment that makes and sells oriental pastries, *baklawa*. This is the bakery referred to above. Inside this establishment's storeroom are remains of the central doorway between the propylaea and the atrium of Constantine's 4th C basilica (of the Church of the Holy Sepulchre). As stated, this basilica opened directly onto the cardo. Sadly, recent building work has made this area difficult to view, although if you are very keen ask the owner if it is possible.

▸ Deir al-Sultan (Ethiopian Monastery)

Ascend the steps by the bakery and at the top walk straight ahead along Aqabat Deir al-Sultan. This entire locality is known as Deir al-Sultan (Monastery of the Sultan), having acquired its rather grandiose title in the 16th century when the Ottoman sultan gave the ruins of the 12th C Latin cloister to the Copts. At that time the Coptic and Ethiopian Churches were very closely aligned, the head of the latter being an appointee of the Coptic Patriarch. Later both split apart and the weaker Ethiopians only managed to retain the "poorer" part of the roof. Disputes between the two over property rights still continue, and some years ago the Israeli courts were asked to intervene in the matter!

don't go home without seeing it!

The area is now shared by the Ethiopian and Coptic Churches, the latter having most of it, but the former far more visitable. About 40 metres along, where the road turns right, is a small entranceway that leads into one of the most delightful places in the Old City – if not the whole of Jerusalem. Delightful not because of the architecture, treasures or anything similar, but because of the people and the tranquillity. For this is the **Ethiopian Monastery of Deir al-Sultan,** a not-to-be-missed corner of a not-to-be-missed city.

no money for taxes

Once upon a time the Ethiopian Church held rights in parts of the actual Church of the Holy Sepulchre, but due chiefly to Ottoman taxation, lost them to the Copts, who subsequently lost most of those for the same reason. The area they now occupy is no more than a cluster of small cells built on the ruins of the medieval cloister.

tranquil haven

Although the monks and nuns (for this is a mixed monastery) who live here are poor, they are among the friendlier people you will meet in this otherwise quite dour church. Up here the noise and activity of the souks below are left behind. I have spent many an hour in this place just enjoying the tranquillity of the site and the enchantment of the scene. Tiny, spotlessly clean, whitewashed cells, each with a green wooden door and a sink with a cold water tap outside, make up the living quarters.

a place in the sun
On a warm, sunny day the monks sit outside their cells studying the Bible or other sacred texts, some dressed in brilliant saffron, scarlet or purple robes. The often weighty tomes are supported by wooden lecterns, and the outside world seems light years away.

The courtyard is on the roof of the Chapel of St. Helena, and the chapel's dome protrudes from the centre of the yard. The ruins you can see on the south and west walls are the remnants of Crusader galleries.

Solomon and Sheba
In the SW is the **Chapel of the Ethiopians**, a simple place adorned by a huge tapestry depicting the meeting of Solomon and the Queen of Sheba (one of her sons, possibly from the union with the Israelite king, became Negus, or king of Ethiopia). As explained earlier, stairs from the chapel lead down into the Coptic **Chapel of St. Michael**, and thence out to the Parvis.

Coptic complex
In the north west corner of the courtyard, a stone doorway leads to the **Coptic Patriarchate**. To the left of this entrance is a column that marks the **Ninth Station of the Cross** along the Via Dolorosa. Besides being the location of the Coptic Patriarch's offices, there is also the **Queen Helena Coptic Church**, and a boys' school. The aforementioned friendliness of the Ethiopian monastery seems to have dissipated somewhat around here!

Return the way you came to the bottom of the steps.

IXth Station of the Cross

The Via Dolorosa

No-one knows precisely when the first processions along a route described as the **Via Dolorosa** or Way of Sorrows took place. Certainly there were occasional such processions in medieval times, when they probably started from the Mount of Olives site where Jesus was arrested, entering the city from the east and continuing to the Church of the Holy Sepulchre. However, if and where they stopped *en route* is unclear. In fact it is likely that there was more than one route, and different groups followed their own agenda.

The approximate route walked today by thousands of pilgrims dates from the 13th or 14th centuries and was conceived by the Franciscans – although we do not know how many stopping points there were. The stations venerated now were established around the early 17th century and, having been cemented in the arts (both painting and music), have virtually become considered factual. Sites such as Pilate's Palace – its position would be vital in establishing where the final walk began – have not been definitely established by archaeologists. But as a clergyman once pointed out to me, "This is a walk of faith and not of exactitude. I believe it happened – a few metres here or there is not important".

Where Next?

This completes the tour of the main sites in the Christian Quarter, but there are a few more places which the inquisitive might like to see, and a route for these continues below in Walk No. 2.

An option would be to turn to Chapter 10 and spend some time just wandering around the souks without having to concentrate on history!

finding your way

To orientate yourself from here: Turning north (left) at the bottom of the steps will lead you to the Damascus Gate. Turning south and walking through the covered souk will bring you to the end of David Street where a right leads to the Jaffa Gate. Continuing straight over will bring you to the Jewish Quarter.

If lunch is on your mind there are several eateries in the Souk Khan al-Zeit, and a highly recommended one in al-Wad Street. See the section on restaurants for details.

▶ **Walk No. 2 – From Souk Khan al-Zeit to the New Gate**

START: **Steps below Deir al-Sultan;** MAIN FEATURES: **Souk Khan al-Zeit – VIIth & VIIIth Stations – Ethiopian Patriarchate – Greek Orthodox Patriarchate – Catholic Patriarchate & Museum – Coptic Khan – various churches – Tancred's Tower;** TIME: **approx. 1.5 hours.**

83

Bustling market street

Along this section of the busy souk are a variety of shops – butchers, haberdashery, and in particular oriental pastry (baklawa) sellers. If you have a taste for such delicacies don't buy here! There are better ones elsewhere!

carrot juice and handcarts

If you're thirsty, it's worth walking back a few metres or so to just before the steps you passed. On the west is a small juice and ice cream shop with a large carrot juice extractor in the open window. For a refreshing drink take a break here and enjoy this really fresh juice. I have been doing so for the past 20 years! Sometimes this section of the street is so crowded that you have to push your way through. Be especially careful of carts as those who push them do so with little regard to the safety of passers by!

Having slaked your thirst continue north along Souk Khan al-Zeit. After c100 metres you come to the cross streets by the **Seventh Station** of the Via Dolorosa (visited in Chapter 4). Turn west (left) into Tariq al-Khanqah. Just 20 metres up on the left, on the wall of the Greek Orthodox **Convent of St. Caralambos**, a cross marks the **Eighth Station of the Cross** (see boxes pp 83 and 85).

After the crowds of Souk Khan al-Zeit, this street will seem almost deserted, but all the same there are a few interesting shops along each side. About 50 metres up on the north (right) side is Aqabat Deir al-Habes, and the same distance along it on the right is the **Ethiopian Patriarchate**. It's not particularly interesting, but the mosaic above the portal is very colourful.

Back on al-Khanqah a further c125 metres up, and just before Christian Quarter Road, is the **al-Khanqah Mosque**.

Sufi convent

This former Crusader structure was built around 1120 as the residence of the Latin Patriarch of Jerusalem. After the reconquest by Salah al-Din in 1187 it was turned into a Sufi convent (or Khanqah). The minaret was added in the early 15th C.

Past the mosque turn left into Christian Quarter Road and continue for about 50 metres where, just under the vaulting, Aqbat Deir al-Rum, or as it is called today Greek Orthodox Patriarchate Road, turns off to the right, while a passage to the left leads to the Church of the Holy Sepulchre. The first part of this street is taken up by the **Great Greek Orthodox Monastery** on the left, and the **Greek Orthodox Patriarchate** on the right.

unofficial visit

The monastery, once the Monastery of St. Thecla, is a maze of buildings, courtyards, alleys and living quarters that extend over Christian Quarter Rd. to the Church of the Holy Sepulchre. Although there is no official visiting, I have often just walked in and looked around. The comings and goings of the black clad monks is almost continuous. The Patriarchate, opposite, contains quite an interesting **museum**.

Continue up to the end of the road, and turn left into Greek Catholic Patriarchate Street (also known as St. Dimitri Road). About 40 metres along on a sharp bend is the **Greek Catholic Patriarchate**

The Route of the Stations of the Cross

(The first seven stations are in the Muslim Quarter, and are visited in that section)

First Station: Where Jesus was condemned by Pilate. This station, at the west end of Tariq Bab Sitti Maryam, about 300 metres from St. Stephens (or the Lion) Gate, is in the 'Umariyya School, the site of the Antonia Fortress.

Second Station: Where Jesus was scourged. At the very beginning of Via Dolorosa (a continuation of Tariq Maryam), in the Monastery of the Flagellation.

Third Station: Where Jesus fell. At the junction of Aqabat al-Wad facing the Austrian Hospital.

Fourth Station: Where Jesus met his mother. In the Armenian Catholic Church on the corner of Via Dolorosa and Aqabat al-Wad.

Fifth Station: Where Jesus stumbled the second time and Simon of Cyrene took the cross (a variation on the Gospel account!) About 20 metres further on the route turns right into Aqabat al-Saray. On the left hand corner is a small chapel. Here on the wall you may be shown a small indent caused, so it is said, by generations of pilgrims placing their hand on the spot where Jesus leaned to break his fall.

Sixth Station: Where Jesus was given a cloth by Veronica. The way now ascends slightly and halfway along is the Convent of St. Veronica.

Seventh Station: Where the warrant ordering Jesus' death was placed. It was then a city gate. Facing the end of Aqabat al-Saray where it joins Souk Khan al-Zeit.

Eighth Station: Where Jesus spoke to the women of Jerusalem. In the Monastery of Caralambos just up Aqabat al-Khanqah, which is almost a continuation of Aqabat al-Saray.

Ninth Station: Where Jesus fell again. In the area of the Coptic Patriarchate. Continue west on Souk Khan al-Zeit for c70 metres then ascend the stairs by Zalatimo's Sweet Shop. Return to Souk Khan al-Zeit.

Tenth Station: Where Jesus was disrobed. At the site of Calvary.

Eleventh Station: Where Jesus was nailed to the cross. Also on the site of Calvary.

Twelfth Station: The site of the Crucifixion. In the Orthodox part of Calvary.

Thirteenth Station: Where Jesus was taken down from the cross and handed to Mary. On Calvary between the two chapels.

Fourteenth, and final Station: Where Jesus was interred. The Tomb.

Many of the events portrayed are, of course, apocryphal. During the Easter season there are constant processions along this route. All year round the Franciscans proceed every Friday at about 3pm. Anyone is welcome to join them.

and museum. Immediately past, turn left into the narrow Aqbat al-Khan, also called St. George St. (Those who are tired can continue ahead for c25 metres to the Jaffa Gate.)

Ottoman style dwellings

Aqbat al-Khan is a typical and attractive back alley of the Christian Quarter, and has the atmosphere of ordinary people in ordinary homes. Where it twists to the left is a Coptic Girls School, the only one in the city. After passing through a short tunnel vault the Aqbat turns right and becomes stepped. Notice the overhanging windows on the upper floor of some houses. This is typically Ottoman, and is very common in the old quarters of Turkish and Syrian towns. Half way down, on the south (right) are the heavy wooden doors of the **Coptic Khan.**

former olive grove

The Copts built this khan in 1837 on the site of an olive grove and press. It was for the use of Coptic pilgrims from Egypt who were mainly very impoverished. Now it is an extremely shabby place, having been taken over by workshops and the poor. Some of the vaulted rooms are now bricked up and unfortunately squalor reigns. Such a place could be restored, as so many similar places have been in other cities. However for a view of a 19th C khan it is still worth visiting. As already explained elsewhere, the rear surveys **Pool of the Patriarch** (Hezekiah's Pool). Facing is the now rebuilt Greek Orthodox **Monastery of the Megale Panagia** originally a 12th C edifice, which in turn stood over a 5th C structure. There is no visiting, and in any case nothing to see.

two more churches

The end of the street is Christian Quarter Road again. Return to it, turn left and walk back to Tariq al-Khankah. Turn left; the street is now called St. Francis Street. Just past the vaulting, on the north (right) side, are two more Greek Orthodox Churches, the **Church of St. Michael**, and the **Church of St. George**. Both these churches were procured from the Serbian Orthodox Church in the late 17th C. The latter is built over ancient foundations.

Further along, where the road bends is the large Latin building complex of the **Custodia Terrae Sanctae** which stretches as far as the city walls. The present building is very modern, giving little indication of the site's long history.

After the fall of Acre in 1291, the last Crusader bastion in Palestine, the Franciscans withdrew from Jerusalem. By 1340 they had returned, settling this time on Mount Zion. They became the Custodians of the (Latin) holy places, as well as taking care of pilgrims. In the mid 16th C they managed to acquire the Church of St. John from the Georgians, who were in difficult financial straits (most Georgian property was sold to other Orthodox churches so this acquisition was quite rare). The church was subsequently renamed. There is nothing to see here, apart from the modern **Church of St. Saviour (Salvador)**, the main Latin Church of Jerusalem, on the first floor.

exiting the Old City

From here you can exit the Old City via the New Gate. From outside St. Saviour turn left and then right into Casa Nova Street. Follow this as it bears left, then take the first on the right towards the New Gate. On the west is the Collège des Frères, a Christian school for youths. Past it, on the left of the New Gate, is a small Ottoman mosque.

▶ ### Tancred's Tower

Also to the left of the gate is what is known as **Tancred's Tower** or Qasr Jalut in Arabic (Castle of Goliath). Tancred was instrumental in the Crusader conquest of Jerusalem in 1099. Although the tower stood on massive foundations of an earlier period, it appears to be a Crusader construction. It was flattened by Suleiman when the walls were rebuilt in 1537 and after.

view from the ramparts

Most of the remnants are within the college, where there is a massive stone substructure, but just outside the city walls, where there is now a pleasant lawn, other sections have been unearthed. (See also Chapter 9, Ramparts Walk.)

The **New Gate (Bab al-Sultan)** is, as its English name implies, the newest gate to the city. It was opened in 1887 to enable the residents of this area to gain better access. As it faced the Israel-Jordan cease fire line it was closed during the period 1948-1967.

6. The Jewish Quarter

INTRODUCTION

Because of its destruction after 1948, the rebuilt Jewish Quarter is the most modern quarter in the Old City, and also the most devoid of visible monuments. That being said it is still an important area to visit and a great deal of effort has been expended to restore or make visible some reminders of the past.

Following the June 1967 war the Israeli government rebuilt the quarter entirely, perpetuating some of its monuments. Modern planning designs were used, assimilating architectural styling compatible with the ancient city. Today it is the most "liveable" part of the Old City; all mod cons have been incorporated into the quarter, from play areas for the bountiful children down to preferential parking spaces for the residents' vehicles – items sorely lacking in other parts of the Old City.

About 4,500 people live in the quarter today, many orthodox students of the religious schools (yeshivot) that abound there.

HISTORY

This part of the city only became known as the Jewish Quarter after the Ottoman conquest, although some Jews were living here as early as the end of the 13th C. In the Fatimid era, prior to the Crusader invasion, the Jewish population of the city resided in the main in the NE section, where they were instrumental in trying to resist the Frankish onslaught.

At other times Jews were either prohibited from living in the city or dwelt in less defined areas.

the beginnings

After the reconquest by Salah al-Din in 1187, Jews, who had been barred from the city by the Crusaders, started in very small numbers to drift back. When Moses ben Nahman (Nahmanides) arrived in Jerusalem in 1267 he found the few Jews who were living there in a state of near poverty. He managed to organise them into a settlement on Mount Zion where he established the first synagogue in Jerusalem for many a century. At the beginning of the 15th C, wanting to live closer to the Western (Wailing) Wall, the present quarter began to develop.

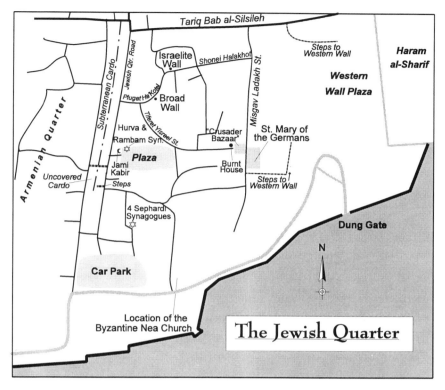

Tariq Bab al-Silsileh

Haram al-Sharif

Steps to Western Wall

Western Wall Plaza

Jewish Qtr. Road

Israelite Wall

Shonei Halakhot

Misgav Ladakh St.

Subterranean Cardo

Pluget Ha'Kotel

Broad Wall

Tiferet Yisrael St.

St. Mary of the Germans

"Crusader Bazaar"

Hurva & Rambam Syn.

Armenian Quarter

Uncovered Cardo

Plaza

Jami Kabir

Steps

Burnt House

Steps to Western Wall

4 Sephardi Synagogues

Dung Gate

N

Car Park

Location of the Byzantine Nea Church

The Jewish Quarter

full to overflowing

In the following centuries the number of Jews in the city grew steadily, although as the overall population of Jerusalem was never large, their numbers were relatively small. By the start of the 18th C, out of a total population of around ten thousand the Jews numbered some two thousand. In the subsequent 60 years this number grew substantially and by the 1860s the Jews accounted for 50 percent of Jerusalem's population of 22,000.

Such a rapid increase brought severe overcrowding to the quarter, and this provided the impetus for the establishment of neighbourhoods without the ramparts. It also led to the acquisition of property, either through purchase or rental, outside the quarter, particularly in the Armenian and Muslim quarters which bordered the Jewish Quarter.

By the 1870s Jews, both within and without the walls, had become the majority in the city, and by the close of the century there were c15,000 people residing in the quarter alone.

expulsion by the Arab Legion

The establishment of neighbourhoods outside the walls relieved the pressure on the Jewish Quarter somewhat, but many of the devout still wanted to dwell as close as possible to the Western Wall shrine. During the 1948 war the Jewish Quarter was besieged by the

89

Arab Legion, and by May of that year severe fighting had broken out which resulted in damage and destruction to many buildings. Unable to withstand the pressure, the Quarter surrendered to the Arab Legion on 28th May, and all the inhabitants were evacuated to the western city.

During Jordanian rule (1948-67) most of the buildings were destroyed or taken over by Palestinians in the same way as the Israelis took over Palestinian-owned properties in the parts of the city they controlled. As explained in the Introduction above, the homes you see today are virtually all post 1967.

THE VISIT

Of all the quarters of walled Jerusalem, religious observance is most pronounced here, and the strict rules of Jewish conduct apply to all. Visitors should respect these, being reasonably clothed and refraining from smoking and photographing on Saturdays and Jewish feast days. Men should be prepared to don a head covering when entering synagogues and approaching the Western Wall. In most cases these are loaned.

▸ The Cardo

As mentioned elsewhere in this book, in Roman Aelia Capitolina, a broad street, the cardo maximus, stretched from the north gate (Damascus Gate) as far as the cross streets (decumanus) of David Street and the Street of the Chain. During the first part of the 6th C Justinian extended this in monumental fashion as far as the southern wall near the newly built Nea Church and it is clearly shown on the Madaba Map in St. George's Church, Madaba, Jordan (see *Jordan Revealed*, by this author, pp 66-68).

over reconstruction?

During renovation and reconstruction work along the Street of the Jews or Jewish Quarter Road (Hebrew, Rehov Ha'Yehudim) in the 1970s, part of this extension was uncovered, and has since been "rebuilt" in a not-too-convincing manner, although there are some points of real interest.

The reconstructed cardo is situated below ground level between Habad Street on the west and Jewish Quarter Road on the east. At various points along the c160 metre length, steps lead up to the latter. Main access is either from the south, in the Jewish Quarter, or from the north by turning south at the eastern end of David Street (see plan).

the very first wall of Jerusalem

Approaching by the latter way, you enter the reconstructed cardo through a gateway. On the west side is a balcony where you can see an excavated section of **Jerusalem's first wall** and you can even approach it down a very long flight of steps. Back on the balcony parts of two pillars from the Byzantine cardo, together with a Turkish cistern are visible. Explanatory plaques, together with a diagram, will assist your understanding.

The shops on either side are placed where ancient shops probably existed. Most of these are aimed at tourists with prices to match! The shrewd shopper can do better elsewhere!

colonnaded street

Further south you enter another section and here there is an impressive row of columns from the street. Naturally these have been extensively restored, but some of the grandeur can be imagined, in spite of much reinforced concrete! Remember, this entire boulevard was originally at street level in the open. Many girders have been installed to support the buildings now above.

In the short open section at the southern end of the restoration are six columns, five fully intact, standing in a row, their Byzantine Corinthian capitals still visible. To the west are recognisable remains of shops cut into the rock wall. This is perhaps the most impressive section of the entire restoration, and where your photographs will be taken.

‣ Hurva and Ramban Synagogues.

Ascending from the cardo, you enter the Jewish Quarter proper. Immediately to the east are the remains of two synagogues, the **Hurva** and **Ramban**. Ramban is another name for the Jewish scholar from Moorish Spain, Moses ben Nahman, generally known as Nahmanides.

History

A saviour from Spain

The Ramban synagogue was the first to be constructed in the Jewish Quarter. Rabbi ben Nahman was instrumental in rebuilding the Jewish community in Jerusalem after the Crusader era, during which they had been banned from the city. In a letter to his son, still living in Moorish Spain he wrote, *"Jerusalem is in... ruin... there is no Jewish congregation...only two brothers who are dyers...and they are joined by a minyan* (a prayer quorum) *of men who pray in their houses on the Sabbath. ...we found a ruined house built upon marble pillars with a beautiful dome and we made it our synagogue...".*

Modern opinion, however, thinks this actually refers to the synagogue built on Mount Zion (see History above) and that the Ramban structure was built c1400 when the community moved to this location. The 15th C edifice was apparently built over the ruins of a Crusader church, St. Martin's, parts of which were probably included in the original Jewish prayer house.

closed by the Ottomans

In 1474 the synagogue either collapsed or was destroyed by fanatics. Shortly afterwards the sultan, Qai't Bey, gave permission for it to be rebuilt. In 1586 the Ottomans prohibited further use of the building as a synagogue. Restoration was carried out after 1967, and there is a series of informative plaques and diagrams.

the new ruin

The newer "Hurva" adjoins to the north. It was built at the beginning of the 18th C by Ashkenazi Jews and called the Yehuda Hassid Synagogue. In 1721 it was destroyed. In the mid 19th C another building was erected on the site and named Beit Yaakov after Baron James de Rothschild who provided the funds. However it soon came to be known as the Hurva, meaning ruin (of Rabbi Yehuda Hassid).

When built it was one of the most important synagogues in Palestine. Like the Ramban synagogue it was restored post 1967.

The nearby minaret belongs to the mosque of **Jami Kabir**, which is certainly older than the Ramban synagogue and was probably built immediately after the Crusader period. It is mentioned by the Arab historian, Mujir al-Din.

▸ The Four Sephardi Synagogues

These are restored synagogues which belonged to the Sephardi community (Jews of Spanish and Portuguese origin).

History

Ottoman immigrants

After the expulsion of the Jews from Spain in 1492 many found refuge in the Balkans and parts of North Africa. When, in the early 16th C, these areas together with Palestine became part of the Ottoman Empire, these Jews, as Ottoman citizens, were free to settle in Jerusalem. Until the influx of Eastern European Jews (Ashkenazim) in the 19th C, the Sephardim formed the majority of the city's Jewish population.

recent destruction

Originally built at a low level because Ottoman law prohibited any structure being higher than a mosque, the rising level of the surroundings over the centuries has made them subterranean. These prayer places were in active use until the 1948 war and the subsequent withdrawal of the Old City's Jewish inhabitants. The ravages of the war and the neglect that followed reduced them to all but complete ruins. They were restored after the Israelis took the city in 1967 and reopened for services in the early 1970s.

From the outside the complex looks like an ordinary building, and it is only the two stone domes on the roof – which can be seen from certain angles – that provide a clue that something more was actually here.

how to find them

To get to these synagogues, from the plaza adjacent to the Hurva and Ramban synagogues, walk south on Mishmeret Ha-Kehuna Street for about 50 metres. The structure that houses them is on the east (left) side. You enter from a sunken courtyard that is reached by steps around to the left. **They are open Sunday to Thursday 09.00-16.00; Fridays till 13.00.** There is an entry fee.

The Visit

The first and largest of the synagogues is the **Yohanan ben Zakai** built at the beginning of the 17th C, and then called in Ladino, El Kahal Grande (Ladino is the Sephardi equivalent to Yiddish and is a blend of Spanish and Hebrew, whereas the latter is a German-Hebrew mix.) The current name dates from the end of the 19th C and was loosely applied to the whole complex.

The layout, common in Sephardi synagogues, places the *bimah* (pulpit) area in the centre and the seating all around. The cross vaulting dates from the 1830s and replaced pillars that supported the ceiling. At the southern end are three arched and recessed windows with further square windows above.

ready for the Messiah

Before 1948 a vial of oil and a ram's horn were placed here, ready for the advent of the Messiah. Now a glass case houses a new vial and horn, still awaiting this occasion. The two stones of the Law above the *Aron Kodesh*, the Holy Cupboard where the scrolls of the law are kept, are from the ancient synagogue in Livorno, Italy.

Elijah comes to pray

Through the doorway at the western end is the **Elijah Synagogue** opened in 1586, and the oldest of the four. Originally called by another name, it acquired the appellation Elijah because of a legend that at one time the worshippers were one short of the ten man quorum needed for congregational prayers. This was filled by the prophet. The embellished chair and the *Aron Kodesh* are restorations of the centuries-old originals that were in the synagogue in Livorno and were damaged by fire during the Second World War.

Returning to Yohanan ben Zakai Synagogue, a doorway towards the centre opens into the **Central Synagogue** built in the mid 18th C for a small congregation. The area was originally that part of Yohanan ben Zakai reserved for women (in Jewish tradition women are separated from men during worship).

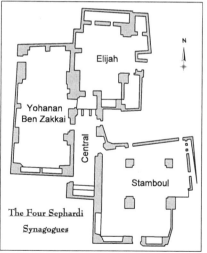

Italian relics

From here you can enter the **Stambouli Synagogue** built in 1764 by Jews from that city. Like the Elijah Synagogue it has a stone dome. Some of the furnishings are also from Italy – the *Aron Kodesh* is from Ancona, and the *bimah*, with four wooden pillars that look like marble, is from the old synagogue of Pesaro.

The pillars at the sides of the *Aron* are inscribed with verses from the Psalms, and these also hail from Pesaro.

▶ Israelite Remains

Retrace your steps to the plaza and turn to reach Jewish Quarter Street above the cardo. Walk north for about 100 metres till you reach, on the right, Plugot Ha'Kotel Street. Turn right into it, and follow the short street till it bends sharply north, left. On the right, and below street level is the first of two wall remnants from the

Israelite period, a carefully preserved section of wall believed to date from the reign of Hezekiah (8th C BC), and called the **Broad Wall**.

▸ The Broad Wall

no cement needed

This very ancient fragment is 7 metres thick and built of quite small stones that were laid without mortar and have stood for 28 centuries! Some scholars think this could be part of a northern defence line against the Assyrian king, Sennacherib, who besieged the city in the early 8th C BC. In spite of being only a small section, it is most impressive.

▸ Israelite Tower

Continue north on Plugot Ha'Kotel street for c50 metres to where it widens at the junction of Shonei Halakhot Street. On the left is a building, number 10, with arches at street level. Enter, and after waking the dreamy guardian and paying the requisite fee you can descend deep beneath the modern city to view the remains of an Israelite tower together with some of the city's defences dating from the Hasmonean period.

vestiges from Nebuchadnezzar's battle

The **Israelite Tower**, c8 metres high and 4 metres thick, has been dated to the 7th C BC. Attempts to identify this tower exactly must be but conjecture, but mounds of cinders and charred arrow heads found there indicate a battle once raged around it. This was probably during the Babylonian pillage of the city under Nebuchadnezzar in 586. The **Hasmonean Tower**, some 9 metres square and clad in dressed stone, is part of the 2nd C wall built by those rulers.

The tour now returns to the Hurva plaza and this is best achieved by walking back to the Broad Wall and just past it turning SE (left) into Tifferet Yisrael Street. Seventy metres or so will bring you into the plaza. Continue east across it, remaining on Tifferet Yisrael Street. Another c70 metres, just before some arches, is our next stop, the **Burnt House**. This is on the left and entered through a very modern doorway.

▸ The Burnt House (Bayit Ha'Saruf)

This relic was uncovered in the early 1970s and subsequently excavated. The house was a Jewish residence incinerated during the Roman rasing of the city in AD 70. The building possibly belonged to the priestly family of Bar Katros (mentioned in the Babylonian Talmud) as this name was inscribed on one of the artefacts found there. Many items of everyday life were discovered and from these an idea of the daily life at the time has been formed.

fully explained

The building comprised four rooms, one of which showed no signs of burning, a kitchen, a yard and a *mikveh* (ritual immersion bath). All the finds have been collated into an exhibition, which is open to the public **Sundays to Thursdays from 09.00 to 17.00, Fridays till 13.00**. There is also an audio visual presentation on this and other discoveries in the Jewish Quarter. An admission fee is charged.

underneath the arches

The vaulted area outside the Burnt House was once part of a **Crusader bazaar**. When the quarter was reconstructed after 1967 the planners decided to restore the arches, and although they have quite a new appearance they are in fact those built by the Crusaders. The area is now an agreeable one of cafés, galleries and shops.

At the eastern end, a few steps take you into Misgav Ladach Street named after a former Jewish hospital nearby. It was also once called Harat Maydan. Directly opposite is an arched entrance which leads into a Crusader hospice, **St. Mary of the Germans**.

▸ St. Mary of the Germans

This very well maintained ruin is built on several levels, the lower ones of which are set in a garden that can be visited if you descend through the garden towards the Western Wall. The structure belonged to the German Hospitaliers Knights of St. John. Just outside the entrance, on the right in an alcove, is a plan of the place. Established to care for the needs of German pilgrims it was situated in a part of the city that was a German locale. The ruin had been very neglected and was only restored to its present condition post 1967.

superb vantage point

One of the nicest things about this place is the view it affords over the Haram al-Sharif towards the Mount of Olives. A photograph of this view from the eastern apse of the church is on the front cover of this book. From here you can make your way to the Western Wall either down the broad steps or through the garden, meeting up with the steps lower down.

Alternatively you could walk north along Misgav Ladach Street, one of my favourite streets in Jerusalem.

get your camera ready

Misgav Ladach Street, or Harat Maydan, is a lovely vaulted alleyway invoking all the atmosphere of Old Jerusalem. Although officially part of the Jewish Quarter, it possesses an oriental ambience that eludes the rest of the modern-feeling quarter. The vaulting along here is original and restored post 1967. Now it is one of the most picturesque streets in the Old City.

Misgav Ladach leads, after about 175 metres, into Tariq Bab al-Silsileh, and you can descend from here to the Western Wall (see Chapter 8).

7. The Armenian Quarter

INTRODUCTION AND HISTORY

The Armenian Quarter lies in the SW part of the Old City between the Christian and Jewish quarters. From the south wall by Mount Zion, it gently slopes down towards the city's centre and covers an area of c10 hectares, making it about half the size of the Christian Quarter.

home of the High Priest

During the Roman period this area included the palace of King Herod, the High Priest's house and other important offices. The legion garrisoning Jerusalem, the Tenth, was also encamped here.

Although not all the residents are Armenian, apart from the very fringes bordering the Jewish Quarter where the two merge, all are Christian. There is but one small mosque in the quarter, right near the parking lot of the Jewish Quarter.

separate identity

Armenians, while being citizens of Palestine, have never been Palestinians and pride themselves on their separate and ancient identity. They are used to living under successive governments. I recently spoke with a 50 year-old schoolteacher who told me that his 92 year-old father, still living, had possessed a Turkish identity card in his youth, then later a British one, that being replaced by a Jordanian card in 1948, and for the past almost 30 years he has held an Israeli one. "Yet", he added, "he, like myself, was none of these; we are Armenian!"

bought from the Georgians

Armenians originally hail from the western Caucasus and in the 4th C were the first nation to officially adopt Christianity as their national religion. They have lived in Jerusalem since at least the 7th C when under the patriarchate of Gregory the Illuminator many Armenian institutions were founded in the city.

The focus of the quarter, the Convent and Cathedral of St. James, was acquired from the Georgians in the 12th C who, due to financial difficulties, were forced to sell many of their properties. Their extensive "rights" in the Church of the Holy Sepulchre were achieved in similar fashion.

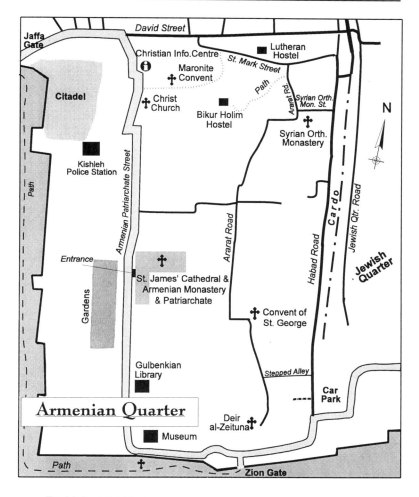

Turkish atrocities

The big influx of Armenians into the city and surroundings came in 1915 when the terrible Turkish massacres that occurred in Anatolia, urged on by the emerging Turkish nationalism, forced many to flee to Syria, Palestine and Jordan as well as countries all over the world. It is said that 1.5 million Armenians and, to a lesser degree, Syrian Orthodox, were slaughtered in 1915-6. As a totally Christian people, the Armenian Orthodox Church, a Monophysite church, is the very centre of their national identity, and few are not ardent churchgoers. A very small number have split away to form an Armenian Catholic Church with allegiance to Rome.

fragrance of jasmine

Apart from St. James Cathedral and the Monastery of St. Mark there are not very many sites to visit, the delights of this quarter being appreciated from just wandering around. This is especially so in summer and autumn when the scent of jasmine pervades the air. The homes are neat and tidy, and the oft-seen mess or spilt garbage of the Muslim and even the Christian quarters is rarely encountered. If a courtyard gate is ajar, peek in to get a glimpse of the potted plants and shady corners. Being a very friendly people, you may be invited in. Armenians are generally well educated and most speak good English.

As elsewhere in the Middle East, Armenians have their own schools; the pupils wear neat uniforms and the girls look especially pretty with their dark complexions and smooth black hair.

pottery experts

Armenians are extremely good potters and decorators, and not only in their quarter, but in many other place in the walled city they have shops with their work on sale.

THE VISIT

▸ Convent and Cathedral of St. James

The most important area in the quarter is the Convent and Cathedral of St. James (Yaakob), which is reached from the Jaffa Gate by walking past the Christian Information Centre and Christ Church, and continuing along Armenian Patriarchate Road to the end of the short vaulted section. The entrance is just here. Spread over a wide area, it occupies in its entirety something like twenty per cent of the quarter.

visiting times

Within the vast complex lies the residence of the Armenian Patriarch of Jerusalem, St. James Cathedral, quarters for nuns and monks, a hospice for pilgrims and various other offices of this closely knit community. **Visiting times are very short, strictly limited to the afternoon service, Monday to Friday from 15.00 to 15.30 or Saturday and Sunday at 14.30.** You will not be able to view the whole complex, but what you can see is very worthwhile. You can always go twice!

the two Jameses

The Cathedral is dedicated to James the Greater, the son of Zebadee, a disciple of Jesus (Matthew 4:21). James was executed by Agrippa in AD 44, and the site of his tomb was thought to be located here. Jesus' brother, James the Lesser, the first Bishop of Jerusalem – and likewise beheaded – is also commemorated here by one of the thrones in the Cathedral (see below).

Egyptian martyr

The earliest church built in this location was in the 5th century and dedicated to Minas, an Egyptian martyr. It was a church and nunnery, with an Armenian as abbot. This structure was destroyed either by the Sasanians in 614 or the Seljuks in 1071.

Byzantine ruins

During the latter part of the 11th C, the Georgian Christians were allowed to build a church to St. James on the foundations of the Byzantine ruins. Parts of that are still present in the cathedral of today. When in the 12th century the Georgians were unable to maintain the building, the Crusaders allowed the Armenians to acquire it.

financial help from Spain

Various changes were made to the complex: a new chapel to Midas was consecrated as were two more dedicated to SS Peter and Paul. During the 15th C communications with the Spanish Church brought much needed financial aid at a time of general difficulties in the city.

Until the mid 17th century an arcade ran along the south wall, but this was closed to create the Etchmiadzin Chapel. The original 12th C door is to the south, although the present entrance is via a porch on the west.

pilgrims pay, but not enough

In 1670 an Armenian Patriarchate of Jerusalem was established, Eliezar proclaiming himself as first patriarch. Throughout the 17th C there was an increased flow of pilgrims which helped fill the coffers of the convent but, for various reasons, including paying for repairs to the Church of the Holy Sepulchre, the convent found itself in debt at the beginning of the 18th C.

In 1720 a new patriarch, Gregory, was appointed, and the convent's debts were settled. Repairs and alterations were carried out over the next ten years, and few changes have been made since then.

The Visit

As stated you may only visit St. James during the afternoon service and many parts are always closed to visitors. Although I have always found the Armenian people very friendly, this does not seem to extend to St. James, especially among the clergy.

wooden bells

On entering the compound you pass into a small courtyard with a 19th C fountain. The church is on the east (right). On the west wall of the yard are various inscriptions dating from the 12th and 13th centuries. Notice on the right of the porch as you enter two *synamids* or wooden bars which sound like gongs when struck. These were used in Ottoman times when the sound of church bells was forbidden.

gloomy interior

The very richly decorated cathedral is dimly lit; only on holidays are all the lamps lit, and even then many areas remain quite dark. This serves to create a somewhat mystical atmosphere, especially when there is a candle-lit procession. Four square piers separate the wide nave from the side aisles, the piers supporting the vaults and dome. At the east end are three apses, the left one dedicated to John the Baptist and the right to the Virgin Mary. The marble floor is covered with carpets and rugs.

Kütahya tiles

The lower parts of the piers and walls are faced with blue on white tiles of floral and abstract design made by the Armenians of Kütahya (Turkey), while the centre areas have 18th C and later canvas paintings of saints. The tiles were originally made for the Church of

99

the Holy Sepulchre in the 18th century, but placed here instead. To the east are three apses each with raised altars.

changed entrance
The original entrance was from the south and the 12th C door is still there, leading into the **Etchmiadzin Chapel**. The west entrance, the one used today dates from the 17th C.

The dome is fairly low, and underneath the vaulting are all sorts of lamps and chandeliers.

James the Lesser's throne?
Just by the NE pier are two Patriarchal thrones, one inlaid with

Armenian Patriarchate, 19th C

ivory. Tradition has it that this was the throne of James the brother of Jesus who as the first bishop of Jerusalem was put to death around the year 65.

To the NE is the cathedral's baptistry, called the **Church of St. Stephen**. At the east are three altars, the north (left), dedicated to St. Cyril, the centre to St. Stephen, and the right to St. Gregory the Illuminator.

red marks the spot
Near the NW corner is the diminutive 12th C **Chapel of St. Makarios**, bishop of Jerusalem from 312 to 334. Very close by another small chapel, this time that of St. James himself, houses the spot – marked by a piece of red marble – which is the traditional site of Jesus' brother's decapitation.

women separate
The upper level has three small chapels. **The Chapel of the Apostles** in the NW is approached by a flight of concealed steps in the NW corner, while those of **SS Paul and Peter** are over the cathedral's apses and reached by stairs in the south wall.

In many eastern churches men and women do not sit together, and a women's gallery was built in the 1830s. Access to this (for those who are permitted), is via the Etchmiadzin Chapel.

Armenian artefacts

Exiting the convent turn south. On the opposite side of the road is a very good Armenian pottery shop which you might find worth taking a look at. This area is the Armenian garden and contains many offices of the community.

About 60 metres along on the left, a gateway leads into a courtyard with the **Mardigian Museum** on the right and the **Gulbenkian Library** opposite. The museum houses a variety of exhibits pertaining to the Armenian presence in the city, including sections of tiled and mosaic floors, frescoes, manuscripts, photographs and other treasures. The library also house a collection of rare manuscripts as well as over 30,000 volumes. **The museum is open Monday to Saturday from 10.00 to 16.30, while the library is open on the same days between 16.00 and 18.00 only**. This occupies an old Armenian school dating from the 1840s.

near Mount Zion

The road now turns east (left) with the Zion Gate and Mount Zion outside the south wall. There lies the **Armenian Church of the Holy Saviour**, described in the Mount Zion chapter. Continue past the Zion Gate, following the road around to the left into Habad Street. The car park for the Habad sect residents of the Jewish Quarter is on the right.

Take the second alley on the left in Habad Street. There is no name displayed but you can't miss it; you enter it through an arch and it is stepped. At the top, c75 metres, turn left, and straight ahead is the entrance to the **Church of the Holy Archangels** also known as the Deir al-Zeituna, the Convent of the Olive Tree. It is really part of the St. James complex, and is no longer officially open to the public, though if you see someone around they may let you in.

another scourging site?

According to Armenian tradition this site has a number of connections. In the 14th C it was deemed to be the site of the house of Annas, the father-in-law of Caiaphas, where Jesus was taken after being arrested (John 18:13). It acquired the name Convent of the Olive Tree because of the tree in its grounds which, according to a minor tradition, is supposed to be a descendant of the tree Jesus was tied to while waiting to be questioned or while being scourged.

mystery of the holy archangels

Surprisingly, I have never been able to find out for sure why it acquired the name Church of the Holy Archangels. I have been told at least four separate reasons, the most recent being that when Jesus was being scourged here, the angels covered their faces so as not to witness the act. At the west end of the church (narthex), in the NE corner is a small chapel, the **Chapel of the Scourging**. Another chapel at the SE end of the convent has a wooden door with the date 1649 inscribed.

▸ Church of St. George

The route continues north on Harat Deir al-Zeit and after c100 metres, by a junction in the lane stands the Crusader **Church of St. George.** This is now a rebuilt modern-looking structure owned by the Greek Orthodox Church.

The lane now bends left then right and continues north for another c225 metres changing its name to Ararat St. After a sharp right turn our next stop is reached.

▸ Convent and Church of St. Mark

St. Mark's is the seat of the Syrian Orthodox Bishop in Jerusalem and the most important church of that denomination in the Holy Land.

site of many occurrences

The Syrian Orthodox believe this was the site of the house of Mark, the writer of the second (perhaps the oldest) Gospel. Their tradition also connects the place with the site of the Last Supper, the utterances of Pentecost (Acts 2:1ff), the baptism of Mary and other New Testament happenings.

This site has been in the hands of the Syrian Church since around the 13th C. There was a church here in Byzantine times and parts of the present one date from the 12th C. The church is small, but beautifully decorated. Near the entrance door is a 6th C engraved plaque discovered during rebuilding in 1940. The guardian will show you a Syriac Old Testament, written on parchment, which is over 600 years old. On the south wall is an icon of the Virgin, which they claim was painted by St. Luke. Down in the crypt are some vestiges of the original building.

The Syrian Orthodox community in Jerusalem is quite small, their main centre being in Bethlehem.

The church is open for visitors every day 9.00 to 12.00 and from 15.30 to 17.30. A guardian with limited English will show you around. An offering is expected.

from hospital to hostel

Outside the convent, Ararat Street continues straight ahead (north) for a short distance. A very short way along take the first turning on the left into Bikur Holim St. At the end is a small building, now a **youth hostel**, which was once the second Jewish hospital in the Old City.

Until the 1850s there were no Jewish hospitals in Jerusalem. Jews who needed medical treatment were compelled to use the medical facilities set up by missionary societies, whose interest in the patient was not confined to the administering of medical aid, but also spiritual, in the hope of converting them to Christianity.

foiling the missionaries

In 1837 the Bikur Holim (Attending the Sick) Society was formed, which initially gave medical help to people in their own homes. In 1864 the society acquired this building in the Armenian Quarter because it was located near a missionary hospital. They hoped that the presence of a Jewish hospital would deter Jews from availing themselves of missionary-provided medical treatment. It opened in 1867 with twelve beds in three rooms. By 1891 it had grown to 36 beds, and by 1914 to 50 beds.

In 1924 a new hospital was purpose-built in the Street of the Prophets (see Chapter 15), but this building continued to serve the chronically sick until 1948. The front part of the building is the original wing. It was turned into a youth hostel in 1978.

Return to Ararat St. and after turning left walk the few metres to the T-junction which is St. Mark's Street.

▶ The Maronite Convent

Turn left and walk upwards past the Lutheran Hostel on your right. The first street on the left is Maronite Convent Street which leads to the convent, on the right, of that name. It is number 25, and above the large iron door is a cross with Mar Maron, St. Maron, inscribed above it. Ring the bell and you will be admitted.

The Maronites are a small Christian denomination with allegiance to Rome. Their main centre is in Lebanon where the majority of Christians are Maronite. The Maronite Church was founded in the 5th C and, often persecuted, its followers found refuge in the mountains of Lebanon. In the 12th C, under the protection of the Crusaders some monks came to Jerusalem and founded a monastery. They acquired this property in the late 19th C and built a church, hospice and school.

stay the night?

Visitors are always welcome, and there is a hospice where you can lodge, but it is often full.

▶ Christ Church

Continue past the convent and after some 50 metres you will arrive again in the square facing the citadel, with Christ Church on the left corner. Christ Church is the oldest Anglican Church in Jerusalem, Palestine and indeed the whole former Ottoman domains.

In the 19th C there was no Protestant church in Jerusalem, and under the enterprise of King Frederick Wilhelm IV of Prussia a joint Anglican/Lutheran Bishopric was established. This church was opened in 1849.

With the building of the Erlöserkirchen, the Church of the Redeemer (see Chapter 5) in 1898, this joint cooperation was terminated.

The church is open every day and also has a well used hospice and hostel.

8. Haram al-Sharif

▸ 1. HARAM AL-SHARIF

Introduction

Known to Muslims as al-Haram al-Sharif, the Noble Sanctuary, and to Jews as Har Ha-Bayit, the Temple Mount, this is an area hallowed to both faiths. Yet apart from the Crusader period, it is and has been Muslim property for almost 1400 years, with all the shrines erected upon it being Muslim. It thereby presents a thoroughly Islamic atmosphere.

Jerusalem landmark

The sanctuary covers some 14 hectares, around 18 per cent of the Old City area. At its heart is a 4.5 hectare elevated platform, about 4 metres higher than the surroundings. In the centre of this platform is the most visual structure in Jerusalem: the golden-crowned Qubbat al-Sakhra, or Dome of the Rock, a monument as instantly recognisable as a landmark of Jerusalem as the Eiffel Tower is of Paris and Big Ben is of London.

most sacred sanctuary

Within the Haram (Sanctuary) are sited, after Mecca and Medina, Islam's most holy mosques: the great congregational mosque of Al-Aksa and the beautiful pilgrimage shrine of Qubbat al-Sakhra. Outside and below is the Western Wall, the site most sacred to the Jewish people.

bewildering spot

The Haram al-Sharif has been the subject of study by archaeologists, historians, architects and many others for nigh on 200 years. Many books have been written on the subject, and I'm sure many are still to come. For any visitor, even those with a particularly inquiring mind, it can be a perplexing subject. Knowing that your trip to Jerusalem will be packed with plenty to keep you busy, I have endeavoured to keep my descriptions to a minimum while retaining the important details. With such a place it is easy to get carried away and forget that, as well as travelling to this city for its historical attractions, you may also be here on holiday! For those who seek greater particulars, I can but refer you to the bibliography at the end of this book.

fascination – and emotion

But with or without an in-depth examination of every shrine, you should find a stroll around the area, with its colourful people and exotic sights, totally fascinating – perhaps the high point of your trip. The sites of the Haram and the Western Wall are much more than mere archaeological and historical curiosities. Both are alive with the presence and aura of their respective faithful, the passionate focus of their prayers and aspirations, national as well as spiritual. As such, the area is permanently charged with a heady climate of emotion. Not always obvious to the outsider, it simmers away, never far below the surface calm.

History

Place of sacrifice

Traditionally this elevated point is equated with the Mountain of Moriah *"Now it came about...that God tested Abraham...And He said, 'Take now your son...and go to the land of Moriah and offer him there as a burnt offering on one of the mountains of which I will tell you.'"* (Genesis 22:1-2). Muslims also accept this story, but their tradition has Ishmael as the sacrificial son.

Solomon builds a house for the Lord

The mount is also identified as the place where David was instructed to *"Go up, erect an altar to the Lord on the threshing floor of Araunah the Jebusite"* and *"David bought the threshing floor...and...built there an altar to the Lord"*. (Genesis 24:18 and 24-25). Here Solomon built the first Israelite Temple which was completed around 950 BC. Nothing of this edifice remains but we are left with the detailed biblical narrative for its description.

destroyed by Nebuchadnezzar

After the division of the Israelite kingdom this temple, as did Jerusalem, became part of the Kingdom of Judah. It stood for a little over three and a half centuries, being totally destroyed by Nebuchadnezzar around 585 BC.

The Babylonians were superseded by the Achaemenid Persians and in 536 the ruler Cyrus II allowed the Judeans to return and rebuild their temple. Though few actually returned, they managed to rebuild a semblance of the original, but by all accounts it was considerably smaller and did not match the former's magnificence. During subsequent centuries, especially in the Hasmonean era, this temple was improved upon.

Herod's magnificent replacement

However, it was left to an Idumean (Edomite) who had converted to Judaism to build what was almost certainly the largest and most elaborate of the temples. Herod the Great commenced work on his structure in 20 BC and although in use some years later, its construction continued into the next century. So monolithic was his enterprise that the whole area was extended by the fabrication of a huge platform, buttressed with vaulting and retaining walls. The Western Wall is part of the retaining wall.

It is Herod's temple which is associated with the life and times of Jesus. A complete model, based on the best archaeological evidence, is on display at the Holyland Hotel in Bayit Ve'Gan, a West Jerusalem suburb..

destruction of the Second Temple

We are not sure whether all Herod's plans for the platform were ever completed, as in AD 70 the whole of the city was rased by the Romans.

Subsequently the site remained in ruins till Hadrian rebuilt the city as Aelia Capitolina when it is thought they erected a temple to Jupiter there. During the Byzantine period no major use was made of the site, it being left in ruins, the focus of reverence in Jerusalem being the Church of the Holy Sepulchre. However, the Madaba Map does show some constructions near its peripheries.

Islamic epoch

In the Koran, Muhammad relates a vision in which he was transported on a nocturnal journey to Jerusalem where he was lifted into heaven to the very presence of God: *"Glorified is He Who carried His servant by night from the Inviolable Place of Worship to the Far Distant Place of Worship the neighbourhood whereof we have blessed..."* (Koran, sura 17:1).

Although not mentioned by name, from the very first, the Far Distant Place was equated with Jerusalem.

finding the Far Distant Place

According to the 10th C Muslim historians Shihab al-Din al-Makdisi and Shams al-Din al-Suyuti, after 'Umar took Jerusalem in 638 the caliph demanded to be taken to the *masdjid*, prayer house, of David, but instead was shown different churches. However 'Umar saw through this duplicity as, according to the historians, the Prophet had described to him the place he had seen on the nocturnal journey; he was then taken to the temple area which he instantly recognised as the right place!

mosque marks the spot

He then had the area cleared of debris and at the southern end built a simple wooden mosque. The presence of this mosque was confirmed by the German bishop Arculf who visited the city around 670.

During his lifetime, and taking a cue from the Jews from who he drew so much of his thought, Muhammad turned towards Jerusalem for prayer. Hence Jerusalem became the third most holy place in Islam, and it is sometimes given preference over the other two, Mecca and Medina, which only really became sacred after the Prophet's death.

construction starts in earnest

In 691 the Caliph Abd-al-Malik built the Qubbat al-Sakhra, the Dome of the Rock. In 715 his son al-Walid reconstructed the simple wooden mosque into the al-Aksa Mosque (details below).

This was followed by many centuries of Muslim building on and around the area. In the 8th and 9th C damage was caused by earthquakes but this was soon repaired. During the Crusader Kingdom alterations were made but most of the main buildings were left as they were – just put to different use! After Salah al-Din's retaking of the city, all traces of Christianity were removed, and the Ayyubids returned them to Islamic usage. It is during this and the subsequent Mameluke eras that the general appearance of the Haram as we see it today, took shape.

status quo preserved

When the Israelis captured the city in 1967, the then defence minister, Moshe Dayan, appreciating the significance of the Haram to Muslims worldwide, turned its administration over to the *Wakf*, the Muslim religious foundation. Because of this, in spite of the political and physical changes in Jerusalem, the Haram remains firmly Muslim property. Palestinian wardens control the area and its buildings, but to the annoyance of all Muslims, the heavily armed Israeli para-military police and soldiers patrol the precincts, and have on occasion (including the summer of 1996) opened fire there.

waiting for the Messiah

From time to time extremist Jewish groups attempt to conduct prayer services on the mount, but these, being prohibited by the authorities, are thwarted. Strangely, the most Orthodox Jews will not step within the walls as they believe they must only do so when the messianic age comes and the Temple is rebuilt. Additionally, as no one knows for certain where the Holy of Holies of the original temple stood, they fear they might stand on its site inadvertently and thus desecrate it.

There are many extremist Jews (and Christians) who would like to eject the Muslims, but wisely, all Israeli governments since 1967 have so far understood the folly of such a move.

The Visit

Entry and visiting information

Visiting times

Access gates for non-Muslims are the Gate of the Chain, Bab al-Silsileh and the Moors Gate, Bab al-Maghariba, inside the Dung Gate. Visiting times are Saturday to Thursday, from 08.00 to midday prayer time, and from the end of these prayers until afternoon prayer time, and then till about 16.00. Prayer times vary according to season, but are around 11.00 in the morning and 14.00 in the afternoon, lasting for about one hour. To visit the site with any degree of thoroughness will require about three hours, so best to get there early in the morning. You'll also be glad of the cooler temperatures.

Admission fees

There is no admission fee to the actual sanctuary, but you do need to buy tickets to enter the Dome of the Rock and al-Aksa. The ticket booth is located between the Moors Gate and the al-Aksa mosque.

Dress

Dress with respect as for all holy places. Women will have to cover their arms and shoulders. A shawl will be provided if necessary.

Skirts should be below knee length; trousers are permitted. Men may be refused entry wearing shorts.

Personal belongings

A major drawback for lone visitors is that in addition to removing your shoes before entering the mosques you are not allowed to enter with bags or cameras. This means that they have to be left outside on the ground. While shoes will always be safe, I can't imagine anyone being brave (or foolish) enough to leave a bag with valuables or a camera unattended! So if you are visiting alone, leave your camera at the hotel if you intend to enter the mosques, returning another time for the outdoor photographs. If you are in company then you can of course take it in turns to go in.

Photography

Apart from inside the Dome of the Rock and al-Aksa you are at liberty to photograph, but please remember many Muslims, especially women, do not like strangers taking pictures of them. Some areas are out of bounds and you will be directed away from these by the wardens.

Tour guides

There are a number of Arab guides who offer their services for quite a large fee. Naturally with such a thorough guide as "Jerusalem Revealed" you should not require their services!

▸ Moors' Gate (Bab al-Maghariba)

My tour begins by entering the Haram area from here, and even if you entered from the Chain Gate I suggest you make your way to this starting point. See map.

Bab al-Maghariba, the Gate of the Moors, is unsurprisingly so called because it was the nearest to the sector of the Muslim Quarter inhabited by Muslims from Moorish Spain and the Maghreb. This was situated where the Western Wall plaza is today and had stood for centuries. Immediately following the 1967 war, the Israelis bulldozed it flat to create a plaza large enough for thousands of worshippers, rehousing the hapless inhabitants elsewhere.

warning for the observant

The gate is approached by a long ramp built by the Israelis after the elimination of the Moors Quarter. It passes above the excavations underneath the Haram's western wall. At the beginning of the ramp is a notice in Hebrew and English indicating that it is forbidden to enter the Temple Mount area. This is not a legal warning but one aimed at Jewish people only, reminding them that strict Rabbinical law forbids entry to avoid stepping on the unknown site of the Holy of Holies, approachable only by the High Priest. Few Jews intent on visiting are dissuaded by such an admonishment!

spiritual milieu

On entering the inner porch of the early 14th C gate, your bags will be searched as a security measure. Once you have passed through the gate into the Haram you will probably be struck by the park-like greenery and the tranquillity. For up here the noise and

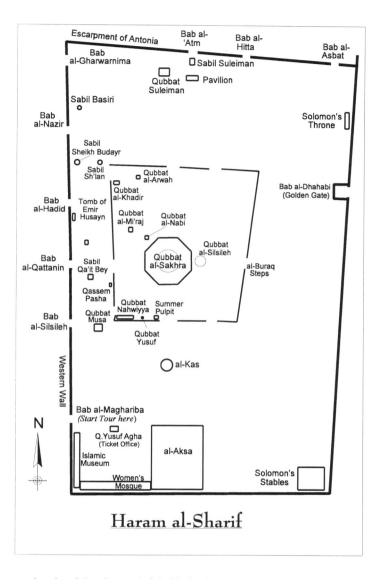

Haram al-Sharif

bustle of the city are left behind. Though you may not be a Muslim, nor of any religious persuasion, few will not find the atmosphere contemplative.

You will see the huge structure of the al-Aksa Mosque about 80 metres ahead to the south, and rising high to the NE the golden dome of the Qubbat al-Sakhra, the Dome of the Rock. However, before we reach these places, there is plenty more to see!

Coptic convert to Islam

Just inside the gate on the south are two entrances with pointed arches. These are entrances to the **al-Fakhriyya Mosque**, the prayer house of the madrassa founded by Fakhr al-Din Muhammad, a Coptic Christian who converted to Islam. The actual madrassa, built up against the SW wall, is made up of a residential area with interior courtyards. In one, a row of columns is topped by six cupolas. Much of the building is made up of recycled Crusader material, and was constructed in the mid 14th C. Above the building is a minaret.

► Haram-al Sharif Islamic Museum

South of this is the **al-Maghariba Mosque**, built in the late Ayyubid period for the use of the inhabitants of the Maghariba Quarter directly outside the gate. In the early 1880s Sultan Abdul Aziz restored the structure and since 1925 it has housed the **Haram-al Sharif Islamic Museum**, an institution worthy of a visit by those with a special interest.

collection of Korans

The anterior area has many items of stone, some from other parts of the Sanctuary, and others from elsewhere. Many of these have nothing to do with Islam, being either Roman or Crusader.

The interior has on display a truly marvellous collection of Korans, some very ancient. There is also a collection of artefacts covering the entire c1400 years of Islamic Jerusalem and of this place in particular.

original copper doors

Among the most outstanding of exhibits are the former doors of the Dome of the Rock covered in copper. These were a gift of the Mameluke Sultan, Qa'it Bey, and were taken down from their original place when the Qubbat was restored some years ago. Also on display are the carved cypress wood roof beams from the Omayyad al-Aksa Mosque of the 8th C.

Along the Haram's southern wall is a vast, now divided, **hall** built by the Knights Templar, during the period of the Crusader Kingdom of Jerusalem. While the western end is part of the Islamic Museum, the eastern end has for centuries been known as the **Jami al-Nasa**, the Mosque of the Women. The hall here measures some 12 by 75 metres. Inside, wide arches supported by pillars form its roof. The facade has a rebuilt Ayyubid entrance way, bordered by Crusader columns and capitals. The building is also called al-Jami al-Baida, the White Mosque.

buy your tickets here

Returning to the pathway that led east from the Moor's Gate, about halfway between it and the al-Aksa is a small domed building, **Qubbat Yussuf Agha**. The history of this is vague but an inscription states that it was restored in the 17th C. This is now used as the ticket office where the tickets for the mosques are bought, and if you intend to visit buy them now.

► Al-Aksa Mosque (Al-Masjid al-Aqsa al-Mubbarak)

We now reach the facade of the **al-Masjid al-Aqsa al-Mubbarak**, the Furthest and Most Blessed Mosque, to give it its full title, one of Islam's most holy congregational mosques. It is also the largest congregational mosque on both banks of the Jordan, and until recent years was the focus of Friday prayers for Jerusalem and the nearby West Bank areas. Nowadays, in the name of security, the authorities often prohibit worshippers from outside the city from attending prayers on the Haram. This makes the Israeli declaration of freedom of worship for all ring rather hollow!

Standing in front of al-Aksa places you before one of the greatest and most ancient prayer houses of the world.

History

According to tradition the site of this mosque is where Muhammad prayed after his nocturnal journey to Jerusalem (see above) and it is generally recognised as the site of the first wooden mosque built by 'Umar in 638. In c715 Walid I built the first stone building, after having just completed the construction of the Great Mosque of Damascus, an edifice that easily outshone the al-Aksa in opulence.

earthquake zone

In 747 the mosque was reduced by an earthquake, and was refashioned on a much larger scale, either by subsequent Ayyubid caliphs or by their successors, the Abbasids. In 1033 an earthquake again devastated the mosque and during the following two years it was restored by the Fatimid Caliph al-Zahir. This is essentially the building which you see today.

nice home for Crusader knight

After the Crusader conquest of Jerusalem in 1099, Godfrey de Bouillon made the al-Aksa his residence. In 1120, Baldwin, the first ruler of the Crusader kingdom, gave the Aksa to the Order of the Knights Templar. Calling it the Palatium Salomonis, they made it their headquarters, turning part into a church topped by a huge cross. Additions were built, of which the present Jami al-Nasa, the Mosque of the Women (see above), built in the great Templar hall, is but one.

Salah al-Din returns

After Salah-al-Din's re-conquest the building was returned to its previous character, and the cross removed. The interior was renovated and in honour of his general, Nur al-Din, a splendid minbar of carved and inlaid wood was installed.

Throughout the Mameluke and Ottoman periods the Aksa was constantly being renovated and extended. In 1927 the mosque was subjected to major reworking and some pillars required concrete reinforcement.

Jordanian king assassinated

After the 1948 fighting, with the whole of the Old City coming under Jordanian control, al-Aksa became the principal mosque of that kingdom. While entering the mosque for Friday prayers on 21st July 1951, with his grandson, Hussein, at his side, Jordan's King Abdullah was shot dead by an assassin.

fanatic sets fire to al-Aksa

When Israel took the Old City in 1967, great care was taken not to damage or violate the mosque. However, in 1969 a fanatical Christian set fire to the building causing severe damage. The beautiful minbar donated by Salah al-Din was completely destroyed. Subsequently, the mosque was closed for some years while major restoration took place. A replica of the pulpit was also made.

During the past few years the formerly silver dome has been darkened, and is now covered with lead.

still splendid

Today the al-Aksa is virtually restored, and in spite of all the alterations, additions, and reconstructions over the centuries, conforms essentially with the ancient structure. Al-Aksa is one of the historic prayer houses of the world, having survived in one form or another for over thirteen centuries. Don't let your journey to Jerusalem pass without seeing it.

The Visit

Built of Jerusalem limestone, the present edifice, while retaining some portions of the original Omayyad and Abbasid structure, is essentially that built by the Fatimid Caliph al-Zahir after the earthquake which struck at the end of 1033. Smaller than the 8th C edifice, it is still of significant size, measuring some 80 by 55 metres.

lucky sevens?

The north facing facade and ante-chamber or porch comprises seven arches corresponding to seven entrances which open onto the al-Aksa's seven naves. Of the seven arches the central one is the highest and widest, and above it is a Mameluke decoration consisting of ornamental pillars and arches.

The Templars, during their occupation (see History, above), executed much building work and the interior of the ante-chamber retains some of their 13th C efforts. The crenellations at the roof edge were added by Qa'it Bey. Seven doors give entry to the mosque's seven aisles, the central ones being the main entrances. These, with their moulded framework, are very early, probably from the original Omayyad and Abbasid construction.

multitude of columns

On entering, one is confronted by a forest of columns and piers. There are about 76 columns and 33 piers. In addition there are many smaller columns at various places around this vast hall.

The columns delineating the central nave were replaced between the years 1938 and 1943 when al-Aksa underwent a thorough renovation. The new ones are made of fine Carrara marble, a gift of the Italian government of the time.

Egyptian ceiling

Above the nave the sculpted and painted ceiling, also a product of the 1938-1943 renovation, was donated by King Farouk I of Egypt. It replaced the huge and ancient roof beams that are now displayed in the Islamic museum (see above, page 110).

mosaics, marble and gold

The oldest part of the building is perhaps the southern section. Here, six small, coloured columns border the mosaic and marble mihrab of Salah al-Din. The gold dedication translates, *"In the name of the merciful and benevolent God, the renovation of this Sacred Prayer Niche and the restoration of the mosque was ordered by... Salah al-Din when he took Jerusalem in the year 583 AH"*. To the east was, until its destruction in 1969, the lovely inlaid cedar wood minbar, also a gift of the great warrior.

Jesus' left footprint

Facing, supported by 14 columns is the platform on which the prayer caller stands. West of the pulpit are two more mihrabs; the first to Moses and the second to Jesus. That of Jesus is supposed to contain his left footprint taken from the Chapel of the Ascension on the Mount of Olives (see Chapter 12).

beautifully decorated dome

The great dome and its supports are the work of the Fatimid Caliph al-Zahir around 1035. However, some vestiges remain of the original Omayyad and Abbasid construction. The upper part was decorated in the 14th C and this is noted in an inscription. The dome, with vaulted windows and arches above, is built on a drum decorated with gold and green floral mosaics which are outstandingly beautiful. These were part of Salah al-Din's late 12th C restoration.

Other restorations to the dome were carried out in the early 19th C and in 1927 when the entire supports were renewed. Not too long ago the outer surface of the dome was recovered in lead, diminishing its historical silver appearance.

three more mosques

To the west of the south wall is the Jami al-Nasa, visited on page 110. To the east is the **Mosque of 'Umar** marking the traditional site of 'Umar's prayers in 638. To the north of this is the **Jami al-Arba'in,** the Mosque of the Forty (Martyrs). This was probably once a Templar chapel, and while it has no mihrab, there is an inscription with verses from the Koran describing Muhammad's night journey to Jerusalem.

which Zechariah?

Adjacent to the Mosque of the Forty is the **Prayer Room of Zechariah**. This 5 by 4 metre room pre-dates the Crusaders and was remodelled by them. In the south wall, the marble mihrab is flanked by two pillars with acanthus leaf capitals. The windows, one round and one rectangular in the east wall are Crusader. The room may be named after Zechariah, father of John the Baptist as some have attributed his death to this spot. More likely, the name refers to the prophet Zechariah, *"...whom you murdered between the temple and the altar"* (Math. 23:25), as the location would be more in keeping. However the truth is lost in history. Both personages are mentioned in the Koran.

When you've seen enough, collect your shoes and continue with the tour.

▸ Solomon's Stables

East of al-Aksa, at the SE corner of the Haram, are subterranean vaults known as **Solomon's Stables**, but in reality they have nothing to do with that king. They were in fact first built by Herod the Great during his rebuilding of the temple, and they were used as stables by the Templars. Perhaps they acquired the title "Solomon's" because the Templar's called their headquarters in the nearby al-Aksa mosque the Palatium Solomonis (see above).

if you could see them...

At this time the stables are closed to the public. Entry, if you could go in, is via a flight of steps. Beneath them is a niche that once most likely held a statue of a Roman deity. Muslims know it as Mihrab Maryam, the niche recorded in Sura 3:37 of the Koran. The steps lead into a vast hall divided into aisles by 12 rows of pillars, 88 in all, which support the vaults and arches, which in turn support the roof.

Rings attached to the walls testify to the fact that horses were once tethered here. They would have entered through a gate in the southern wall, the Single Gate, later blocked up by the Ayyubids.

▸ Al-Kas Ablutions Fountain

Between al-Aksa and the central platform is **al-Kas** or the Cup. This is an ablutions fountain for use by worshippers before prayers. Muslim ritual requires all to wash their hands, face and feet before performing their *salut*, prayers.

addition of taps

Al-Kas is a circular basin, two metres in diameter and cut from a single piece of stone. Surrounding it is a decorated railing and several taps. The worshippers sit on the stone stools while carrying out their duties. Al-Kas was built by the Emir Tankiz in 1320, although the mosaic in the centre is from the Ottoman period. The taps are newer. On the west of the fountain is an ancient olive tree, *zeituna al-Nabi*, associated with the prophet Muhammad.

From here 22 steps lead up to the elevated platform and the **Dome of the Rock**. At the top is a *qanatir* or arched arcade. Who will not be photographed on these steps!

▸ Central Platform

We have now ascended to the central raised area on which stands the Dome of the Rock and several other structures. It was built either just before or at the same time as the huge edifice, towards the end of the 7th C. Covering an area of c4.5 hectares, it stands about 4 metres above the rest of the Haram. The sides are irregular, the north measuring c155.5 metres, the south c127.5 metres, the east 161.5 metres and the west 167.5 metres.

scales of justice

There are eight flights of steps from the lower level: two on the south side, one on the east, two on the north and three on the west. Each flight is topped by a *qanatir*, or arcade, comprising of a number of arches. These arcades, which all must pass through to reach the great mosque, are metaphorically called *mawazin*, meaning scales. Islamic tradition has it that on Judgment Day every person's actions will be weighed by these illusory scales.

‣ Summer Pulpit (Minbar Burham as-Din)

At the top steps and immediately to the west is the **Minbar Burham al-Din**, the Summer Pulpit. Acquiring its name from the late 14th C Qadi Burham al-Din, the exact use of this marble minbar is uncertain. The structure was built or adapted from Crusader material, and you can see Crusader capitals on the pillars which support the dome. It was restored by the Ottomans in 1843.

I will now come to the main edifice on the platform leaving the others till later.

‣ The Dome of the Rock (Qubbat al-Sakhra)

> *"There is no more wonderful structure to look upon...save the Dome of the Rock in Jerusalem."*
> Ibn Jubayr, medieval traveller, when looking at the
> Great Mosque of Damascus, AD1184.

Islam's third most holy shrine, and the second place of pilgrimage, **Qubbat al-Sakhra**, the Dome of the Rock, is a building of outstanding beauty with its sumptuous colours and golden dome shimmering in the brilliant Jerusalem sunlight. One of the world's most famous and imposing buildings, it represents the ultimate example of Byzantine/Islamic architecture, and is the structure that most symbolizes Jerusalem. What newscast from this city would be complete without it as the backdrop!

rock of ages

The mosque is built over a rock, revered by Jews, Christians and Muslims as the summit of Mount Moriah, where Abraham was willing to offer one his sons as a sacrifice, and as the site of the threshing floor purchased by David where the Temple of Solomon (and its successor) was built. For Muslims it possesses an additional significance in that it is also the traditional site from where Muhammad ascended to heaven.

There are other reasons why the mosque was built besides the obvious one of the sanctity of the site – it served as a counter to the Church of the Holy Sepulchre and as a balance to the prominence of Mecca, which lay so far from the Omayyad capital, Damascus.

centre of pilgrimage

The Dome of the Rock is not a congregational mosque as is al-Aksa, but more a centre of pilgrimage. Although a journey here is not requisite for the Muslim faithful as is the *haj* to Mecca, for those who are able to come here it is their next priority.

History

Due to the complete destruction of Jerusalem by the Romans in AD 70, it is very difficult to know exactly what stood here before then. The sanctity of the site has made meaningful archaeological excavations out of the question. What is clear, though, is that there is no record of a structure here from that time until the Muslim conquest. How it became associated with the Prophet's ascension is lost in tradition.

no expense spared

Built in 691-2 the architects drew on the design of the Church of the Holy Sepulchre and other great Byzantine buildings for inspiration. However, in the case of this mosque very intricate geometry, of which the Arabs were then the masters, was used in the planning. No expense was spared in the construction, and craftsmen of many nationalities were employed. The dome was especially costly, being completely gilded. During the Fatimid era an earthquake caused considerable damage to the dome, and it was rebuilt by the Caliph al-Zahir.

souvenir rock

During the Crusader occupation of the city the Qubbat al-Sakhra was converted into the Templum Domini, the Temple of our Lord, and a huge cross erected on the dome. Other facets of Christianity, such as an altar, were installed. Christian pilgrims made their way here, many of whom would chip at the rock for holy souvenirs. So much so that the Augustines erected an iron barrier to prevent approach to it. Salah al-Din's reconquest of the city in 1187 returned the building to its rightful use.

sumptuous decoration

Until the early Ottoman period the mosque was faced with exquisite mosaics but, severely damaged by the ravages of time, these were replaced with marble and glazed tiles. (Some of these mosaics are on display at the Islamic Museum, see page 110) From time to time other renovations were carried out, such as those on the entrances and the repair and replacement of tiles and marble facings. Sultan 'Abd al-Hamid II re-carpeted the floor, and installed a belt of tiles with verses from Sura 36 of the Koran around the upper part of the octagon.

shaken by earth tremors

During British rule the lower part of the dome was repaired with tiles from Kütahya in Turkey. Earth tremors in 1927 and 1936 both caused damage, with world events delaying restoration until the Jordanians took control in 1948. The damage already sustained, together with the excessive weight of the lead roof and wear and tear of the ages, had made renovations very urgent.

all that glitters...

New carpets were laid, and the mosaics restored. The foundations were strengthened with concrete, and the entire outer surface recovered with specially fabricated Kütahya tiles. Most of all, the huge dome was encased in lightweight, gilded aluminium.

The Visit

The regulations for entering are the same as for al-Aksa, so please refer to the general information on page 107.

looking at the exterior

Qubbat al-Sakhra is an octagon. Each side is 20.5 metres long making it 53.5 metres in diameter. The whole building stands 43 metres in height. Each side has seven tall, arched decorated panels and five somewhat pointed windows. Above is an etching in Arabic glorifying God. The lower part of the facade is covered in white and grey marble. Above this, the octagon is covered with the Kütahya tiles, mainly blue, green and white. These date from the Jordanian restoration of the late 1950s, recorded on a plaque to the right of the entrance.

four entrances

The mosque has four doors, one at each compass point. The west entrance, the **Bab al-Gharb**, is today's main portal. The north one is known as **Bab al-Janna**, the Gate of Paradise. Above it is the inscription recording that the Qubba was restored by Suleiman I. The southern door, the **Bab al-Qibla** faces al-Aksa and the direction of prayer, while the east entrance, the **Bab al-Silsileh**, opens to the Dome of the Chain (see below).

At the top of the panels, and stretching all around the facade is the row of tiles contributed by 'Abd al-Hamid II in 1876 containing part of the 36th sura of the Koran. The earlier tiles were placed by Suleiman II in the mid 16th C and some of these are on display in the Islamic Museum (see page 110).

story of the night journey

At the top of the walls, the roof inclines towards the dome-supporting drum which is buttressed from inside the building. The tiles that cover the drum replaced the original mosaics. Around the circumference are sixteen windows and at the top a blue and white banding with verses from the Koran's 17th chapter which describes Muhammad's Night Journey.

all that glitters...

The dome has a double wooden frame dating back to the Fatimid Caliph al-Zahir's building of 1022. It has been encased with gold-coloured aluminium since 1960.

Inside the Dome of the Rock, 19th C

117

going inside

You will now be walking either barefoot or in your socks, and carrying nothing except this book.

The design and ornamentation of the interior is most impressive, made more striking by the dimness of the light.

Two colonnades, one inside the other, surround the mosque's main feature, the Rock, which is at the building's centre. The outer colonnade, parallel to the building's sides, is comprised of eight six-sided pillars, one at each of the mosque's angles. Between each pillar are two columns. The inner colonnade is made up of a series of arches resting on four pillars and twelve columns.

imposter's plaque

Many of the columns have been recycled from other, Roman and Byzantine structures and are thus dissimilar. The pillars are surfaced with marble, and the columns decorated with mosaic floral and geometric patterns. Above the mosaics, is an inscription attributing the construction of the Dome of the Rock to al-Ma'mun, 813 to 833. However, Ma'mun usurped this honour by erasing the original inscription which testified that 'Abd al-Malik was the founder, and replacing it with his own name.

Other parts of the inscription include the section of the Koran which rejects the Christian belief that Jesus is the son of God, indeed the whole concept of the Trinity:

> *"People of the Book, overstep not the bounds of your faith, and of God speak only the truth. ... Jesus the son of Mary, is only a messenger [prophet] of God and His Word... Believe therefore in God and His prophets, and say not three... God is only one God. Far be it from His glory that He should have a son."* (Koran, Sura 4:169)

the centre of the universe

At the very centre of the mosque, beneath the dome and in the middle of the colonnades, is the *raison d'être* of the building, the hallowed piece of rock. Measuring about 12.5 by 17 metres it is surrounded by a highly decorative wooden partition with inlaid and carved panels. Here, tradition has it, is the spot where Abraham offered to sacrifice Isaac (or Ishmael), and where the Holy of Holies of the Temples may have stood; and from this rock Muhammad and his horse are said to have ascended to heaven, passing on the way, among others, Moses, Abraham and Jesus.

According to a Jewish tradition expounded in the Talmud, the rock is the centre of the world and the foundation on which the entire universe was created. It is therefore called the *Even Hashetyya*, the Foundation Stone.

Naturally there is no evidence to connect this rock with any of the traditions attributed to it!

Muhammad's hairs

At the SW corner of the rock is a tower-like shrine supposedly containing some of Muhammad's hairs. To the SE a marble entrance leads to a cave beneath the rock. This appears to be of Crusader origin. Steps lead down to the cave which was used by the

Crusaders. There are two shrines here: one to Abraham, the other to the prophet Elijah. On the south wall are two prayer niches.

We'll now leave the muted illumination of the shrine and return to the other structures on the platform, shimmering in the brilliance of the Jerusalem sunlight. I suggest you refer to the plan to orientate yourself.

▸ Dome of Joseph (Qubbat Yusuf)

Just west of the Summer Pulpit is a small domed cube-like structure called **Qubbat Yusuf**, or the Dome of Joseph. It was built at the end of the 12th C by Salah al-Din, whose first name was Yusuf. It was renovated in 1681, recorded by a carving in Turkish (Arabic letters) on a plaque. On the south side is a mother-of-pearl inlaid mihrab.

▸ Dome of the Learning (Qubbat Nahwiyya)

Further west is the **Qubbat Nahwiyya**, Dome of the Learning. This is a rather long building of three rooms, built in 1207 by the then Ayyubid governor of Damascus.

We now reach another arcade and flight of steps. As these lead to the Bab al-Silsileh, this one is known as the **Mawazin Bab al-Silsileh**. Turning north, and facing the entrance to the Qubbat al-Sakhra is the western *qanatir* or *mawazin*.

▸ Dome of the Prophet (Qubbat al-Nabi)

Now comes a series of small domed structures. The first, and nearest to the mosque is **Qubbat al-Nabi**, the Dome of the Prophet. Named for the prophet Gabriel, this edifice dates from early Ottoman times. Its lead-covered cupola measures some three metres in diameter, and is carried on eight marble columns above which are stone arches.

▸ Dome of the Ascension (Qubbat al-Miraj)

To the NW of the Dome of the Prophet is the spot where Muhammad is supposed to have prayed before his ascension to heaven. It is therefore called **Qubbat al-Miraj**, the Dome of the Ascension. Built originally as a baptistery by the Crusaders it was Islamified by the Ayyubids after the re-conquest. This octagonal structure (the Church of the Ascension on the Mount of Olives is also an octagon), is capped with a leaded cupola supported by eight columns. On the south side is a mihrab. Almost behind is a rectangular building used for Koranic studies.

▸ Dome of St. George (Qubbat al-Khadir)

Very near the **NW** *qanatir* is **Qubbat al-Khadir**. This refers to St. George (although some say the prophet Elijah). St. George is known to Arabs as al-Khadir, the Green or Evergreen. The small dome rests on a hexagonal drum with six marble columns topped by arches. Immediately north is the NW arcade.

▸ Dome of the Spirits (Qubbat al-Arwah)

To the east is the octagonal **Qubbat al-Arwah**, the Dome of the Spirits. Eight marble columns support a 4 metre dome which is

119

surmounted by a finial with the Muslim crescent. In Muslim tradition the spirits of the dead are assembled here. Behind and to the north is the triple-arched arcaded north *mawazin* which leads to **Bab al-'Atm** (or Faisal). East of that is the *mawazin* which leads to **Bab al-Hitta**.

▸ Al-Buraq Steps

Turn now to the east side of the platform and the five arched eastern *qanatir* or *mawazin*. The steps leading down to the lower level are particularly wide, c11 metres, and are known in Muslim tradition as the **al-Buraq Steps**, after the horse that brought Muhammad from Mecca to Jerusalem. He was supposed to have entered the city through the eastern gate opposite. From here you can enjoy a wonderful view of the Mount of Olives, particularly enchanting when seen through the graceful arches.

▸ Dome of the Chain (Qubbat al-Silsileh)

Between these and the Dome of the Rock is the second most important edifice on this elevated area, **Qubbat al-Silsileh**, Dome of the Chain. For the past few years this building has been under renovation, and at the time of writing it still is.

Thought by many to be a prototype for the Dome of the Rock, it was built at the beginning of the 690s, just prior to the great mosque. The edifice is an eleven-sided building with concentric arcades made up of 17 columns, mostly re-cycled Byzantine material. The outer arcade comprises of eleven columns with arches. The inner arcade has six columns which support the hexagonal drum on which the cupola rests. The mihrab is decorated with marble and mosaics, the latter being a late addition.

place with many possibilities

Many traditions are associated with the place. One, from which it acquired its name, relates that it was the Mahkama or Tribunal. A chain was suspended from the ceiling and at the time of ruling the truthful could touch it whereas the guilty could not. Another says it was the treasury of the second Temple. There is a Jewish tradition that it was where the Ark of the Covenant was kept. During the Crusader occupation the building was converted into an oratory and dedicated to Jesus' brother, James the Lesser.

▸ Lower level of the Haram

Descending by these steps I will now guide you around the lower area of the sanctuary, moving in an anti-clockwise direction.

keep to the path!

The eastern wall of the Haram is also the eastern wall of the Old City, and for most of its length is out of bounds due to it being part of the Muslim cemetery that is mainly visible outside the wall. Any attempt to approach it will be thwarted by the wardens! Below the steps of the eastern *mawazin* is a pathway, and visitors are expected not to stray east of it.

▸ Golden Gate (Bab al-Dhahabi)

About 100 metres north you come level with the eastern gate of the

Haram, **Bab al-Dhahabi**, the Golden Gate. Actually it is a double gate, and the name applies to the whole. The northern entrance is called **Bab al-Rahma**, the Mercy Gate, while the southern is **Bab al-Tawba**, the Repentance Gate. Since the 13th C the entire opening has been blocked up.

With a c18 metre wide facade, Bab al-Dhahabi is a highly ornamented structure, and has recently been renovated. More than just a gate it is a building in its own right and is approached by a descending pathway. Inside there is a large chamber with six cupolas, and columns with Ionic and Corinthian capitals..

gateway for the Messiah

As the gate opens directly on to the Temple area many myths and traditions surround it. Jewish tradition believes that when the Messiah comes he will enter Jerusalem via this gate. Christian lore gives it a similar significance: it is thought to be the gate where Jesus entered the city with his triumphal procession, and the gate by which he will re-enter on his Second Coming. Some say that Muslims placed a cemetery outside in order to prevent this, as he would not pass through a burial ground. (The actual reason for the cemetery's position is that Muslims, like Jews, believe that it is here that the Day of Judgment will occur.)

The messianic implications of the gate provide a possible reason for its having been sealed: many false messiahs were prone to pass through it, and its closure halted this phenomenon.

the red heifer was here

Other legends associate the gate with the ceremony of the Red Heifer (Numbers 19:1ff) as enacted when the Israelites had their Temple. Yet another story is that when Heraclius returned from the Persian capital with the "True Cross" which had been stolen from the Church of the Holy Sepulchre in 614, he entered the city via this gate. As such, in Crusader times it was opened especially for the feast of the Exaltation of the Cross.

▸ Solomon's Throne (Kursi Suleiman)

Just north of Bab al-Dhahabi is a twin domed building known as **Kursi Suleiman**, or Solomon's Throne. Its origin is uncertain but it may have been built by Suleiman the Magnificent in the 16th C. If so, this could be the origin of its name though various Muslim traditions have it otherwise. One surmises that the wise king sat here to watch the temple being built. Others are more far-fetched!

▸ Gate of the Tribes (Bab al-Asbat)

At the NE corner of the esplanade is the **Bab al-Asbat** or Gate of the Tribes. A diagonal path leads to it. In Crusader times it was called the Paradise Gate. The present edifice was constructed in the early 19th C using Crusader bits and pieces. It is a main entrance for Friday worshippers, as it can be approached by car.

▸ North Wall

West of the Bab al-Asbat is the *riwaq* or portico that extends along most of the Haram's northern wall. Comprised of stone arches supported by pillars, it is open to the south. The construction is mainly Mameluke and along its length are many madrassas (theological schools), most named after their founders. Some are really no more than classrooms.

release from sins

There are two gates along the north wall, and these have already been covered in the tour of the Muslim Quarter. The first is **Bab al-Hitta**, the Gate of Remission (see page 45). Built during the early Fatimid period, it was reconstructed in 1220 by the Ayyubid al-Mu'azzam. Its name is derived from the Koranic scripture which relates how the Israelites were required to ask for remission of their sins before being allowed to enter Jerusalem.

Faisal's tomb

The second gate, less than 100 metres further west, is **Bab al-'Atm,** the Gate of Darkness (see page 45). It is suggested that its name refers to the dark, vaulted lane outside, but I wonder, as surely it was not always so! This wooden gate dates from the early 13th C. Nowadays it is often called Bab al-Faisal because King Faisal II of Iraq, cousin of King Hussein of Jordan, killed in the revolution of 1958, is buried in a nearby chamber.

another of his fountains

Just south of the Bab al-'Atm is a *sabil*, fountain, known variously as **Sabil Suleiman** or Sabil Bab al-'Atm. Nearly all the fountains now visible in Jerusalem were the product of this enlightened leader's building programme, and this one, under the care of the *wakf,* is better cared for than others. From the south there are steps that descend to the decorated fountain. To its immediate south is an early 19th C **pavilion** used by Sultan Mahmud II.

too late for Solomon

About 80 metres to the west is the 12th C **Qubbat Suleiman**, or Solomon's Dome. An octagonal domed structure originally built by the Crusaders in the 12th C as an oratory. Later a mihrab was added and it became a small Muslim prayer place. Each side of the facade has an arch, over which is a round drum with eight windows. Its main name is derived from a legend that King Solomon prayed here on completion of his Temple.

In the west part is a rock enclosed by a fence. This rock gives the structure an alternative name, Qubbat Sakfat Sakhra, Dome of the (small) Piece of Rock. A Muslim tradition holds that this broke away from the rock inside the Qubbat al-Sakhra.

appreciating Antonia

To the north you can see the outside of the large windows of the *iwan* in the 'Umariyya School, the First Station of the Via Dolorosa (see page 47). Now you can appreciate the high escarpment on which the Tower of Antonia once stood. In the very NW corner is the towering 'Anum minaret. On the west wall, as on the north, a portico open to the east runs for most of the way.

▸ The West Wall

Just prior to the Bab al-Nazir is a small fountain, the **Sabil Basiri** dating from the mid 15th C. This is built over an ancient rock cistern, and water was dispensed to the needy via outlets on three sides with the entrance on the fourth.

To the SE at the base of the raised platform is the **Sabil Sh'lan**, an early 13th C fountain. An arched open structure, it is capped by a low dome.

Many of these water fonts had prayer areas, presumably for giving thanks to God for the liquid. Prayers require a mihrab and there is one here.

Immediately west is the **Sabil al-Sheikh Budayr**. An 18th C construction, this small place has its windows covered by grilles. The prayer area, slightly elevated, is open on the south side.

two western gates

The gate nearby, slightly north, is **Bab al-Nazir**, the Gate of the Inspector (see page 53). Although the Omayyads built the first gate here, this one stands on the foundations of a Crusader one that was called the Gate of Michael. Rebuilt by the Ayyubids, their record can be seen at the top. In later Ottoman times it was also called Bab al-Habs, the Gate of the Prison, for the prison just outside.

Less than 100 metres further south is **Bab al-Hadid**, the Iron Gate, already visited from the other side (see page 54). It was built in the 1350s by Arghun al-Kamili, who also built the madrassa outside.

Arab revolt leader's tomb

One of the rooms just south of it, and clearly visible from the outside as it is permanently brightly lit, is the **Tomb of Emir Husayn ibn Ali**, the great grandfather of King Hussein of Jordan (see *Jordan Revealed* by this writer, pp 17 & 21). The tomb in the centre of the room is covered with a gold and green embroidered cloth.

A very short way further south is an open prayer area with a mihrab.

former glory

Next we come to the **Bab al-Qattanin**, the Cotton Merchants' Gate (see page 54), sited at the end of the once important souk of the same name. Although dating from the building of the souk in the first half of the 14th C, it was erected over an earlier substructure. Possibly the finest of the Haram's entrances, it stands right before the steps leading up to the west door of the Dome of the Rock. Above the entrance is a stone rosette in alternating black and white. An inscription records that it was built by the then Governor of Damascus in 1337. The actual doors have splendid carved wooden panels. Due to the fallen fortunes of the Souk al-Qattanin the gate has lost much of its grandeur.

Adjacent to the gate, and attached to it by an outer passageway, is the **Bab al-Mat'hara**, the Ablution Gate. Outside are the Haram's ablutions (see page 55).

another fine fountain

Slightly SE of the Cotton Merchants' Gate is one of the most enchanting of the small structures of the Haram, **Sabil Qa'it Bey**, the Fountain of Qa'it Bey. It stands to the NW of an open prayer area with an unattached mihrab on the south. The lower part is rectangular with marble-silled windows covered by grilles on the north, south and west sides, with the entrance on the eastern side. The stonework is red and off-white, making the edifice outstanding in brilliant sunlight. In each corner there is an engaged column with typical Mameluke decoration for the capital.

Fountain of Qa'it Bey   *Wilson , Picturesque Palestine, 1865*

water for the righteous
At the top of the rectangular base there is a band of very fine lettering that indicates not only the restorer, Qa'it Bey, but also the name of the actual builder of the 1450s. There are also verses from the Koran and an invitation to the "righteous servants of God (Allah) to satisfy their thirst". Above, the unusual drum gradually leads up to the high stone dome, topped with a crescent.

The water reached the fountain from a cistern, filled by an aqueduct which brought water from pools south of Bethlehem.

one more fountain and one more dome
Two more structures are worth noting before the Bab al-Silsileh. The first, just south of Sabil Qa'it Bey is an octagonal edifice with a lead cupola supported by eight columns. Known as **Sabil Qasem Pasha** and, according to the inscription on the western wall, built by that gentleman in 1527. Inside a marble-faced cistern is enclosed by an iron rail.

Further south and almost directly east of the Bab al-Silsileh is **Qubbat Musa**, the Dome of Moses. This is a square chamber supporting a low octagonal drum with a cupola on top. The entrance on the north side is marked by an inscription recording that it was built by al-Malik al-Salih Ayyub in 1250. On the southern side is a raised prayer area. There is no apparent reason why it carries the name of Moses.

main gate

We have now reached the double gate known as the **Bab al-Silsileh** (see page 56 for a description). Just north of the gate is a minaret, the **Minaret of the Chain**, first erected in Abbasid times but rebuilt in 1330 by the Emir Tankiz.

The continuation of the west wall now runs above **Wilson's Arch** area and the **Western Wall**.

▸ 2. THE WESTERN WALL (Ha'Kotel Ha'Ma'aravi)

History

The Western Wall, Ha'Kotel Ha'Ma'aravi in Hebrew, is the exposed section of the great west wall that supported the platform on which Herod built his temple.

remembering the Temples

Since Jews returned to Jerusalem both to dwell and visit, they have stood by this Herodian vestige, the closest they could get to the site of the actual temple, to offer prayers and to lament, particularly on the 9th day of the Hebrew month of Av when they commemorate both temples' destruction. These, often weeping, lamentations gave rise to the appellation "Wailing Wall".

access denied

The Muslim Maghreb Quarter formerly stood in this location, and there was only a narrow lane in front of the wall with no proper prayer area. Throughout the centuries limitations were placed upon Jewish worshippers as to when they could go there to pray. In latter Ottoman times right through the British Mandate this was an especially sensitive spot, as more and more Jews came to live in the city, many having nationalist ideals which were at odds with the local populace. The vast plaza as seen today was created after 1967, when the Maghreb Quarter was demolished.

The Visit

In accordance with Jewish custom the prayer area is divided into two; the larger to the north is for men, and that to the south for women. If you wish to approach stick to your area. Men will be required to wear a head covering, and there are some paper ones at the entrance.

plenty of good portraits

The very orthodox may come here to pray every day, perhaps several times, while others do so only once in a while, often travelling from other towns. Photographing is permitted except on Saturdays and Jewish festivals. The men, sitting or standing by the massive ochre wall, make evocative subject matter for photographs.

Draped in prayer shawls with phylacteries strapped to their arms and foreheads, they pore over their well-worn prayer books, oblivious to all around them.

incredible feat

The entire length of the west wall was c500 metres; however most of what would still be above ground is concealed by the buildings against it. The exposed section at the Western Wall Plaza is c58 metres. Seven courses of un-mortared Herodian blocks of dressed stone are visible, the lower two exposed since 1967. Some of these weigh 100 tons! A further 18 or 19 are thought to lie beneath, reaching down to bedrock. Over the exposed courses are several rows with smaller stones dating from the early Arab period, and atop those is a stone wall built in Ottoman times.

The wall is estimated to be about 5 metres thick, and behind it stretches a series of vaults, cisterns, and passages which were all part of the platform infrastructure.

By the Western Wall   *J. I. Porter, Jerusalem, c1860*

120 ton lintel!

At the southern end, in the section reserved for women, is a sealed entranceway, known as **Barclay's Gate**, after the architect who examined it in the mid 19th C. Above, partially concealed, is a massive lintel made from one piece of stone. Almost eight metres long, it is estimated to weigh in excess of 120 tons!

▸ Wilson's Arch

At the northern end of the plaza is a vaulted men's prayer section, originally an open archway above ground, known to history as Wilson's Arch after its 19th C excavator. You can access this famous discovery either from the north of the men's prayer area, or more suitably from the entrance just outside and west of it. There is a sign.

History

The Gate of the Chain stands directly above this arch, which was originally discovered by the German T. Tobler in the first half of the 19th C. However, it was Charles Wilson who, realising that this was a notable discovery, set out to excavate it.

As already noted above, Herod the Great in building his temple greatly expanded the area of the Temple Mount platform. Much of this expansion took place to the west and a great deal of construction was required for support. This was mainly in the form of vaults and the huge retaining wall.

digging deep

The important approach to the Temple Mount from the west, the Upper City, was over the Tyropoeon Valley, which was then much more pronounced than it is today. The arch formed part of the bridge that crossed this valley to the entrance of the elevated Temple area.

Continuously built upon over the centuries, the remains of the bridge, road and the surrounding buildings became submerged and lost. The huge cavern formed by the arch was turned into a cistern which held water for use on the Haram.

In investigating the vault, Wilson discovered part of an ancient street, the one that once ran beneath the present Street of the Chain. Remnants of a Herodian street that paralleled the wall were also found at this level.

Then in the mid 19th C, C. R. Condor, who mapped the city for the Palestine Exploration Fund, discovered a tunnel there that he believed ran from outside the Damascus Gate to bring water to the Haram.

did you say 400 tons?

Since 1967 further and more thorough excavations have been conducted, and these have revealed passages, rooms, and further sections of the west wall where the stone blocks are more massive than those exposed at the Western Wall, some as long as 60 metres and weighing an incredible 400 tons!

traversing the tunnel

Condor's tunnel, which was indeed a rock hewn aqua channel, was further excavated and opened in September 1996 amid great controversy (which resulted in riots with many dead on both sides) for tourists to traverse. However, it proved to run north and not east, to where the Sisters of Sion Convent on the Via Dolorosa now stands.

The Visit

The main entrance to these underground antiquities is just west of the men's prayer area. There is a sign. Because of prayers, visiting hours are restricted as follows: **Sunday, Tuesday, Wednesday 08.30-15.00; Monday and Thursday 12 noon-15.00; Fridays and eves of Jewish festivals 08.30-12 noon. Closed Saturday and Jewish festivals.**

room of the freemasons

You enter the underground passageway and pass vaulted chambers built close to the west wall. The route twists and turns, passing various spaces that were used for stables, storage and later as rubbish dumps. One of the most notable areas is called either the **Masonic Room** or **Hasmonean Room**. In his explorations, Wilson concluded that it had once been used by Masons as they associated the place with King Solomon. The chamber measures about 14 by 25 metres and has now been partially restored. Semi-columns were found along the walls, and a double entrance in its east. Whatever it was used for, it certainly must have been a splendid room.

books and scrolls

You then come to the chamber of Wilson's Arch, leading out to the south to the men's prayer area of the Western Wall. The chamber itself is now part of that area, providing not only an extension of the wall for prayers but also a useful shelter in inclement weather. In the chamber is a shaft driven by Warren, a collaborator of Wilson, in the course of his investigations. This has been sunk about 13 metres and actually reaches the foundations of the wall. Parts of the chamber are lined with bookshelves for Jewish prayer books, and there are also a number of cupboards to house the Torah (Pentateuch) scrolls that are used in services at the Western Wall.

North of Wilson's Arch is an Herodian gate discovered by C. Warren and named after him, **Warren's Gate**. Very similar to Barclay's Gate (see above), it is located just south of the Ablutions Gate of the Haram.

problem tunnel

Further north is the tunnel that figured so prominently in the events of September 1996, when its opening was opposed by the Palestinians. As mentioned above this can be traversed by those with non-claustrophobic tendencies, for about 100 metres exiting along the Via Dolorosa.

▸ 3. ARCHAEOLOGICAL EXCAVATIONS

Below the southwestern and southern walls of the Haram is a vast archaeological area, at the time of writing still being turned into a park. Here, during the last 150 years, a great deal of digging and investigation has been undertaken yielding significant finds and information. It would be beyond the scope of this book to attempt but a brief outline of it and, as with the Haram, those who require a more detailed and in-depth explanation of the area should consult either my bibliography or other sources.

significant excavations

Since the area came under Israeli control in 1967, most extensive excavations, headed by Professor Mazar of the Hebrew University, have been conducted and these, together with the earlier finds, make a tour very interesting.

History

Solomon's city centre

The site is presumed to be the Ophel mentioned in II Chronicles 33:14, and other places that lay between the Temple Mount and the site of the original city to the south. It is called by Josephus Ophlas, and was the city centre of the Jerusalem of Solomon.

Herod the Great developed the area extensively, adding a broad paved section with steps and gates which led onto his rebuilt Temple Mount.

The Visit

Entry is from near the Dung Gate and a charge is made. **The park is open Sunday to Thursday 0900-1700, Fridays and eves of Jewish festivals 0900-1500; closed on Saturdays and Jewish festivals.** There are guided tours in several languages and information on these can be obtained either at the ticket office or most government tourist offices.

arch across the valley

From the ticket office a path enters the park and soon splits, with one going north and the other east. Take the northern one which runs beneath the very southwestern part of the Haram's west wall, where a huge pier, part of the springer of an arch, juts out from the wall. First identified in 1838 by the American explorer Edward Robinson, and since named after him, this is **Robinson's Arch**. The arch was part of an overpass that, like Wilson's Arch, connected the Temple Mount with the city over the Tyropoeon Valley. In recent excavations to the west of the arch a series of smaller piers were uncovered which carried a flight of steps that began from the south, turning east at the top where the arch spanned the valley.

Herodian shopping mall

Paving stones belonging to the Herodian road which ran along the Temple Mount's western wall, passing beneath the arch, together with some of the shops that lined it have also been unearthed. This road would have continued south towards the Pool of Siloam, at that time within the city walls (see map, page 16).

words of encouragement

On the lower part of the west wall just north of the arch, and now safeguarded by a housing, a two line inscription in Hebrew has been discovered. It is believed to originate from the second half of the 4th C AD and is taken from Isaiah 66:14, *"And when you see this, your heart shall be glad, And your bones shall flourish like the new grass"*.

Below the arch are two channels hewn along the wall, cut in early Muslim times to convey water to the area south of the Haram's walls.

south of the Haram

Return now to where the path split and walk east. Though this area was extensively built upon before, and especially during the Herodian era, following the Roman rasing of the city it was not redeveloped until after the Arab conquest.

vast palace

The path passes through what was once the porticoed inner courtyard of a large **Omayyad Palace** probably erected by Mu'awiyya and his successors. It formed the inner court of a complex which took up the entire area between the southern walls of the Haram and the city; in fact the southern wall of the palace acted as the city wall and was built upon by Suleiman for this purpose. The palace was two storeys high and was connected to the Haram by an elevated bridge which afforded the residents easy access to al-Aksa. What survived until the 11th C was destroyed by the Fatimids.

About three quarters of the way along the path, a side path leads off north and reaches some steps that lead up to a **tower**, built by the Crusaders and rebuilt by Salah al-Din who left an inscribed date of 1191. The eastern part of the tower is outside the Ottoman walls, and seals an ancient entrance, the **Double Gate**.

the biblical Ophel

Return to the main path and pass through the recently opened opening in the city walls here. This is the area of **Ophel**, and while excavated earlier, has been the subject of a very thorough investigation since 1967. Here you will find many Herodian, Byzantine and Omayyad remains, perhaps the most visible being the Herodian gates to the Temple Mount and their approaches.

Some remains have been partly restored, and walkways and steps installed to make a traverse of the excavations fairly straightforward, though it does involve quite a number of stepped ascents and descents. The direction takes you south then east then north to the Haram's south wall, before returning to the opening in the city wall. (If you are short on time (or strength) you can skip this bit and go straight to the Haram's southern wall by turning left inside the gate and ascending the stone steps.)

happy home

After passing through the city wall descend the steel steps just to the south. Here you enter rooms, some with scraps of mosaic. In one room near the top is an inscription in Greek *"Happy are they that live in this house"*. The entire structure housed a number of Byzantine dwellings. Nearer the bottom are some baths and cisterns. Descending further, an area that was probably once a pool is entered. Notice the stuccoed walls.

palace of Queen Helena?

The way now turns east and then SE, partly along a path and partly down steps. You pass remains of more Byzantine dwellings and part of an 8th C Omayyad structure. Further along, past more

Byzantine houses, and almost at the SE corner, are remnants which may be a **palace of Queen Helena** of Adiabene (see page 186, Tomb of the Kings) who built many palaces in and near the city.

earliest remains

Turn north and to the right are the vestiges of a **tower** and **walls** that are the most ancient remains found at the site. They date from the 7th C BC or earlier.

Continuing north briefly the path turns NW and ascends steps towards the southern wall of the Haram. Here you enter a large **courtyard**, once columned. Dating from the Omayyad period, this was part of a public building or palace. Some of the marble and red granite pillars have been restored and re-erected, but most are lying in fragments on the ground. Crosses engraved on some pillars indicate that they were reused from Byzantine churches.

discovery of Herodian gate

From this court stone steps lead into a sort of plaza and yet more steps lead towards the blocked up **Double Gate** or West Hulda Gate. Built by Herod the Great, this gate is not recorded in history, and was only discovered by excavations. It was an important entry-point to the Temple Mount from the city below, which then extended way beyond the present walls (see map page 16). It was preceded by a paved road ending in steps. Most likely destroyed in AD 70, it was rebuilt by the Omayyads, but was finally sealed in the 11th C.

The gate is about 13 metres wide, and lies some 12 metres below the Haram's surface. The arch is Omayyad, and above its right end is a stone bearing the following and very difficult to read inscription "TITO AE HADRIANO ANTONIUS AVGPIO PPONTIFAVGVR DD". Obviously a reused stone from a Roman temple in the vicinity.

another sealed gate

Following the reconstructed wide road that runs east below the al-Aksa, you come to the likewise sealed **Triple Gate** or East Hulda Gate. Originally Herodian, the portals as seen today were built by the Omayyads and, like the Double Gate, were sealed up in the 11th C. This is probably the gate called Hulda, mentioned in the *Mishna*, the commentary on the Jewish Law.

Further east, but not approachable, is yet another gate with but a single portal. Evidence points to this being of Crusader construction.

You can exit by returning to the Double Gate and descending the steps towards the gate you entered by.

9. The Ramparts Walk and Old City Gates

INTRODUCTION

One of the best improvements made for travellers to the Old City since 1967 is the restoration and paving of the city's ramparts, making it possible to walk atop them. You can view almost the entire city this way, the only inaccessible section running between St. Stephen's Gate and the Dung Gate, i.e. the part that also forms the eastern and southern walls of the Haram al-Sharif.

Suleiman's magnificent walls

The present walls were either built or repaired by Suleiman the Magnificent soon after the Ottoman conquest in 1516. They follow the line of the previous, but partly dismantled, walls. Although there are many ancient city walls still standing around the world, it would be fair to say that these of Jerusalem are among the most exciting and distinctive. When so many other formerly walled cities of the Middle East have had their walls pulled down in the name of progress, it is gratifying to know that these will not suffer the same fate. When travelling in renowned Middle Eastern cities such as Aleppo, Diyabakir, Sana'a and others, I always lament that their great walls are no longer intact.

Another post 1967 feature is the construction of an attractive garden around the outside of the walls, thereby isolating them from the modern part of the city. Each section of the garden was built with funds donated by people from abroad, and their names are prominently displayed in each section. (I find the plaques somewhat mar the effect; posterity in this city used to be earned, not bought.)

not easy to breach

The walls are c4.5 kilometres in circumference, and about 3.6 kilometres of them can be walked upon. They vary in height from 5 to 15 metres. At ground level they are a massive three metres thick. There are 35 square towers and 15 machicolations. Numerous inscriptions in honour of Suleiman are recorded on them, together with geometric and other decorations.

THE VISIT

Good exercise

While it may not appear so, a walk along these ramparts can be quite strenuous, especially in the hot months; there is no shade and there are numerous steps to ascend and descend. A fee is charged, but as this is valid all day you can break your journey at any suitable point and continue after a rest. I reckon it will take an average person about three hours to do the circuit.

tickets and visiting times

The Ramparts Walk is open Saturday to Thursday from 09.00 till 17.00 and on Fridays from 09.00 till 15.00.

You can buy tickets at the Damascus Gate, Jaffa Gate or Citadel. If you want to make the walk on a Saturday or Jewish religious holiday, you must purchase tickets in advance. This regulation applies even for the sections that pass in their entirety through Arab vicinities. The section that runs south of the Jewish Quarter is almost at ground level, from inside the city, and is free.

distances between sections

The approximate distances are as follows: Jaffa Gate to Damascus Gate – 1 km. Damascus Gate to St. Stephen's Gate – 1.2 km. From the Citadel to the Zion Gate – 0.6 km, and from the Zion Gate to the Dung Gate – 0.8 km.

▸ From the Jaffa Gate to the New Gate

▸ Jaffa Gate (Bab al-Khalil)

Named after God's friend

The Jaffa Gate is called Bab al-Khalil (Gate of the Friend) in Arabic. Muslims call Abraham *Ibrahim al-Khalil*, as he was said to be the friend of God, and he is often just referred to as al-Khalil. In Hebrew the gate's name translates literally, Sha'ar Yafo. It has also been called the Bethlehem Gate, the Pilgrim's Gate, the David Gate and Bab Mihrab Daoud (the Gate of David's prayer niche). The last two came about because of the erroneous association of the adjacent citadel with King David.

The names that prevail link the gate to the roads leading to Jaffa (Yafo) and Hebron (al-Khalil, the city of God's friend).

Built by Suleiman the Magnificent in 1538, an inscription on the facade records this for posterity. The gate, with its massive wooden door, contains a right-angled turn to prevent horse-mounted attackers charging in. Defensive measures included a portcullis, barbican tower, and machicolations.

making way for the king

The section of the city wall between the citadel and the gateway was demolished in 1898 to enable Kaiser Wilhelm II to enter the city with his carriage. General Allenby also entered the city in 1917 this way, but on foot.

From 1948 to 1967 the gate was closed, as the armistice line ran just outside. It is the main entry point from the western "new" city.

walking on the top

The first part of this short section runs in a NW direction and provides views over the NW part of the Christian Quarter, which are not of great interest, the sights outside the Old City being more attractive. After about 280 metres, while overlooking the **Collège des Frères** to the right, the walls turn NE and then north. At this NW corner of the city and outside the walls is a grassy area with signs of excavations. Here are some of the remains of a tower known variously as **Tancred's Tower** or Qasr al-Jalut, the Castle of Goliath. Most of the remains lie inside the grounds of the college and are not accessible. The remnants outside the walls were discovered during excavations in the early 1970s.

warlord of Antioch

In spite of other theories, the tower is almost certainly Crusader, incorporating material from an earlier date. Tancred, an important Crusader warlord, played a leading part in the taking of the city and later became ruler of the Crusader principality of Antioch. Why a tower here should bear his name is unclear as his attack at this NW point failed, and he only gained entry much further east, near Herod's Gate via a tower built by Godfrey de Bouillon.

When al-Malik al-Mu'azzam dismantled the city's defences in the early 13th C, the tower was included, and it was not restored by the Ottoman rebuilders. Just inside the New Gate is a small 16th C mosque, **Masjid al-Qaymari**.

▸ New Gate

Bab al-Sultan in Arabic, and Sha'ar Ha'Hadash in Hebrew, this gate was constructed by the breaching of the walls in 1889. Like the Jaffa Gate during the period 1948 to 1967, it faced the armistice line and was closed during those years.

▸ From the New Gate to the Damascus Gate

From the New Gate, the walls have been erected above remnants of earlier constructions, Byzantine, Muslim and Crusader. As you walk on top you'll get good views inside the Old City of the **Terra Sancta** complex. On the outer side you pass the **Notre Dame** complex and eventually the Damascus Gate parking lot and bus station. As you approach it, you get a fine vista of the gate's distinctive and impressive ornamentation.

▸ Damascus Gate

The Jerusalem experience

The Damascus Gate, together with the immediate area inside and outside of it, constitutes the commercial hub of Palestinian Jerusalem. Flocks of people and honking traffic teem in and out of the nearby bus and service taxi stations; men for hire with their battered trucks or seeking jobs as porters, painters and handymen, line the road alongside the taxis. The broad, steep steps leading down to the gate are bright with the bustle of the crowds and with vendors selling everything from felafel to frying pans, from shoelaces to

Damascus Gate, c1920

sheepskin rugs. Come down from the walls (or come here again) and take some time out to sit on one of the steps, drink in the atmosphere and watch the fascinating world around you.

other names

The gate's Arabic name is Bab al-Amud, Gate of the Pillar, and the Hebrew is Sha'ar Shekhem (Nablus Gate). The Crusaders called it St. Stephen's Gate, as at that time it was the traditional stoning site of Stephen.

entrance to the cardo

While both the Western and Hebrew names refer to its direction, the Arabic refers to the Roman column that stood here in Roman and Byzantine times. This column, at the northern end of Aelia Capitolina's cardo, was erected in honour of the Emperor Hadrian, and stood in the semi-circular plaza inside the gate. The gate and the cardo are clearly shown on the Madaba Map, and the gate is depicted with two flanking towers.

During the following centuries the gate was rebuilt many times, specifically by the Crusaders. In the early 13th C it was destroyed, probably on the orders of al-Malik al-Mu'azzam, and the aperture blocked up.

recent improvements

The gate as seen today was built by Suleiman, and his name is (unsurprisingly) inscribed above it. The bridge leading to the gate was constructed in the 19th C and, until 1980, when the present outside plaza and steps were laid, the approach was quite plain.

The actual gateway is set back within a pointed arch with ornamented voussoirs. Above the arch is a decorated window, with turrets on both sides.

struggling through

You enter the gate through wooden double doors into the vaulted passageway; it first makes a turn to the east (left) and then south (right), into the busy souk area beyond. The fact that the Damascus Gate is the main entry point from the Palestinian city and leads to the main souks, often makes it a struggle to get through. The inflow and outflow of people, together with peddlers hawking all manner of merchandise, squatting at the sides or carelessly pushing barrows, makes for very slow progress! In the actual passageway there are even money changers and shops.

ancient remains

Outside and below the gate are the remains of some ancient structures, and these can be visited every day of the week. At the bottom of the steps on the west side of the bridge are the remains of a **Crusader chapel** and to the east the remains of the **Crusader wall**. Further steps descend to a paved area and the arch of the Roman gate. This gate is part of the **Hadrianic triumphal arch** that stood without any supporting wall. It consisted of a central gate with smaller ones to the east and west. The surviving one is the eastern gate.

view from the top

From atop the Damascus Gate there is an amazing rooftop scene over the Old City southwards, and you also get exceptional views of the very busy area just inside, as well as the outer plaza. Although my favourite local haunt is a seat on the plaza steps, this vantage point adds a special perspective. On occasion access to it is closed, as the Israeli para-military police also use it as an observation station.

▸ **From the Damascus Gate to St. Stephen's Gate**

One king's quarry is another's hiding place

This part of the walk continues to pass parallel to the busiest area of Palestinian Jerusalem. Inside the city is the **Spafford Orphanage** founded by Anna Spafford (see page 189). On the outside (you can't see it from the top of the ramparts) is the entrance to a cave known either as **Solomon's Quarries** or Zedekiah's Cave. This rock hewn cave was undoubtedly an ancient limestone quarry, but whether it can be linked to Solomon is questionable. According to some Jewish traditions it was the escape route used by King Zedekiah when he tried to elude Nebuchadnezzar during the conquest of Jerusalem.

The entrance was sealed by Suleiman when he rebuilt the walls and remained so until the early 1850s when it was discovered by J. T. Barclay. The walls now run parallel to Suleiman Street, the main thoroughfare of the Palestinian city.

▸ **Herod's Gate**

The appellation "Herod's" was given to this gate by medieval Christian pilgrims because it led to Deir Abu Adas, the Monastery of

136

the Father of Lentils situated near the bottom end of Shari'a Dawish, thought to have been the site of the Palace of Herod Antipater. The Muslims call it Bab al-Zahira or Zahra, roughly meaning the Gate where they Stay Awake. Al-Zahira was the name of a Muslim cemetery (now gone) opposite, where those who had undertaken the *haj* to Mecca were buried. According to the Koran, these will be the first to be resurrected. In Hebrew it is known as Sha'ar Ha-Prakhim, the Gate of Flowers, due to its floral decoration.

Crusader's entry point

Between Herod's Gate and the NE corner of the walls is the location where in 1099 the Crusaders under Godfrey de Bouillon managed to break into the city. A likely spot is marked by a plaque. The tower in the NE corner is known as the **Stork Tower**, or Burj Laqlaq in Arabic. This tower was built by Suleiman in the late 1530s, and the inscription is on the second storey over a small pointed arch. Below the tower a lively Arab **sheep market** is held every Friday morning.

From here the walls turn south and below is a Muslim cemetery. This part of the Old City was until the 19th C quite sparsely populated and even today it is not as crowded as other parts of the city.

▸ St. Stephen's Gate

At St. Stephen's Gate you have to descend. Christians call it St. Stephen's Gate because it was thought to be one of the possible locations where Stephen was stoned to death (Acts 7:54-60). Today, the main Palm Sunday processions from Bethany over the Mount of Olives enter the Old City through this gate.

Muslims call it Bab Sitti Maryam, Lady Mary's Gate because it led to Mary's tomb at the foot of the Mount of Olives. In Hebrew it is Sha'ar Ha'Arayot, the Lion's Gate, because of the carved lions at the sides of the arch. In Old and New Testament times it might have been the Sheep Gate mentioned in Nehemiah 3:1 and John 5:2. The Crusaders named it the Jehoshaphat Gate as it led into the valley of the same name (Wadi Kidron), while the early Ottomans knew it as Bab al-Ghor, or the Valley Gate, as it was the way to the Jordan Valley, al-Ghor in Arabic.

Suleiman makes his mark again

As seen today, it was built by Suleiman the Magnificent in 1538. Again a faded inscription on the inside of the gate records this fact. The original design incorporated a right angled turn which exited to the south, but during the British Mandate the west wall was removed, eliminating this and permitting cars to enter.

▸ From the Citadel to the Dung Gate

Ascend the ramparts from the promenade outside the Citadel. On the city side is the Citadel, described in Chapter 11. This is one of the finest stretches of the walls and they are particularly impressive seen from the pathway below (see Chapter 13, Mount Zion). From the ramparts, high above the Hinnom Valley, the views to the south are excellent. Turning east at the SE corner, you can see most of the sites on Mount Zion.

▸ Zion Gate

Battle-scarred

Called in Arabic Bab al-Nabi Daoud, the Gate of the Prophet (King) David because it led to his supposed tomb, it is known to Jews as Sha'ar Tzion of which Zion Gate is a translation. It was built by Suleiman in 1540. Closed between 1948 and 1967, the gate and adjacent walls are badly pock-marked by bullets from the wars of those years. The entrance way is positioned below a pointed arch with machicolations at the sides. Like other gates, the Zion Gate has a right-angled turn, but this one can (just about) be negotiated by reasonably sized cars. It was here that the Israeli army broke into the Old City in 1967.

bird's eye view of the past

Passing over the Zion Gate, the walls run downwards towards the Tyropoeon Valley. On the outside is a fine landscaped **archae-ological park** which extends all the way to the Dung Gate, and is worthy of your exploration at a separate time. Numerous plaques sited there give ample explanations.

On the city side, just past the Jewish Quarter parking lot, is a depression at the base of the walls, where recent excavations have taken place. Here are the remains of a tower that may have been part of an **Ayyubid gateway** of the 13th C.

Slightly further east a short stretch of the wall turns north, and on the outside is a projecting tower known as the **Sulphur Tower** or Burj al-Kibrit in Arabic. An inscription on the south facade dates it to 1540, although it was built on the site of an earlier construction, probably 12th C.

significant find

With the walls still running in a northerly direction, on the west are gardens, where beneath were discovered the **water cisterns** of the Nea Church, the great Byzantine church which stood at the southern end of the cardo, and is clearly defined on the Madaba Map.

saving the best till last

The walls now turn east again and run along the roadway, parallel to the Jewish Quarter. From here you get truly magnificent views across the valleys towards the Judean Desert, and even if you do not do the entire ramparts tour, try to walk this part. Its free!

After a slight turn to the NE the walkway ends just prior to the Dung Gate.

▸ Dung Gate

This, the lowest of the city gates, is called in Arabic either the Bab al-Maghariba, the Gate of the Moors, or Bab al-Silwan, as it leads out to the village of that name. In Hebrew it is called Sha'ar Ha'Ashpot, the Gate of Garbage, a slight elevation from its Western name! Both the Western and Hebrew versions seem to be of comparatively recent origin, perhaps commemorating a gate of similar title that stood far to the south near the Siloam Pool when that area fell within the city walls.

The gate dates from c1540 when it was a square postern in a tower of the wall. Above it is a pointed arch decorated with a motif. The gate was enlarged during the 1950s to enable motor traffic to enter.

10. The Old City Souks

INTRODUCTION

Until the end of the last century, the souks and bazaars of the Middle East were where most commercial activity and shopping took place. With the gradual spread of these cities beyond their walls, the souks lost the importance they once enjoyed. One has to visit a city like Aleppo in Syria to see these oriental shopping centres as they were in former times.

more than souvenirs

With the influx of tourists into Jerusalem, many eager to acquire "souvenirs" and the now assembly-line products of local Arab craftsmen, many of the souk alleys have become tourist bazaars. This is especially true of David Street (Souk al-Bazaar), Street of the Chain and parts of the route of the Via Dolorosa.

That being said, some of the remaining souks in the Old City of Jerusalem are still full of atmosphere and in spite of the plethora of digital watches, portable TV sets and almost every other mod-con that can be sold in such a confined space, allow you to enter the world of the traditional Middle Eastern souk.

THE VISIT

The main souk of the city, and the one where the locals shop is **Souk Khan al-Zeit,** or Tariq al-Zeit as it is also called, which starts inside the Damascus Gate and runs south through to the centre. A leisurely walk along this route will bring you into a world of tiny shops, delightful colours, pungent aromas, care-abandoned noise and an open display of foods that would set the hygiene inspectors of our sanitised society busy scribbling reports.

Although you will cross parts of this street a number of times during your sightseeing, if time allows you may find it best to take a special stroll along this longish souk in order to appreciate its character.

colourful crowds

Start from outside the Damascus Gate where the plaza, on many days of the week, also becomes a bustling bazaar, mainly selling trinkets and clothes. On the broad bright steps vendors display such a variety of merchandise that passage down to the gate is often impeded. As mentioned in the Ramparts chapter, to sit on these steps and watch the comings and goings is an enthralling experience. Palestinian village folk, the women in their distinctive embroidered dress, the men, many wearing the traditional *galabiya*, the long loose robe, Christian clerics of myriad denominations, and the occasional Orthodox Jew making his way from Mea She'arim to the Western Wall. I love to sit here watching, and never tire of the unfolding scenes.

Although this plaza, and the stepped street within, are post 1967 the more characteristic and simple affair that preceded them attracted the same typically Arab commercial initiative. Over the years the Israelis have made repeated attempts to bring some sort of order into this trading but to no avail. A thousand and more years of tradition is hard to change.

a tight squeeze

Sometimes so many people make their way in and out of the city here that the way through the confined double "L" gate passage becomes a log-jam of people pushing and shoving. In these crowds hang on to your possessions. Although theft is not a serious problem there may be the odd rogue or two among the throngs.

At the bottom of the stepped street inside, also a virtual emporium of makeshift stalls and barrows, the way forks left and right. Left is al-Wad street and right is Souk Khan al-Zeit, the main souk street of the city.

from perfume to pickles

Once a broad porticoed Roman cardo, the centuries and changing population have reduced it to a narrow alley hardly wide enough for the throngs that often fill it. Where once was arrayed the grandeur of Roman and Byzantine opulence, now you will find all manner of emporiums, some large but most very small. Bright perfumeries with a western high street appearance stand next to typically oriental grocery shops where sacks of rice, pasta, and pulses, sold by the weight are stacked all around. There are specialist shops that sell olives, pickled eggplants, lemons, peppers and the like. The red purée often seen in these places is ground hot red peppers, and the purple pickle – called *lefet* – is pickled turnip coloured with beetroot. All these are oriental favourites and are served with almost all meals.

sticky delights

There are a number of shops that sell Middle Eastern pastries, *baklawa*, but some are better than others. The one I like best is just up on the right (it's the second one you come to). Called Jaffar Sweets their pastries are definitely worth trying. For an unusual one – and the most popular among Palestinians – try *knafeh*. This delicacy is made from cracked wheat (burghul), a special stretchy white cheese and lots of syrup. Beloved in Syria, Lebanon and Jordan as well as here, it is best eaten on the spot, fresh and warm. You can see it in huge trays being kept warm over a low flame. A portion is 250 grammes, and is often enough for two. The server, who has been doing it for years, will cut off piece after piece with a spatula and it will always be within a few grammes of 250. They are particularly busy on Fridays after morning prayers.

deep into the bazaar

About 300 metres along the street the souk becomes partially vaulted and the light very dim. Here the souk meets the route of the Via Dolorosa, and the next 150 metres, till it turns right, is part of that processional way. Now Tariq al-Zeit ends and you enter the main medieval souk area of the city. This, the great covered bazaar of Jerusalem, was built by the Crusaders and involves three parallel alleys built over the route of the Byzantine cardo. Orientalised after the Crusader departure, the shops are but alcoves under the roof vaulting.

heady spices and heads of sheep

These alleys extend into the centre of the city, and once upon a time each supported a specific trade, as their names imply. The central one, **Souk al-Atarin**, the Spice Market, is now a *pot pourri* of merchants, though there are still a few spice vendors among the stores, perfuming the air with the scents of cardamon, cumin, cinnamon, coriander and a host of other Middle Eastern cooking staples.

Parallel, and to the west, is **Souk al-Lahamin** the Butchers Market, and this is what it remains. Along here you can see meat butchery Arab fashion, with whole carcasses of sheep dangling from hooks. Another sight – and perhaps not for the squeamish – is the display of sheep heads.

Also parallel, but on the eastern side, is the much quieter **Souk al-Khawajat,** Merchants' Market, and today the merchants sell mainly carpets and drapery. It is also known as the Goldsmiths' Market.

authentically ancient

The alleys merge into the centre of the city meeting David Street and Tariq Bab al-Silsileh which traverse the path of the Roman E/W decumanus. Remains of the tetrapylon erected at the crossroads here were found beneath a Turkish cross-shaped building. In Crusader times it was Jerusalem's main bazaar and has hardly altered since.

In this area you will find many very short alleys, all inter-connecting. If there is any part of the Old City that has remained quite unchanged for countless centuries it would be here. Just wander around and try to avoid being pestered by the overkeen marketeers!

A few tens of metres ahead (south) is the recently reconstructed section of the Byzantine cardo (see Chapter 6).

11. The Citadel

INTRODUCTION

On the south side of the Jaffa Gate lies one of Jerusalem's most famous sites, **the Citadel**, or al-Qala'a in Arabic. Situated at a commanding height of 780 metres above sea level, its towers offer magnificent views across the Hinnom Valley and the city itself. Today it is the **Museum of the History of Jerusalem**, with very detailed explanations, and an excellent audio-visual presentation. I recommend you visit it.

HISTORY

Although there is evidence of prior occupation, the history of the site really starts with the Hasmoneans who fortified the area against the Seleucids. However, it was Herod the Great who first built substantially.

According to Josephus Herod erected three large towers on the site, and these were possibly on the fortifications of earlier Hasmonean ones. To these he gave names: Mariamne, after his wife; Hippicus, after a friend and Phasael, after his brother – most likely the NW tower that can be seen today. To the south, the tyrannical king built his palace, which is amply recorded by Josephus in his *Wars V*. This palace stretched east from the citadel almost the entire length of the present south wall. After the destruction of the city practically nothing of this palace remained.

probable site of Jesus' condemnation

Following Herod's death the palace became the Praetorium of the Roman procurators, who, having their official residence in Caesarea on the coast, would use it on their visits to the city. Most now believe that this was the site where Pontius Pilate condemned Jesus.

dastardly deed

Josephus relates how during the First Jewish War the Roman garrison took refuge in the towers and was besieged by the Jews. After agreeing to surrender, they were perfidiously massacred – an act which certainly contributed to the Roman Emperor's decision to level the city. The towers may have been spared as the area became the camp for the Tenth Legion. Remains have been found in the form of bricks and clay pipes bearing the Legion's stamp.

usual name confusion

During Byzantine times the fortifications were renewed, and one

143

of the Herodian towers appears on the Madaba map. The origin of the stronghold's more common names, "Citadel" and "Tower of David" may have been conceived in this period, with the title being applied to the large Herodian tower, but this is far from certain. At one time the Muslims called the Jaffa Gate after David (see Ramparts Walk, page 133), and clearly there was a confusion. Following the Muslim conquest other fortifications were constructed, including four towers.

Fatimid's last stand

In 1099 after the Crusaders broke into the city, the Fatimid soldiers made their final stand in the Citadel. The Crusaders made many additions to the fortress and it was used by Baldwin II as his palace. The fine inner entrance gate is Crusader and Ottoman.

During Mameluke times the citadel took on its present appearance, and among their works are the splendid Hexagonal Hall, the mosque and tower in the SW corner and the eastern tower.

minaret of David

Further additions were made during the lengthy Ottoman rule. Suleiman rebuilt the outer entrance, and his inscription above it can be seen. In fact there are other dedications to the great sultan by the mihrab in the Open Mosque, south of the entrance, and on the guardrail on the stone bridge. During that period, in 1635, the minaret was erected, and it is that which is known as "David's Tower" now.

spoiling the myth

Nineteenth century explorers of the city constantly referred to the citadel as the Citadel of David, although Ulrich Seetzen did call it the Citadel of Jerusalem. The most famous picture of it, a lithograph by David Roberts, clearly uses the title David's Tower, as does the drawing in Wilson's *Picturesque Palestine*. It is only in this era of thorough research that any association with that Israelite king has been laid to rest. Strangely, the street that leads from it east into the Old City was only called David's street in modern times.

still a stronghold

During the 19th and 20th centuries Ottoman troops were stationed inside the stronghold although the main barracks, the Kishleh, abutted it to the east (this is now a major police station).

During the Mandate, the British restored the site and archaeological research was undertaken. During the period 1948 to 1967 it was on the front line and again reoccupied by soldiers.

THE VISIT

Entry is either from the east inside the walled city facing the Christian Information Centre or from the west, outside and just south of the Jaffa Gate. There is a not-so-small charge for entry. **The Citadel is open Sunday to Thursday from 08.30-16.30, Friday 08.30-14.00; closed Saturdays and Jewish Festivals.** During the summer months the sound-and-light presentation takes place every evening except Friday, in a variety of languages. Details can be obtained from Government Tourist Offices or the Citadel itself.

As exhibits and layout are always changing I will not attempt to lead you around. In any case the detailed explanations and routes are clearly shown.

Gate to Citadel, 19th C

12. Mount of Olives

INTRODUCTION

Seeming to tower over the city, the Mount of Olives is one of the most delightful areas of Jerusalem to explore, especially if you do so after having spent some time in the restricted alleyways of the Old City. Like most of this land, the mount is at its best in the springtime when wild flowers cover much of the slopes. Allow plenty of time, as I'm sure you'll want to sit for a while just absorbing the stupendous panorama of the city which the elevation affords.

The Mount of Olives is part of a c4 kilometre north/south ridge that lies just east of the Old City, and separated from it by the Kidron Valley. This ridge forms part of the Judean mountains, falling steeply into the Jordan Valley to the east, and more gently towards the coast.

three peaks

Three crests crown the ridge: the northern crest, Mount Scopus, Ras al-Musharif in Arabic, the central crest directly facing the Old City, which is the part generally called the Mount of Olives and the southern crest, sometimes identified with the High Place which *"...Solomon built for Chemosh the detestable idol of Moab on the mountain which is east of Jerusalem."* (I Kings 11:7).

Mount Scopus

Mount Scopus, in Hebrew Har Ha'Tzofim, means Observation Mountain. At c820 metres it is the highest of the ridge's peaks and the summit provides an admirable view over the city from the northeast. Josephus records that it was here that Cestius made camp in AD 66 prior to his failed attack on the city. In AD 70 Titus also pitched camp here before beginning his siege of Jerusalem.

Today it is the site of the original buildings of the Hebrew University opened by Lord Balfour in 1925, and the Hadassah University Hospital, opened in 1934, then the largest and most modern medical facility in the Middle East.

There is also a First World War British war cemetery near the hospital.

Israelis remained

During the 1948 war all the area around Mount Scopus fell to the Jordanians, but the University and Hospital buildings remained in Israeli hands, creating an "island" of Israeli territory within the Jordanian-held area. This meant that from 1948 to 1967 the facilities of the two institutions could not be used, and replacements were constructed in the western city. After 1967 when the territory was captured by Israel, the buildings were restored and are, today, in full and fruitful use.

UN presence

Slightly south is the crest (814m) on which sits the Augustus Victoria Hospital, built by Kaiser Wilhelm II on land given to him by the sultan in 1898 and named after his wife, Augusta Victoria. It first opened as a hospital and Lutheran hospice in 1910. It is now a hospital for Palestinians run by UNRWA. Its 60 metre high tower provides a superb vantage point and is open to visitors between noon and 1600 every day.

actual mount

It is the central part, at an altitude of 816 metres and facing the city, which is generally known as the Mount of Olives, though in ancient times this appellation may well have applied to the entire ridge. From here the ridge falls away to the south to Ras al-Amud, with the Palestinian village of Silwan on its western slopes (see page 177).

the Resurrection starts here

Besides providing an expansive view across the city, this hill is the site of numerous New Testament happenings, most of them commemorated by churches. The Jews, taking their cue from Zechariah 14:1ff, believe that the messianic era – and consequentially the resurrection of the dead – will begin here, thus making the slopes a very desirable place to be buried. It is therefore not surprising that large tracts of the southern slopes are covered in Jewish graves. (Christians interpret the same scripture to refer to the Second Coming of Jesus.)

Arab village

Atop the mount sits the Palestinian village of al-Tur, a name derived from the Syriac Tura Zita, (*tura* = mountain, *zita* = olives). The village is now incorporated into greater Jerusalem, though parts still preserve a very Palestinian village atmosphere. A stroll around some of the back lanes will reveal a very different world from the one in the city below.

HISTORY

From Ascent to Mount

First mentioned in the Bible as the Ascent of Olives – Ma'aleh ha-Zeitim in Hebrew (II Samuel 15:30), its summit was where David used to worship God (verse 32). In Ezekiel 11:23 the mount is alluded to when *"the glory of the Lord went up from the midst of the city, and stood over the mountain which is east of the city"*. It is in Zechariah 14:4 that the actual name Mount of Olives appears for the first time.

The Mount of Olives figures prominently in the final chapters of the Gospels. Although translated as either the Mount of Olives or Olivet, the literal translation from the Greek is more probably "mountain of olive trees".

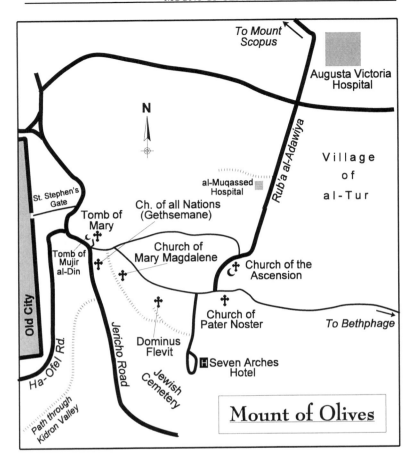

Mount of Olives

from Jericho to Jerusalem

The ancient road from Jericho to Jerusalem (still there, though recently asphalted) passes over the hill, and it was from here that Jesus' entry into the city at the start of the final week of his life began. Here it was that Jesus found the donkey that was to convey him to Jerusalem (Matthew 21:1ff). On the way he looked down on the city and, foreseeing its coming destruction, wept over it (Luke 19:41). At the foot of the hill, in the Garden of Gethsemane (Gethsemane being a corruption of the Hebrew *Gat-Shemanim*, meaning olive press), he spent the night in prayer prior to his arrest the following morning (Mark 14:32ff). And tradition has it that it was from the summit of the Mount of Olives, 40 days after his resurrection, that Jesus ascended to heaven.

Roman then Muslim camp

During the Jewish revolt and the subsequent siege of the city, the Roman Tenth Legion (Fretensis) camped on the mount and according to Muslim tradition, 'Umar, the second Caliph, received the surrender of Jerusalem in 638 while encamped there. In the Byzantine era, when Jerusalem was thoroughly Christian, many churches and monasteries were built over its slopes, and their vestiges – or modern reworkings – remain today.

VISITING THE MOUNT
How to get there

The climb to the top is very steep, and during the hot months can be tiring. Best therefore to travel up by bus or taxi and explore it on the descent, and this is how my tour will go. Bus 75 from the Damascus Gate will take you there, as will, of course, any taxi. If you have a car the main route up (the same route the bus takes) is from the NE corner of the Old City walls. The road first descends into the Kidron Valley, then turning sharp right makes a very steep ascent. At the junction on the summit a turn to the left leads to the Augustus Victoria and Mount Scopus, and to the right towards the part of the Mount of Olives proper. Straight over lies the village of al-Tur, and the narrow road eventually joins up with the new highway to Jericho and the Dead Sea.

▸ Chapel of the Ascension
How to get there

Turning south (right) at the junction, a straight road leads you through the outer fringes of al-Tur, and past the al-Muqassed Palestinian Hospital. After c700 metres, just on a left bend, you will find the Chapel of the Ascension preceded by a parking area or "square". To the left is a small minaret signifying that this is Muslim property. **It is open at most times of the day and there may (rarely) be a small admission charge.**

History

Pious Poemenia

The first site to be accepted as the place from where Jesus rose to heaven was a cave just south of this chapel where the Church of the Paternoster is today. By the end of the 4th C the location had moved here. After the Emperor Julian (r.361 to 363) failed to stamp out Christianity, a wealthy woman of Jerusalem, Poemenia, endowed a church on this spot, recognising it as the place of the Ascension.

the footprints of Jesus

Like much else it was destroyed by the Sasanians in 614, later being rebuilt by Modestus. The building was visited by Arculf (a German bishop who travelled extensively in the Holy Land) in the late 7th C. He records that it was round, open to the sky, and on the floor were the footprints of Jesus.

sequestered by Saladin

By the beginning of the 12th C the edifice had been severely damaged and was restored by the Crusaders. After the reconquest of the city by Salah al-Din in 1187, it was acquired by Muslims. Jesus is recognised in Islam as an important prophet, in fact second only to Muhammad, and his ascension is accepted —*"for did not Muhammad himself depart this world in a similar fashion?"* Since that time this has been a Muslim property, although the actual chapel is no longer used as a mosque.

removal of the left footprint

In the early 13th C the building underwent reconstruction and the "left footprint" of Jesus was removed to the al-Aksa Mosque, where it remains to this day.

The German explorer Seetzen who visited in 1806 records that the place was in ruins, and the keys were kept by a Muslim. In the mid 19th C other travellers note that the actual chapel was being used a mosque.

The Visit

The right footprint?

You enter the site from the west, at the southern corner of the square. This opens onto a courtyard with the Chapel of the Ascension in the centre. The chapel is octagonal and topped with a stone dome. Around the walls are small marble Crusader columns with crafted capitals. On the south wall is a mihrab and on the floor, enclosed by a frame, is a shallow depression said to be "the right footprint" of Jesus. The bits of columns etc, strewn outside and round about were part of the 12th C Crusader monument.

During the Feast of the Ascension Palestinian Christians come here to celebrate.

closed tomb

To the south (right) of the entrance is a courtyard and small mosque built in 1617, but closed to visitors. To the south of the mosque you can see a tomb (likewise closed to visitors) which shoulders many traditions.

which lady lies in the tomb?

The Jews hold it to be the tomb of Huldah, the prophetess consulted by King Josiah (c 640 to 609 BC) in order to ascertain the significance of the discovery of the Books of the Law (II Chron:34:21ff).

The Christian tradition will have none of this saying that the tomb is the resting place of St Pelagia, a penitent young lady from Antioch who, renouncing her life as an "entertainer", became a recluse on this spot. But according to the Muslims, both Jews and Christians have got it wrong and the tomb is really that of Rahibat bint Hasan, a 9th C female Muslim saint. Your choice!

At one time a Dervish monastery was situated in the vicinity of the tomb.

▸ Church of the Paternoster

About 25 metres south of the Chapel of the Ascension, just by a road junction and on the left, is the Church of the Paternoster. This church is visited primarily to view the more than seventy translations of the "Our Father" prayer which decorate its walls. **Open Monday to Saturday 08.30-11.45 and 15.00-16.45**. There is no entrance fee.

History

A cave on the site was once associated with Jesus' Ascension (see above). The same cave was also revered as the spot where Jesus taught his disciples the Lord's Prayer (Luke11:2-4).

the Olive Church

The first church here was built by Constantine for his mother Queen Helena around 328. It was called the Church of the Disciples, although the travelling nun Egeria called it in her journal "Eleona", the Church of the Olive Grove (*elaion* = olive, Gr.) It was about 70 metres long and 30 metres wide with a single apse, an atrium and a narthex. The cave was located underneath the apse. The Ascension was remembered here until 363 when it was moved some sixty metres north (see the Church of the Ascension, described above).

cave baptisms

Egeria recorded in her journal that during the Easter season the Bishop of Jerusalem officiated here every day. She also adds that every afternoon during that season, newly baptised children were brought to the grotto.

Destroyed in 614, it was rebuilt more modestly by Modestus, but the grotto remained hidden by debris until the early 20th C.

In spite of this, memories of the site persisted, and pilgrims would come to the ruined church to pray.

Danish enlargement

In 1102 the Crusaders built a small oratory amidst the ruins, and in the mid century the structure was enlarged by the Sveinsson brothers from Denmark, one of whom was Bishop of Jutland, when they came on a visit to the Holy Land around 1140. They were eventually buried there. Following the Crusader withdrawal in 1187, the church fell into disuse. In 1342 a visiting Franciscan discovered a section of the wall of the then ruinous building – a large stone on which the Lord's Prayer had been inscribed. Another visitor in 1582 found only a single column standing among the ruins and, even worse, by 1676 a passing Jesuit found only rubble!

purchased by a princess

In 1856 Aurella, the Princesse de la Tour d'Auvergne, came to Jerusalem on a pilgrimage. Finding only the rubble, along with a few poor Arab houses amongst them, she dedicated herself to the rebuilding of Constantine's basilica to Queen – or by then Saint – Helena, and to the finding of the cave. To this end she devoted the greater part of her fortune and seventeen years of her life. It took her eleven years – from 1857 to 1870 – just to secure the purchase of the land, some six hectares in all. During this time, and with the help of Clermont-Ganneau (1846 to 1923), they searched without success for the cave.

grotto finally found

In 1870 work on building the cloister began. It comprised a rectangular enclosure 30 by 20 metres, made up of two sections. The whole area was surrounded by a portico divided into 28 bays, nine on each side. Each bay was decorated with ceramic panels inscribed with the Lord's Prayer in different languages. It was completed by 1872.

It was not until 1910 that excavations unearthed the foundations of the original Church of the Disciples and the cave (or grotto) was discovered under what had been the apse. After clearing out the centuries of debris, it unfortunately partly collapsed, and concrete supports had to be implanted.

bungled basilica

In 1920 an attempt to rebuild the basilica in its original form was started. In order to place the apse over the grotto, part of the cloister constructed at great cost by the Princesse de la Tour d'Auvergne had to be demolished. The grotto, which was to be the crypt of the church was also "restored" with marble and other furnishings. After a while the undertaking had to be halted, and it was never completed. In the meantime, the princess's cloister was rebuilt and the vestiges of the never finished basilica dot the grounds.

The princess died in 1889 and was first buried in Florence, but in 1927 her remains were moved to the cloister.

The Visit

Greek, Urdu, Gaelic and all the rest!

You enter via a gate and then down steps to the main convent entrance from the north. Just inside to the east of the gate is the Lord's Prayer engraved in Hebrew and Aramaic on the north wall. All around the courtyard of the cloister – and in fact on every available perpendicular surface – are tiled plaques with translations of the Pater Noster prayer in every conceivable (and inconceivable!) language.

diverse dialects

Even variations of dialect and local versions of languages are represented. For example there is Spanish, Basque, Catalan, Marllorquin, Papiamento. If you know the difference you will find Russian and Muscovite, French and Provençal. Altogether there are upwards of 70 languages and more are always being added. The plaques are all locally produced by Palestinian ceramicists. This is the ideal opportunity to practice your language skills, ancient or modern!

On the south side of the cloister is the tomb of the princess, moved here as mentioned above, 38 years after her death.

▸ DETOUR to BETHPHAGE

From here you can make a there-and-back detour off the main route to visit the monastery of Bethphage, about three quarters of a kilometre away.

"And when they had approached Jerusalem and come to Bethphage, to the Mount of Olives, then Jesus sent two disciples, saying to them, 'Go unto the village opposite you, and immediately you will find a donkey tied there and a colt with her. Untie them and bring them to me.'"

(Matthew 21:1,2)

How to get there

Turn east down the road outside the Church of the Paternoster. This road, winding at first, leads past the **Russian Orthodox Convent of**

the Ascension on the left which is normally closed to visitors. The church was built in the second half of the 19th C on a site that the Russian church identifies with Jesus' ascension. The location of this happening is marked by a stone in the courtyard. The church also houses a spot where the head of John the Baptist was said to have been found – but then it has been discovered in so many places!

can be seen from Jordan

The tower, six storeys high, is reached via 214 steps, and is the highest structure on the Mount of Olives. It can be seen on a clear day from the heights above the Dead Sea in Jordan.

Keeping straight on, the road runs along the side of the mount with a dramatic view to the right. You will arrive at the **Monastery of Bethphage**, or Bethfage, after some 700 metres, on the left.

History and visit

Palms and psalms

This modern Franciscan monastery was built in 1883, and is supposed to mark the spot referred to in Matthew 21:1 as the start of Jesus' entry into Jerusalem for the final week of his life. The monastery was erected over the remains of a medieval church discovered a few years earlier. The church contains a painted stone depicting the raising of Lazarus (John 11:40-43) on the south side, the untethering of the white donkey (Matthew 21:2&7) on the north and the Palm Sunday procession (Matthew 21:8-8) on the east. The annual Palm Sunday Procession begins here, winding its way, with singing, prayer and the waving of palm fronds, down to St. Stephen's Gate.

From Bethphage a path leads to **Bethany**, (see Chapter 18).

End of Detour, return to the Paternoster Church the way you came.

spectacular scene

Turning left past the Paternoster leads you to the wide open area with the Seven Arches Hotel to the east, the only 5 star hotel in Jerusalem that is not kosher or governed by Jewish religious practices. The glorious panorama viewing point over Jerusalem, mentioned at the beginning of this chapter, is on the west.

stunning sunset

Almost every visitor to Jerusalem comes up here if only for this wonderful vista. Although there are other points around the city where excellent – and varied – views of the city can be obtained, none is as memorable as this, and it will be one of your finest recollections of the city. For a really striking view come up here especially about an hour or so before dusk, and watch the sun set over the city spread out beneath. The changing red and gold tones enhance the scene, suffusing the city with an almost surreal aspect. But remember, in these latitudes there is little twilight and dark falls rapidly.

As this is an exposed place, and Jerusalem can be cool at night even in summer, bring a light coat or sweater.

prettier than a picture

As well as taking your own photographs, which in many cases

may not do justice to the scene, you might want to buy one of the panoramic posters of the view from one of the Palestinian hawkers or from almost any souvenir shop in the city. I have one above my desk as I write and, although I know the city as well as any other, it never fails to inspire me.

priests prohibited

From this vantage point and immediately over the protecting wall is the Jewish cemetery, extending all the way to the bottom and around to the south east. Orthodox Judaism forbids certain Jews, those who are believed to be descended from Israelite priests or Cohanim (usually identified by their names, Cohen, Levy, or anything similar), to stand on ground that is used as a cemetery. As the road beneath cuts across the slopes of the mount, and therefore was once part of the cemetery, they are, by religious law, prohibited from travelling that way – as they are likewise forbidden to stand where you stand now! Some years ago, before the new road was built to the Dead Sea, this caused problems for those adhering to the law.

► Tombs of the Prophets

A few metres to the north (right) is the start of a lane that descends the mount ending at the **Garden of Gethsemane**. About 10 metres down, on the left and in the back yard of the guardian's house, are the **Tombs of the Prophets**.

prayers for the prophets

Although this quite large hypogeum dates only from the first century AD it is the traditional site of the tombs of the prophets Hagai, Zechariah and Malachi. Inside you will find a round chamber with semicircular corridors leading to the burial niches. Inscriptions above these niches show that they were used, or perhaps reused, in the 4th and 5th centuries.

Jews, in particular, used to pray at the cave. An 1847 report said that they flocked there in great numbers.

Visiting times: Monday to Friday 09.00-15.30. A flashlight is essential.

► Church of Dominus Flevit

Where Jesus wept

As Jesus made his way down the Mount of Olives, *"He saw the city and wept over it"* (Luke 19:41). Less than 50 metres further down the steep decline, on the right, is the Church of Dominus Flevit (The Lord Wept). The land on which it stands was acquired in the late 19th C by the Franciscans who erected a chapel there. In 1954, excavations were undertaken and a cemetery was dis-

Dominus Flevit

covered dating from the middle of the 2nd millennium BC. This spot was used again for the same purpose between the 1st and 4th C AD and you can see some tombs from this period in the grounds.

Further excavations revealed the ruins of a 5th C monastery. As recently as 1955 a new church was built over the ruins and a portion of the ancient apse was preserved in the modern design.

tricky photography

The view of the Dome of the Rock from the window at the rear of the altar is particularly attractive, and has been the subject of numerous photographs. But unless you are an experienced photographer and have come equipped with a tripod, don't expect it to turn out as it looks!

You may visit Dominus Flevit every day from 08.00-12.00 and from 14.30-17.00. There is no charge.

▸ Church of Mary Magdalene

KGB spies?

Further down the lane and on the right you come to the Russian Orthodox Church of Mary Magdalene (in Arabic sometimes called the Moscobiyya, as during the Cold War it was said to be the eyes of the Kremlin in the area).

This rather lovely church in its garden setting was built by Tsar Alexander III in 1888 as a memorial to his mother, Maria Alexandrovna.

lovely inside and out

The seven golden "onion" domes leave no doubt as to which nation this beautiful building belongs. The grounds, together with the fine church interior with its iconostasis and icons, definitely merit a visit.

Mary Magdalene

Open to visitors Tuesday and Thursday 09.00-12.00 and 14.00-16.00. Services are daily at 06.00 and 16.30

▸ Garden of Gethsemane and the Church of all Nations

History

At the foot of the mount you come to the Garden of Gethsemane and the Church of all Nations (Basilica of the Agony). The entrance is on the left just before the main road. Built by the Custodia Terrae Sanctae in 1924 on the site of many former structures, the church's name testifies to the numerous countries who aided its construction.

"Then Jesus came with them to a place called Gethsemane, and said to his disciples, 'Sit here while I go over there and pray'".
(Matthew 26:36)

155

Early Christian tradition places this and the subsequent events that ended in Jesus being led away, to have been enacted in this locale. According to Egeria there was a church on this site in the late 4th C, and its remains are beneath the modern one. It was built by Theodosius I as early as 385 and destroyed in the mid 8th C, probably by an earthquake.

ancient trees and rock of prayer

In the 11th C the Crusaders built a small chapel here and in 1170 enlarged it into a more substantial structure, but by the 14th C the site appears to have been abandoned. Excavations were conducted in 1909-10 when the Custodia acquired the land. The rock on which Jesus is supposed to have sat while he prayed was enclosed within both these former churches, and it has also been assimilated into the modern one.

The garden is beautifully maintained, and some of its gnarled massive-girthed olive trees are said to date back a thousand years or more (is this possible?).

a dozen domes

Take the path around the garden which ends by the porch at the western end of the church. This porch, which is clearly visible from the road and the east side of the Haram, has a mosaic decorated facade depicting the suffering of Jesus. The porch is the anterior of the basilica which is roofed by 12 domes. The aisles and apses also have mosaic decorations. The light is very dim and atmospheric due to the purple glazed windows. At the east end is the "rock".

less visited

Outside the garden and across the road, a gate that is nearly always locked leads into the other part of the garden (the road is a modern division of the property). This section is a really delightful place, perhaps closer in appearance to how it may have looked 2000 years ago. At the back is the roof of the Cave of Gethsemane (see below). Only special groups are allowed in here, but you may be able to sneak in by mingling with them as they enter. It is a very worthwhile place to visit.

▸ Tomb of Mary

Exit the Garden of Gethsemane and turn left, which will lead you almost immediately to the main road. Just before the main road a sharp turn to the right will bring you to the **Tomb of Mary**. Dominated by the Greek Orthodox Church, the Armenians, Copts and Ethiopians also have "rights" here.

History

Perhaps neither here nor there?

Two locations vie for the honour of being the spot where the Virgin Mary died (fell asleep) and was buried: Jerusalem and Ephesus. According to John's Gospel Jesus entrusted his mother to the Apostle's care (John 19:26-27). In the Ephesus tradition John brought her to Ephesus where she died and was buried. On a hill not far from the ruins of that ancient city is a small chapel, said to be built over her house.

The more accepted (or convenient) tradition places Jerusalem as where she spent her last days, Mount Zion as the place of her Dormition and this site as the site of her burial.

tomb discovered

The first church built here was on the lower level and dates from about the middle of the 5th C when a rock-cut tomb of the Roman period was discovered and held to be that of Mary. This was based on earlier traditions that she had been buried in the Kidron Valley, i.e. the Valley of Jehoshaphat.

more palatial

At the end of that century a more sumptuous upper level was constructed, described in the late 7th C as containing four altars with the lower level having a single altar at the east, with the tomb of Mary on the right.

Crusader Queen

The church was rebuilt on its Byzantine substructure by the Crusaders in the 12th C and Queen Melisande, the Crusader ruler from 1131, was interred here in 1161. The upper church was demolished after 1187, but the lower remains as it was built.

The traveller I. Norov who visited in 1835, described it thus:

"At the foot of the Mount of Olives, one could see the Tomb of the Holy Virgin, located in a courtyard reached by some ten to twelve steps. To the right of the entrance was the cave in which Jesus had prayed before Judas' betrayal. The number 1635 was inscribed on the wall, apparently the year in which this underground chapel had been built. A Catholic chapel, it had a simple altar and a picture of Jesus and the disciples. Light entered through an opening in the roof. The cave of the Virgin's Tomb was adorned with a Gothic facade and pointed double arch above the door. Some 50 steps led down to a dark crypt, in which natural light filtering in mingled with the light of candles from below. After 15 steps one reached, on the right, two cave-tombs - those of Mary's parents. On the left, Mary's husband Joseph was buried. Down below, to the right of the stairs, there were rows of gold and silver hanging lamps and strong light from the entrance illuminated the cave. The tomb, faced with marble like the Holy Sepulchre, was lit by more than twenty lamps, which burned continuously; the tomb itself was enveloped in silk curtains. The Virgin's Tomb was the property of the Greeks and the Armenians. The altar was underground in the wall of the cave-tomb close to the entrance. The underground gallery extended beyond the tomb and led to another altar, which belonged to the Greeks. On the other side of the Gallery was an Ethiopian altar".

Reise nach dem heilgen Lände in Jahre 1835.

Another 19th century German traveller, one H. Scherer, reported that the place was very crowded over Easter and visitors had to wait a long time. He also added that the Greeks had wrested control of the place from the Latins in the 17th C (*Eine Oster-Reise ins Heilige Land in Briefen an Freunde*, 1860).

The Visit

Open Monday to Saturday from 06.00-11.30 and 14.00-17.00.
Entry is down a few steps into a courtyard where a splendid facade of an arch supported by marble columns can still be seen. This was part of the Crusader portal. From here you take a long flight of marble steps down to the lower level.

confusing the tombs!

About half way down to the right is the tomb of Queen Melisande, its arched vault entrance engraved with a flower design. Curiously, in later years this tomb was identified as being that of Joachim and Anne, Mary's parents, and this is how it is recognised by many today. Almost facing, is another Crusader tomb, later to gain a tradition as being that of Joseph, Mary's husband.

dim light

The lower church is c11 metres below the entrance and is very gloomy, the main light being provided by dim electric lamps. In the centre of the eastern apse, which is rock hewn, is a small chapel which contains a rock bench that is venerated as Mary's tomb. It could possibly date from the first century AD.

Behind the chapel is the Greek Orthodox altar, and to the left the Armenian Orthodox.

Caliph prayed

To the south (right) of the altar is a mihrab built when Muslims also had a stake in the monument. Remember Mary is also venerated in Muslim tradition, the second sura of the Koran being called Sura Maryam. It is also said that after receiving the surrender of Jerusalem in 638, the Caliph 'Umar prayed here.

The western apse is a natural cave. In the front is a water cistern. Behind that is the Ethiopian altar.

Franciscan cave

Ascending to the courtyard and turning east (left) along a passage is the **Cave of Gethsemane**, belonging to the Franciscans. It is rarely open. Here, according to some, was where the disciples sat while Jesus withdrew to pray on the night before his arrest (Matthew 26:36). Part of an enlarged natural cave, it was first a Byzantine church and later a Crusader chapel.

This is really part of the Garden of Gethsemane, and it only appears divided.

Muslim memorial

Just south of the Tomb of Mary, on the corner, a cupola supported by columns marks the **Tomb of Mujir al-Din**, a respected Arab historian who lived between 1456 and 1522. His best know work is a history of Jerusalem and Hebron (al-Halil).

Stephen's memorial

Across the main road, on the south side of the road that skirts the Haram, is **St. Stephen's Church**. This is a modern (1968) Greek Orthodox Church. It marks one of the reputed sites of the killing of Stephen, Christianity's first martyr (Acts 7:58). Inside is a chapel built on the site of the event.

13. Mount Zion

INTRODUCTION

The southwestern part of the Old City of Jerusalem, now outside the city walls, has been known since Byzantine times as Mount Zion. Although this appellation is now firmly established, the Zion of the Bible referred to the actual Jebusite and Davidic city which was situated more to the south east of the present walls.

lost meaning

It is clear from the Old Testament that the name Zion (the etymology of the word is obscure, though it may come from an Aramaic word meaning "dry") is just another name for Jerusalem:

"Now David and his men went to Jerusalem, and the inhabitants said to him that he shall not enter. Nevertheless, David captured the stronghold of Zion, that is the city of David." II Samuel 5:6-7 (author's rendition)

heavenly Jerusalem

Over the following centuries the name Zion or *tsiyon* in Hebrew, became synonymous with the spiritual Jerusalem and the Holy Mountain of the Lord (the Temple Mount, not this one).   Unaware of the origins of the city, and as this plateau had the appearance of a "stronghold", 4th C Christians named it Mount Zion or Sion. Then, as in gospel times, it lay within the city walls and close to the Mount of Olives, so it was easy for these early Christians to conclude that here was the location of the New Testament events mentioned below. Indeed, from Hasmonean times through to the Roman destruction, this area was located within the city walls, although the Roman city of Aelia Capitolina did not incorporate it.

In the 5th C when Theodosius' wife, the Empress Eudocia, settled in Jerusalem (444) she had the walls extended so as to include not only the mount but the lower parts of the Tyropoeon Valley. Since Crusader times the mount has been outside the walls, but must still be reckoned as part of the Old City.

Even the title "mount" is something of a misnomer; it is essentially an extension of the southern sector of the city, with the Hinnom valley to its west and southwest, and the Tyropoeon valley to the southeast. The area that is built upon and abutting the walls is a flat table which falls away suddenly at the southern end.

spiritual spot
The locale is congenial to visit, being almost devoid of commercial establishments, and nearly all the buildings have a religious character. A visit here can be combined with your tour of the Armenian and/or the Jewish quarters.

HISTORY

Venerated by Christians
Mount Zion has, since at least the 4th C, been held to be where Caiaphas the High Priest had his house (Matthew 26:57). It is also believed to hold the room of the Last Supper, the same room where the Apostles later waited for the Holy Spirit (Acts 1:13). Since the end of the 5th C Mount Zion has been the accepted location of the home and death of the Virgin Mary, although some traditions place that event in Ephesus (see page 156).

wishful thinking
A 12th C Christian convention, latched onto by Muslims and Jews, places the tomb of King David here, although this is most certainly not the case, as explained later.

first churches
The first church erected on the mount was the mid 4th C Church of the Apostles. Egeria, the late 4th C traveller and pilgrim, visited it and recorded that it stood on the site of the Pentecost occurrence. By the year 417 it had expanded into a great basilica, the Hagia Sion, Holy Zion, also known as "The Mother of all Churches" *(mater omnium ecclesiarum).* This building is clearly identifiable on the 6th C mosaic map of the Holy Land at Madaba, Jordan.

By the mid 5th C a Church of St. Peter had been built by Eudocia on the "site" of Caiaphas' house adjacent to the north.

Assumption of Mary
It was at this time that the convention pertaining to Mary's death on Mount Zion began to appear, notwithstanding the then established Ephesus tradition. Towards the end of the 5th C, Church ruling decreed Jerusalem to be the spot but some Orthodox traditions continue to adhere to the Ephesus version.

pilgrim's plan
The Church of Holy Sion was destroyed in 614 by Sasanians. The rebuilding by Modestus is confirmed by Arculf who visited in 670 and made a plan of it. It was rectangular and in three of the corners were chapels commemorating the Last Supper, the Descent of the Holy Spirit and the Dormition of the Virgin. In the centre was the Column of the Flagellation.

By the 12th C this building had crumbled, and Mount Zion had long been outside the city walls.

Crusaders build cathedral
The Crusaders built a new complex, the Monastery and Church of St. Mary on Holy Sion, or the Sion Cathedral. This monumental edifice, c55 metres by 28 metres, was divided into three naves. To the north stood an edicule commemorating the Dormition, and in the SE was the Cenacle, built on two levels. The top level represented

the upper room of the Last Supper and Pentecost, while in the lower a tradition began to take hold that the tomb of David was situated there.

The walls of the monastery extended north and included the site of the house of Caiaphas, where a small church was built over the ruins of the 5th C edifice.

terrible Turkomen

After the Muslim recapture of Jerusalem in 1187, and the departure of European Christians from the city, the monastery and church gradually declined, eventually being destroyed in 1244 by the Khwarizmian Turks.

Jewish population

In 1267 Moses ben Nahman (Nahmanides) arrived in Jerusalem and organised the tiny Jewish population into a settlement on Mount Zion. This lasted until the beginning of the 15th C when they moved to the present location of the Jewish Quarter.

Franciscans buy the Upper Room

In 1333 the Franciscans began to return and negotiated the purchase of some of the land on Mount Zion. They established a pilgrims' hospice and later were able to acquire the site of the Upper Room which included the so-called Tomb of David. But during the 16th C they were expelled again.

"David's Tomb" then became a mosque, and non-Muslims were not permitted to enter.

cease fire line

During the time Jerusalem was divided, 1948 to 1967, Mount Zion was the nearest point Israel held to the Old City, and was thus on the front line. Most of the buildings were used by the Israeli army, and were frequently damaged by gun fire from the Jordanian side.

no compulsory donations!

Since 1948, and more so since 1967, Jews have taken over many of the buildings on Mount Zion. In particular, a private Jewish theological school, the Diaspora Yeshiva, has staked claim to almost everything they can lay their hands on, and almost everywhere you go their presence is felt. Living mainly on donations, they use every opportunity to extract "contributions", often in a manner that might make the visitor believe they are compulsory. Do not feel obliged to give anything if you do not wish to!

HOW TO GET THERE

You can reach Mount Zion either by exiting the Old City through the Zion Gate, or via the ascending road that turns east from the Bethlehem Road by the Sultan's Pool, skirting the Hinnom Valley or, best of all, by a delightful walk along the city's outer walls from the Jaffa Gate.

walk with a view

To do this take the rising path south from the gate (ie turn left outside the gate if you are exiting the Old City), walking below the massive ramparts. Over the past couple of decades the Jerusalem municipality has turned this area into a very attractive park, making the route particularly enjoyable.

Although these ramparts were built by Suleiman, sections retain earlier Herodian and Ayyubid foundations, and these are marked with explanatory plaques. Below the road to the west (on your right as you walk) is the part of the Hinnom Valley known as **Sultan's Pool**, now an amphitheatre. Beyond, and above the pool, is **Mishkenot Sha'ananim**, the first Jewish area to be built outside the city walls, now refurbished, and the **windmill** built by Sir Moses Montefiore (see Chapter 16). At the southwest corner of the walls the path turns east. Straight ahead leads to a Greek Orthodox monastery and the American Institute for Holyland Studies. Take the path to the east (left) and continue up a short flight of steps. The Zion Gate is less than 100 metres further on.

THE VISIT

▸ Church of St. Saviour (House of Caiaphas)

If you have approached Mount Zion along the route described above, about 60 metres from the top of the steps an entrance on the south (right) leads into the grounds of the Armenian **Church of St. Saviour**. If you came through the Zion Gate, turn west, and this entrance is about 30 metres along on the left.

to pay or not to pay

As you will find in Jerusalem, Armenian churches are very difficult to visit, and this one is no exception. You will be fortunate to find it open, and even if you can get into the grounds, you may still be unable to go into the church. But a visit to the grounds is still very worthwhile. If it is open, the guardian will tell you that there is a fee to pay for entering, but as there are no tickets this is not correct. (To the best of my knowledge the only Christian shrine where a fee is payable in Jerusalem is the Church of St. Anne.) To placate him you can give him a few shekels, but it's up to you.

Entry is into attractively landscaped grounds. To the east a new church is being built, a very slow ongoing project. Walk down the path towards the arch.

no, no, no

Some Christian convention recognises this as the site of the house of Caiaphas, the High Priest (Matthew 26:57). It was here that Jesus was held and where Peter denied him three times (Matthew 26:69-75). The present (old) church dates from the 12th C and was part of the Monastery of St. Mary. It was built over the ruins of Eudocia's 5th C edifice. It became an Armenian possession in the 15th C when it was rebuilt as a church and cloister.

room where Jesus was held

The church has a single nave, with an elevated altar in the apse. Groin vaulting supports the roof. The lower part of the walls are partly covered in blue and white tiles. In the SE corner is a tiny area that is said to be where Jesus was held while in the house. You can see this by walking around the outside of the building if it is closed.

Turkish blue tiling

Under the porticos in the courtyard are the tombs of former

Armenian patriarchs, who were buried here until the site became inaccessible in 1948. Note again the blue and white tiles for which Armenians are known. These come from Turkey and the shade of blue is distinctive. Similar tiles made in Jerusalem cannot reproduce the exact hue.

Exit the way you came in and turning east (right) brings you to the Zion Gate.

▸ The Zion Gate

Bab al-Nabi Da'oud, (the Gate of the Prophet David) in Arabic or Sha'ar Tsiyon in Hebrew, this gate was built by Suleiman in 1540. Above the decorated arch which surrounds the gate is a turret braced by stones in the form of leaves. On either side of the actual entrance are decorated panels re-used from Mameluke times. The gate chamber has a sharp right-angled turn, and although cars are allowed to use it this makes the process tricky.

marred by warfare

Being on the front line between 1948 and 1967, and the point at which the Israeli forces broke into the Old City in June 1967, the gate was badly damaged. Although since restored, the bullet and shell marks remain as a reminder.

marked by mezuzah

As this gate leads directly into the Jewish Quarter, a mezuzah, an oblong object containing the handwritten words of Deuteronomy 4:4-5, is fixed to it (on the inside). All doorways in Jewish households are supposed to have such an item affixed to them, taking literally the injunction, *"And you shall write them* [the words of the above scripture] *on the doorposts of your house and on your gates."* (Deut. 4:9).

▸ Dormition Abbey

Walk south, with the car park on your left, and after c30 metres bear to the right (a sign points to the coenaculum). A further 20 metres along the path forks, left to the **Cenacle**, and right to the **Dormition Abbey** or Dormitio Beatae Mariae Virginis.

In 1898 Kaiser Wilhelm II made a visit to Jerusalem to open the Erlöserkirchen, the Church of the Redeemer, which had been built on land given to his father in 1869. Abdul Hamid, the Ottoman sultan, presented him with another piece of land, this time on Mount Zion. Having given one site to the German Protestants, this one was donated to the Catholics who built the Dormition Abbey, which was consecrated in 1908. During the work, remains of former structures were uncovered including the entrance of the Crusader Church of St. Mary.

fine mosaics

The Abbey was erected in Romanesque style from the design of Heinrich Renard, and includes a tower and cupola that make it a landmark for the entire vicinity. The inside is beautifully decorated with mosaics on the walls, floor and cupola. The upper part of the apse has an especially fine golden mosaic of the Madonna and Child, and below mosaics depicting the prophets. The crypt is the **Chapel**

Original plan of Dormition Abbey

of the Dormition and has an effigy of Mary sleeping, and above a splendid mosaic of Jesus receiving her in heaven. Around the statue are small chapels donated by different countries. One, the **Chapel of the Holy Spirit**, has a mosaic showing this descending on the waiting Apostles.

Although the Abbey suffered damage during the years 1948-1967 this has all been repaired.

You may visit the Dormition Abbey every day from 08.00-12.00 and from 14.00-18.00.

▸ The Room of the Last Supper (Upper Room) (Cenacle)

Return to the fork and turn right. A few metres down on the left, a pointed arched entrance leads to the Room of the Last Supper, or Cenacle, or in Latin *coenaculum*, meaning refectory. Ascend the steps immediately ahead. The lower area belongs to the Diaspora Yeshiva mentioned above. Go straight through the room at the top along the short open passage. You then enter the Cenacle.

History

Double Greek

The Cenacle is the traditional location of the Last Supper (Matthew 26:26-35). The name is derived from the Latin which is used in the Vulgate. It is a translation of two Greek words; one was used in Luke 22.12 and referred to the upper room of the last supper, while the second was used in Acts 1:13, also written by Luke, and alluded to the upper room of Pentecost. Both words translate similarly.

Crusader vestige

In the church rebuilt after 614 by Modestus, the sites of the Last Supper and Pentecost were positioned in opposing corners of the building. The Crusader Church of St. Mary, built on two levels, placed them in a chapel on the upper level, while beneath it was the supposed tomb of David.

With the recapture of Jerusalem by the Muslims and the departure of the Franciscans, the Crusader edifice fell into ruins, but veneration of the place was continued by the few visiting pilgrims. Eventually, with the return of the Franciscans the shrine was restored, and later rebuilt in the Gothic style.

The Visit

Pillars of pecking pelicans

You pass through a pointed archway dating from the 16th C into the Cenacle. The large room, c15 by 10 metres, restored in Gothic style, originally dates from Crusader times. Three pillars support the vaulted roof. In the SW corner, steps (now closed) lead down to David's Tomb. Above these stairs is a dome supported on small columns with curious capitals depicting pelicans pecking at the flesh of each other. On the south wall is a carved mihrab that dates from the 16th C. The coloured windows are Turkish.

▸ David's Tomb

Exiting the Cenacle turn left and immediately in front is an arched entrance leading to David's Tomb..

History

Bogus belief

Despite the fact that many religious Jews and Muslims will tell you that this is the tomb of King David – it can't be. At least not if you follow the biblical narrative. This tells us: *"Then David slept with his fathers and was buried in the city of David."* (I Kings 2:10). As the city of David was located on the ridge SE of the Dung Gate this, therefore, cannot be the place. It is probable that the notion he was buried here stems from the mistaken naming of this area Mount Zion (see the Introduction to this chapter).

astonishing find

The first reference to a tomb of David did not occur prior to the 11th or 12th C when it was part of the memorial commemorating the Upper Room and the Dormition of Mary. The Spanish Jewish traveller, Rabbi Benjamin of Tudela (c1173), mentions a story relating to the miraculous discovery of David's tomb on Mount Zion.

Muslims sequestrate

After the Franciscans rebuilt the shrines in the 14th C, including the "tomb", both Muslims and Jews took the site very seriously. So much so that in the second half of the 15th C the Muslims managed to seize it from the Christians. The chamber was sealed from the other parts of the building, and it was made into a mosque, a cenotaph was installed representing the tomb of Nebi Da'oud (the prophet David), and only Muslims were permitted to enter. By 1550 Sultan Suleiman had banished the Christians entirely from the region.

now a synagogue

Muslims remained in charge of the place until 1948 when it was taken by the Israeli Government. By then, the most holy of Jewish shrines, the Western Wall, was closed to Jewish worshippers, and this "tomb of David" was about as close as they could get to it. The place then developed into a major religious site and continues to be so today. Today it is an exclusively Jewish place administered by a rabbi, and subject to the usual Jewish customs (men should cover their heads). You should avoid visiting on the Jewish Sabbath and holy days.

The Visit

Inside you will be able to borrow a paper head covering. If a payment is solicited, do not feel obliged to give, you may visit this site free of charge! Turn left under the arch and just through the iron gate turn left again into a hall which was once the lower part of the Crusader Church of St. Mary, later a mosque and now a synagogue. The first part is used as a congregational prayer hall. Pass through into the second part which contains the cenotaph.

floral decoration

On the south wall is a mihrab dating from the 15th C, confirming that it was once a mosque. Framing this are floral patterned tiles. A dividing wall with a central doorway separates the main room from the small tomb chamber which is on the north side. On the east side of this wall are more decorative tiles.

Muslim monument

The marble cenotaph placed here by the Muslims takes up almost the full width of the tomb chamber, and is draped in a black cloth now embroidered with the Star of David. Weeping, wailing worshippers, pray close to it.

The area above the tomb is very blackened and is thought to be part of the 4th C church.

David's Tomb, 19th C

▸ Protestant cemetery

On the west side of Mount Zion is the **Protestant cemetery** and the **Bishop Gobat School**, now the American Institute for Holyland Studies.

The cemetery is normally closed to visitors, but if you really want to visit it this can be arranged through St. George's Cathedral. The burial site was established in the late 19th C and continued in use until 1948. Among those interred here are the British archaeologist, Sir W. M. Flinders Petrie who undertook much excavation work in Palestine, Conrad Schick, the noted Jerusalem architect, the Spaffords, American philanthropists and founders of the American Colony (see page 189), and many more names of note.

▸ Bishop Gobat School

This was the first building to be erected on Mount Zion in the "modern" era, in 1853, during the period when the Anglicans Lutherans had a combined presence in Jerusalem. Samuel Gobat founded the school as a missionary establishment for Arab boys. It is now the American Institute for Holyland Studies.

During construction of the school remains of the 2nd C BC **city wall** were discovered, and in the rear courtyard remnants of a **tower** in the wall can be seen.

road for Pope's visit

From outside the school a winding path leads down to the bridge that spans the Hinnom Valley. In the period 1948 to 1967 this path was the way up to the mount. The road route was built in 1964 when Pope Paul VI made a visit to the divided city.

▸ St. Peter in Gallicantu

Crowing cock

On the eastern slope that reaches down into the Hinnom Valley stands the modern church of **St. Peter in Gallicantu** (St Peter at the Place Where the Cock Crowed), named after the event recorded in Matthew 26:34, *"Truly I say to you that this very night, before the cock crows, you shall deny Me three times"* .

This is an alternative position for the house of Caiaphas, but one that has little probability. At the time of Jesus this area was outside the walls of the city and therefore does not meet an important criterion for the site of the high priest's house.

abandoned by Armenians

However this has been an alternative site since the late Byzantine era, when a church was erected. In late Crusader times there appears to have been an Armenian presence here, but it seems they abandoned it when their present St. Saviour's was acquired in the 15th C; after that there is no record of a structure here.

In the early 20th C the Assumptionist Fathers took over the site and excavations revealed remains of the former building, some of which you can find around the modern church, which was built in a neo-Byzantine design during the late 1920s.

panorama to the southeast

To its east is a large terrace from which you'll get a fine view to the SE, encompassing the Tyropoeon Valley, Silwan, the area of the Davidic city and the SE corner of the Haram.

crossing the valley

Ancient stone steps located just to the north of the church descend into the valley below. These are the remnants of a Byzantine route that led to the Pool of Siloam and beyond. Some like to think that this could have been the way that Jesus and his disciples took across the Kidron to Gethsemane – the tourist guides especially so, as from a simplistic point of view this site is easier to visualise as the position of Caiaphas' house than the other. As a result, more people visit this church than the more likely Armenian Church of St. Saviour.

14. The Ancient City and the Kidron Valley

INTRODUCTION

Many people coming to Jerusalem are surprised to learn that the original Jebusite and Davidic city stood outside the walls of the present Old City. David's city was situated on the rocky spur which protrudes between the Kidron and Tyropoeon valleys, SE of the Dung Gate.

Excavations were carried out here during the second half of the 19th C, confirming for the first time that Jerusalem was initially sited here. Later the city was enlarged northwards in an elongated shape, stretching towards, and eventually including, the Temple Mount. This is the area that archaeologists call the City of David.

Nearly all these excavations are now fenced off in a small archaeological park.

▶ City of David Archaeological Park

How to get there

Just east of the Dung Gate, a road with a large car park on the corner leads off south (left). You can either enter the park from a path c40 metres east of here on the main road, or turn down this road, which leads down the Tyropoeon Valley, and take the first path on the left, c100 metres.

The Visit

The City of David Archaeological Park is open every day between 09.00-17.00, and there is no admission charge.

biblical accuracy confirmed

There is not a great deal to see, but what there is can be quite fascinating and should not be missed by anyone who wants a comprehensive grasp of Jerusalem. Many of the finds have verified biblical descriptions of the region.

If you go in from the north you will see a large sign on which each item is distinguished by a number, and explained by a corresponding sign at the location. The signs are not always too visible, and you may have to search for them. To make it easier for you, they are listed as follows:

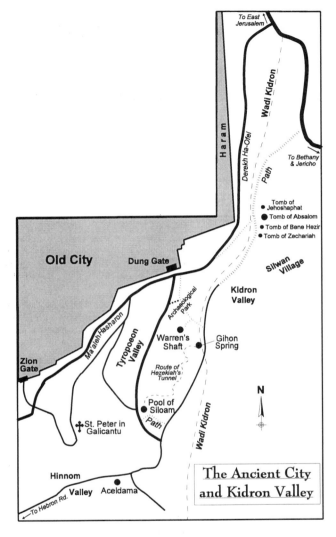

The Ancient City
and Kidron Valley

1. This is at the top of the slope, and is a remnant of the **city wall** first built in the 5th C BC by Nehemiah and subsequently rebuilt during the Hasmonean period.

2. This is a **northern tower** of the wall, and measured some 17 by 5.5 metres.

3. Another **tower**, but substantially smaller, c5.5 by 1 metre.

4. This **stone ramp** dates from David's time through the next couple of centuries, and its remains were used for later constructions. It is about 17 metres high.

5. A Judean house from around the 7th C BC, and has been named the **House of Ahiel**, a name derived from an inscription found on a piece of pottery. This reconstructed house is typical of the

Judean houses of the period, having stone pillars to support the roof and walls.

6. The **Burnt Room** is the remains of another house, probably devastated during the Babylonian destruction of the city. Remains of charring are still visible.

7. Dating from the period of the late Judean kings, 51 clay seal impressions (bullae in Greek) were found in this, the **House of the Bullae**. The seals bore various biblical names. One such name was Gemaryah son of Shaphan, a scribe mentioned in Jeremiah 36:10.

8. **Jebusite fortress** consisting of the remains of walls and masonry from a podium of the Jebusite city's citadel. Could this have been the stronghold of Zion recorded in II Samuel 5:7, and of which nothing has ever been found?

▸ Warren's Shaft

Leave the archaeological area from the south and follow the descending path to a junction where a sign points right to **Warren's Shaft**, a truly remarkable site.

Acquiring it's name from the archaeologist who discovered it in 1867, this is an innovative piece of ancient ingenuity. It was further explored in 1909 and 1911 by Charles Parker, also from Britain, and in 1978 a research team led by Yigal Shiloh of the Hebrew University re-examined it, clearing away the debris and making a visit today possible.

engineering feat

This shaft was part of the Jebusite city's water supply and enabled the inhabitants to draw water safely from the Gihon Spring below, without having to exit the city walls. At some period before the 10th C BC the inhabitants of this ancient city exploited a natural fissure in the rock, enlarging it to form a tunnel and shaft that provided access to the water of the spring and to the east.

The basic concept was this: an entrance within the city walls would lead, via a tunnel which passed under the walls, to a vertical shaft from which water could be drawn up by a vessel attached to a rope.

read all about it

To see it you pass through a small building where, after paying the entrance fee, you may browse around an exhibition which explains the site and displays some artefacts found here.

After descending some iron steps into a vaulted chamber, you negotiate a stepped and descending path which leads past a side opening, on the right, to the vertical shaft now protected by railings. From here a 13 metre perpendicular drop ends at a natural tunnel and the waters of the Gihon Spring which was outside the city walls.

unlikely story

Some scholars believe that this could have been the passage by which David's men were able to enter the city: *"And David said... 'Whoever would strike the Jebusites...let him reach... through the water tunnel* [Heb. *sinnor*]'" (II Samuel 5:8). But an examination of the features makes this unlikely.

Warren's Shaft is open daily from 09.00 to 17.00 hours.

Entrance to the Gihon Spring

Return to the fork in the path and descend to the **Kidron Valley** below, and the **Gihon Spring**.

▸ The Gihon Spring

Intermittent flow

The life blood of ancient Jerusalem was the Gihon Spring (Heb. *Ein Gikhon* from *l'hagi'ach*, to gush forth). In Arabic it's called *Ain Umm al-Daraj*, the Spring of the Mother of Steps, as it is approached down a steep flight of steps.

The Gihon Spring's flow is cyclic, gushing forth 4 to 6 times a day in the wet season, and only once or twice in the dry (hence the Hebrew name). In ancient times it was the only reliable water source for Jerusalem.

down into a cave

You reach the actual spring by descending the steps which date originally from Byzantine times, into the cave where the spring is located. To the west a gallery leads to Warren's Shaft (now blocked off with access only from the Archaeological Park) and this is the beginning of **Hezekiah's Tunnel** (see below) which leads to the Siloam Pool to the south east. To the south began the earlier Siloam Channel, which led to the lower pool of Siloam, (see Tyropoeon Valley, below).

When Hezekiah's tunnel became mostly obstructed, the Gihon waters flowed into the Kidron and the source of the water disappeared from sight.

where Mary washed clothes

When the spring was rediscovered in the late 14th C, Christians decided it was the place where Mary had washed the infant Jesus' clothes, and named it the Virgin's Fountain, a name still used today.

> ## Hezekiah's Tunnel

Alluded to by Isaiah

Around the time of King Ahaz, (c730) there were two reservoirs (pools) at the southern end of the city, in the area called Siloam. As one was higher than the other they were simply known as the Upper Pool *(ha'brekha ha'elyona)* mentioned in Isaiah 7:3 (the Pool of Siloam), and the Lower Pool *(ha'brekha ha'takhtona)* of Isaiah 22:9 (see Tyropoeon Valley, below). These pools were fed by an open rock-hewn conduit *(ta'ala,* in Hebrew).

threat from the east

Hezekiah, who succeeded Ahaz, realising the threat of siege from the Assyrian king, Sennacherib, decided to build a more secure channel to bring the Gihon water into the city. This resulted in his famed tunnel, a masterpiece in ancient engineering.

Beginning at the Gihon Spring it followed a twisting route, 533 metres under the hill on which Jerusalem was built, and when finished sloped c2 metres from the Gihon to Siloam, providing plenty of gravity for the flow. So sound was its construction that it flows until today! The tunnel was dug from each end, but as the level was slightly miscalculated, the floor level had to be lowered to permit the water to flow. The tunnel can be assigned to Hezekiah on the basis of II Kings 20:20.

record found

In 1880 a Hebrew inscription was discovered chiselled from the rock near the south end of the tunnel. Although there are several gaps in the text, which also uses obscure phrases, it describes the event in the tunnelling when the workers, tunnelling from either end met, and the water began to flow; by filling in the gaps in a logical manner it has been translated roughly as follows:

"When the tunnel was being bored through, this was the manner in which it was bored through. While...the pick-axe, each man toward his fellow, and while there were still three cubits to bore through, there was heard the voice of a man calling to his fellow, for there was a fissure [?] in the rock on the right and on the left. And when it was bored through, the quarrymen struck towards each other, pick-axe against pick-axe, and the water flowed from the spring toward the reservoir for 1,200 cubits; and the height of the rock above the heads of the quarrymen was 100 cubits".

Catholic Encyclopaedia

The stone is now in the Museum of the Orient, Istanbul.

It is possible to walk through the tunnel, although you will get wet in the process. This should, in any case, only be done in the company of a knowledgeable person.

I have heard rumours that a major touristic undertaking is in the pipeline that will make such a walk easier. For the time being, this is for the future.

▸ The Lower Tyropoeon Valley and the Pool of Siloam

The Tyropoeon Valley (Gr. Valley of the Cheesemakers), bisects the Old City of Jerusalem, running in an almost straight line from the Damascus Gate south to the Dung Gate, then descending sharply to its confluence with the Kidron Valley. Apart from the southern and extra-mural section, it has been so built upon over the centuries that it is barely discernible as a valley (see page 49 Muslim Quarter).

How to get there

To reach the Pool of Siloam from the Gihon Spring will require a walk of c600 metres. Follow the Kidron Valley road south to its confluence with the Tyropoeon Valley, then turn NW. The pool is c150 metres on (this is included in the 600 metres), near the end of the valley.

The name Siloam is derived from the Hebrew *shiloakh*, the sending (of the water), and its Arabic version, *Silwan* has the same meaning, a name also given to a nearby village.

The pool is flanked by the remains of an Ottoman mosque with a lowish minaret, built at the end of the last century on the ruins of a then just discovered Byzantine church. You reach the pool from a path to the left.

History

This was certainly the location of Hezekiah's reservoir, as his tunnel terminates here. This could also be the pool mentioned in Isaiah 22:9 (see above). Verse 11 of that chapter *"And you made a reservoir between the two walls"* confirms this, as it indeed lies just west of the 6th C eastern wall.

Jesus heals

Hezekiah's pool was still there when Nehemiah rebuilt the city walls (Neh. 3:15) and survived into the first century AD as the place where a blind man was healed by Jesus: *"And as He passed by, He saw a man blinded from birth...and he said to*

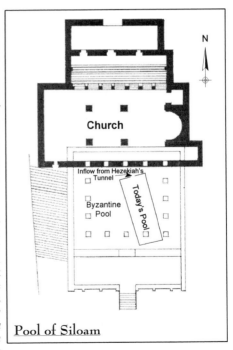

Pool of Siloam

him, 'Go, wash in the pool of Siloam' And so he went away and washed, and came back seeing." (John 9:1 & 7).

In the Roman/Byzantine period a more elaborate pool was constructed, surrounded by arcades. This was considerably larger than the present one, and was used for bathing and medicinal purposes. The enlarged pool was seen by the Bordeaux Pilgrim on his travels here around the year 333 (Itinerarium Burdigalense).

At its northern end, Eudocia, wife of Theodosius, then resident in Jerusalem, built a church and hospice. This was visited and described by the Piacenza Pilgrim, the "Anonymous of Piacenza" in 580.

Although the Muslims at first considered the water to have healing properties, they soon after abandoned them and the pool fell into disuse.

The Visit

Faded glory

Today the Pool of Siloam, a mere shadow of what it must once have been, is long and narrow, c18 by c5 metres. Hezekiah's Tunnel flows into it from beneath an arch at the northern end.

The pool is approached down a flight of stone steps, through a gate that is often kept locked. However the guardian is always nearby and will see you coming and open it. Descending, be careful at the bottom as the last step is very low, and easily missed! There is not much to see except the pool itself and some remains of stone pillars.

replaced by garden

Further south at the bottom of the valley, where this valley and those of the Kidron and Hinnom meet, is the now walled garden that was formerly the Lower Pool (see above), known to the Palestinians as Birket al-Hamra, the Red Pool. The well-watered gardens belong to the Palestinian village of Silwan.

In the late 19th C, archaeologists F. J. Bliss and A. C. Dickie found large sections of the city walls here. They had been used to dam the mouth of the Tyropoeon Valley, thus fortifying this, the lowest part of the city. Part of these hail from the Byzantine period. Although outside the walls of Aelia Capitolina, the walls of Jerusalem were extended to include this area by Eudocia in the second half of the 5th C. Now, with the area quite built up and roads laid, there is little to see, and the character is quite different.

the field of blood

About 200 metres further south is the eastern end of the Hinnom Valley. On the southern side is a rocky terrace known as **Aceldama**, a corruption of the Aramaic for Field of Blood. According to some traditions this is the piece of land that the priests purchased with the 30 pieces of silver that they were going to pay Judas Iscariot for betraying Jesus.

In 1892 the Greek Orthodox **Convent of St. Onuphrius** (a Byzantine anchorite) was built over the site and some ancient burial caves.

The entire area is covered with the ruins of cave tombs and it is thought that this was a cemetery where unnamed pilgrims and

175

perhaps criminals were buried. The explorer I. Norov described this part of the Hinnom Valley as being desolate and full of ruined tombs. Some of the entrances had decorated lintels and chambers with burial niches inside. Some bore inscriptions in Greek and other languages (I. Norov, *Reise nach dem heiligen Lände,* 1838). Then as now shepherds grazed their flocks over the hillsides which become very verdant in spring. Many olive trees also grow over the area.

Above is the hill of Abu Tor, sometimes equated with the Hill of Evil Counsel, where traditionally Caiaphas and others conspired to do away with Jesus.

▸ KIDRON VALLEY

Numerous names

Its Hebrew name, Nakhal Kidron, the Kidron stream, is derived from the word *kadar,* meaning shady or dark (alluding to its depth). The Arabs have various names for it. Wadi Sitti Maryam, Wadi Far'un and Wadi Silwan. A deep ravine section in the Judean Desert where the Monastery of Mar Saba overhangs (see Chapter 20) is known as Wadi al-Nar, the Valley of Fire, because of the intense desert heat.

car repair region

The wadi actually starts slightly north of the Old City, just east of the American Colony. The wadi and surroundings here are known by the locals as **Wadi Joz**, but in reality form the beginning of the Kidron Valley. The area is an oily jumble of small garages and workshops where you can bring any car of any age and find someone to fix it.

road to Jericho

After running east towards the Mount of Olives the depression turns abruptly south, and becomes the divide between the eastern elevation of the Old City and the Mount of Olives. The road to Jericho and the eastern Palestinian villages of Jerusalem passes through it.

Here the valley becomes deeper, or appears to because of the heights to the east and west, and more confined, separating the city from the Mount of Olives. In late Old Testament times this section was known as the Valley of Jehoshaphat (see below).

passing David's city

The valley then continues south. To its west rises the ridge where the original Jebusite and Davidic cities stood. Above it, to the east, is the sprawling village of Silwan, clinging to the rock side, one of the poorest areas of Jerusalem and often a trouble spot for the Israelis.

Further south is a confluence with the two other valleys, the Tyropoeon and Hinnom.

quite a grand canyon

The Kidron then flows in a southeasterly direction for a while, veering south again briefly before finally heading east, cutting its way through the arid hills of the unbearably hot Judean Desert. Close to the Monastery of Mar Saba (Chapter 20) it enters a striking, rugged-sided canyon on its journey to the Dead Sea, where it empties some 3.5 kilometres south of Ra's al-Fashkha (Ein Fashkha).

CAVES AND TOMBS OF SILWAN

The area of Silwan village is filled with caves and ancient tombs. In bygone eras and even the recent past they formed the bulk of the habitations of the people of the village.

Numerous 19th C accounts describe the village of Silwan. U. J. Seetzen who visited in 1806 reported that the village houses were pitiful, built either in or adjacent to caves. There were few well-constructed houses and the villagers dwelt together with their sheep and goats under the same roof!

R. R. Madden wrote in 1825 that Silwan was a clutter of tombs, caves and houses, one beside the other and on top of each other. According to the Baedeker guide of the 1870s many of the caves on the rock side were once the abodes of monks and hermits.

Between the dwellings are many very ancient tombs, the most important of which – but hardly worth the effort to see – is the **Monolith of Silwan**, more commonly called by the locals the Tomb of Pharaoh's Daughter. Dating from the period between the 9th and 6th centuries BC, its present-day flat roof was topped by a pyramid. An inscription in ancient Hebrew characters was discovered over the doorway.

the Kidron sewer

For centuries the part of the wadi below the Gihon spring has been used as an open sewer, first by the city and lately by the villagers, and until recently it was quite disgusting and smelly. This part has now been covered up, relieving an incredible eye and nose sore. However, by the time it reaches the Dead Sea it somehow manages to collect all kinds of effluents, making its final stretch still far from pictorial!

shaping the city

It is the Kidron and its concourses which have determined the contours of the area on which Jerusalem was built and, together with its spring, the Gihon, emanating from the western slope, has fixed the exact location.

History

Biblical beginnings

The Kidron makes its first appearance in the Bible when King David, fleeing from his usurping son, Absalom, crosses it on his way to the desert (II Samuel 15:23). In the early 7th C BC, King Asa burned his mother's idols in the Kidron (I King's 15:13) and in the late 5th C Josiah commanded the high priest to bring out of the temple all the vessels that were made for Baal, *"and he burned them outside Jerusalem in the fields of the Kidron"* (II Kings 23:4 (also verses 6 and 12)).

Jeremiah, in prophesying a new covenant between Israel and the Lord, included the Kidron in the area that was to be holy.

waiting for Judgment Day

In later OT times it was also called the Valley of Jehoshaphat (especially the part below the Mount of Olives), meaning 'God judges': *"For behold in those days and at that time...I will gather all nations, and bring them down to the valley of Jehoshaphat, then I will enter into judgment..."* (Joel 3:2). For some that name took root and in Byzantine times Christian ascetics and hermits lived in the Judean Desert, in caves in the wadi's walls, waiting for the day of judgment to strike (see Mar Saba, Chapter 20). The Jewish cemeteries on the Mount of Olives extend into the valley for the same reason.

Islam holds a similar tradition as detailed in the Kitab Ahwal al-Qiyama, the Book of the Stages of Resurrection.

How to Get There

The monuments of the Kidron Valley, which are tombs, are situated adjacent to one another in the part just south of the Jericho Road. They can be approached either as a continuation of the tour to the Gihon above, or after your visit to the Mount of Olives, or separately.

As my route is a continuation of the tour above, if you select one of the last two options you will have to work backwards in my book. You can approach the valley either from the road that skirts the southeastern city walls where a new stepped path has just been built (c300 metres east of the Dung gate), or from the Jericho Road, where a couple of hundred metres south of the Church of All Nations, along the main road, you'll find a new paved path leading off to the SW (right). (Buses 43 & 45 from the East Jerusalem bus station).

Haram raised high

If you made the detour to visit the Pool of Siloam, return to the Gihon Spring, and continue NE. As you walk the 450 or so metres along the valley to the tombs, you'll get an unusual perspective of the Haram. From this low position it appears to be considerably higher than it actually is. To the east spreads the hodgepodge of houses that make up the village of Silwan.

no longer agricultural

There are no longer any fields along this part of the valley, and the most rural sight you will encounter will perhaps be a few sheep grazing under the watchful eye of a young shepherd, most likely from the village above. This contrasts with the reports of 19th C travellers, when substantial flocks of sheep grazed the valley and fields and orchards were quite plentiful.

doubtful origins

The tombs, situated just below the Mount of Olives, are of a style and age that could not possibly fit the traditional names applied to them, and this is recognised by most authorities. In spite of this, the names persist, perhaps in lieu of anything better. They are nevertheless of great age and interesting to see.

▸ Tomb of Zechariah

Approaching from the south the first tomb encountered is the **Tomb**

of Zechariah. Dating from the late 2nd or early 1st C BC this tomb became associated with the prophet who King Joash had stoned to death (II Chron. 24:22).

This cube-shaped solid structure is crowned by a plain pyramid, and stands on a three stepped dais c12 metres high. Along the sides are semi-engaged columns topped by ionic capitals.

▸ Tomb of the Sons of Hezir

Next to it (to the north) is the **Tomb of Bene Hezir** (Sons of Hezir) which actually forms part of a tomb complex with the Zechariah tomb. It is approached via a flight of steps from its north side. The rock hewn tomb has a facade with two engaged end columns and two free standing ones towards the centre that support a Doric frieze. Behind this facade is a portico. From here a doorway leads to a central burial chamber with three more chambers leading off it. The chambers have bench-like niches in which the bodies were laid. As a family tomb this structure was probably used for quite a few generations.

getting the name right

In the mid 19th C an ancient Hebrew inscription was uncovered which gave the names of six brothers from the priestly family of Hezir as being buried here. The first biblical reference to this family is in I Chron. 24:15 when the duties in Solomon's Temple are detailed. The second reference is in Nehemiah 10:21 when the names of those responsible for duties in Nehemiah's rebuilt temple are detailed. It could be assumed that the brothers who were buried here were descendants of these, as the monument also dates from the end of the 2nd C BC. The appellation given to this particular tomb is therefore probably accurate.

In the 12th C or thereabouts, a Christian tradition developed that this was the tomb of St. James the Lesser, the brother of Jesus.

▸ Tomb of Absalom

The next monument, slightly further north, is the most famous of the Kidron tombs, the so-called **Tomb of Absalom** (also referred to as Absalom's Pillar), with behind it the **Tomb of Jehoshaphat**.

The former is the most conspicuous of all the sepulchres, but has nothing to do with the personage of Absalom. The idea that it did, came about through the biblical story that *"Absalom in his lifetime had taken and set up for himself a pillar which is in the King's Valley...and it is called Absalom's monument to this day."* (II Samuel 18:18).

missile bombardment

In the past when the monument was believed to be the tomb of David's would-be patricidal errant son, Jews, Christians and Muslims alike would throw stones at it and offer curses!

conical roof

The impressive structure, standing in a court c12 metres long, is hewn from the cliff and dates from the first C BC. The lower part is cut from the rock while the upper is an added construction. Standing on a dais, each side has two semi-engaged Ionic-capitaled columns on which rests an architrave and a Doric frieze. A cornice above supports a round drum which in turn rises to a concave conical roof. The height is almost 17 metres.

The original entrance was high on the south side where steps led down into the two hewn burial chambers in the lower section.

confusing connotations

To the north and on the east side of the court is the **Tomb of Jehoshaphat**. Stone steps lead up to the entrance which is topped with a decorated pediment of acanthus leaves, vines and fruit. The doorway, which is now closed, leads into a hall and passage which in turn opens into a number of burial chambers, some of which have bench burial niches.

The tenuous linkage to King Jehoshaphat is due to the biblical record that *"Jehoshaphat slept with his fathers and was buried with his fathers in the city of David..."* (I Kings 22:50), coupled with the fact that this part of the Kidron Valley was called the Valley of Jehoshaphat (which word also means 'God judges', see above). It can all be very confusing!

15. North of the Old City

INTRODUCTION

The area north of the Damascus Gate is especially interesting, and even if you don't have time to explore the entire "outside-the-walls" city, you should try to allocate a few hours here.

The route covering this section starts at the corners of Nablus Road (Derech Shechem in Hebrew) and Sultan Suleiman St., directly opposite the Damascus Gate. Most of this area developed in the late 19th C, mingling history rich sites of antiquity with those of the later period.

I have divided the area into two walks. If you combine them, depending on how long you linger at the various sites, it will take you a good half day or more. The first part takes you through Palestinian areas of the city, most noticeable around the bus station near the beginning of Nablus Road. The atmosphere here has a strong Middle Eastern flavour, with many of the throng in traditional garb and all manner of street vendors offering all manner of produce.

THE VISIT

> ### Walk No. 1 - Nablus Road to the American Colony

MAIN FEATURES: **Garden Tomb – Church of St. Stephen – Cathedral of St. George – Tomb of the Kings – American Colony – Tomb of Simon the Just.** TIME: **2-3 hours.**

The walk begins at the corner of Nablus Road almost facing the Damascus Gate. Usually there are one or two felafel vendors on this corner, the smell of the frying falafel being more enticing than the unhygienic conditions in which they are cooked. Buy at your risk (I often have)! Equally tempting and tasty are the freshly-baked, sesame-covered bread rolls, usually sold with a hard-boiled egg and a newspaper-screw of *zarta*, an aromatic thyme-like herb.

▸Schmidt School for Girls

The turreted, castle-like building on the corner of Nablus Rd. and Sultan Suleiman St. is the **Schmidt School for Girls**. In the 1870s the Palastina-Verein der Katholiken Deutschland, the German

181

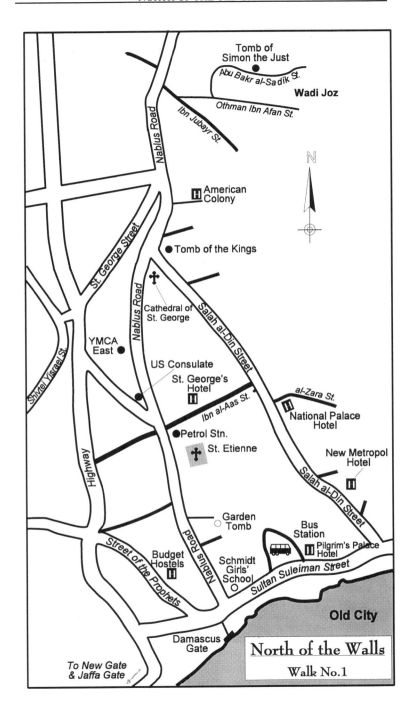

Catholics in Palestine, decided to build an institution of their own in Jerusalem. One of their leading members, Father Ladislaus Schneider had managed to buy some land on today's Bezalel St. in west Jerusalem, quite some distance from the Old City. In the late 1880s two buildings were put up there, a pilgrims' hospice and a girls' school which initially had less than 30 pupils.

closer to the walls

In 1890 a Lazarite priest, Father Wilhelm Schmidt, arrived in Jerusalem and was made head of the school. Although the school flourished the hospice did not, being rather distant from the Old City. Accordingly, the German society looked for a more suitable plot. This was found in 1899 at the present location and a new hospice, named for St. Paul, was built on the site together with a boys' school. These buildings, completed in 1910, were consecrated at the same time as the Dormition Abbey in the presence of the German Crown Prince, Friedrich. The hospice was large and palatial and housed many works of art.

headquarters of the RAF

During the First World War the institution served as the divisional headquarters of the German military, and during the British Mandate was used for government offices. It also functioned as the HQ of the RAF.

The building now belongs once more to the Deutscher Verein vom Heiligen Lände and is again a hospice as well as the location of the girls' school now named after Father Schmidt.

▸ The Garden Tomb

Continue up Nablus Road for a few tens of metres until you reach a lane, Conrad Schick St., on the right, and a sign pointing to the **Garden Tomb.**

more realistic

For many Protestants, especially Evangelicals, this is the site, or at least the preferred site, of the Tomb of Jesus and Calvary. As you will have gathered by now, most biblical locations in Jerusalem are identified mainly by tradition, and there is certainly no tradition to support this place as being that of Calvary – the archaeological evidence is weak and more fanciful than anything else. Be that as it may, many people, believers or not, understandably find this grassy, open air location more analogous to the Gospel narratives than the gloomy, ceremony-bound complex inside the city walls. This charming spot is something of a placid haven in this turbulent city. Often overlooked, it certainly merits a visit if only for this unusual characteristic.

History

The place of the skull?

The site is sometimes called "Gordon's Calvary", after the British General, Charles Gordon who in 1883 publicised this location as being that of Golgotha and the Holy Tomb. A popular story has Gordon standing on the ramparts of the Old City, looking north and noticing the rock promontory (it's at the rear of the bus station about

100 metres further east on Sultan Suleiman St.), and being struck how it resembled a skull. (The name "Golgotha" means "Place of the Skull".) However there were others before him who had toyed with a similar notion.

first century tomb

As early as the 1840s some digging had been undertaken on the site and at some time, probably around 1870, the discovery of a rock hewn tomb together with a cistern showed that the area had been in use in the first century AD. The tomb is hewn from the scarp inside the garden, and although it may originally have been cut in the 1st C, it was reused in Byzantine and Crusader times. A semi-circular furrow around the entrance is said to have been made by the round sealing stone.

The Visit

Soothing and serene

Belief being what it is, the plot was purchased by the specially founded Garden Tomb Association, and it was landscaped to its present design. The result is one of the most beautiful and serene places in all of Jerusalem, and it is easy to understand why many hold it so dear. Guided tours are provided by the very evangelical staff, and many Protestant groups come here to pray. On Easter Day a very large service is held.

▸ The Church of St. Stephen

Leaving the Garden Tomb, return to Nablus Road, turn right and continue north. The wall to your right is that of the **Dominican Convent** and in the grounds is the **Church of St. Stephen** and the **École Biblique et Archéologique Française**. The entrance gate is further along and is kept closed. By the side is a door with an intercom. Press the bell and tell the sister who answers that you wish to see the church. No one will greet you and it is most likely that you'll be the sole visitor. Few realise that entry is permitted. **You may visit daily from 07.30-13.00 and from 15.00-18.00.**

History

Mix-up of gates

St. Stephen, St. Etienne in French, is a new basilica built on the foundations of a 5th C Byzantine structure. No one knows the location of the stoning of Stephen (Acts 7:58-60), Christianity's first martyr. Early tradition placed it outside the northern gate, now the Damascus Gate. In Crusader times this was actually called St. Stephen's Gate. A later tradition placed the occurrence outside the eastern gate which we now name after St. Stephen, although Jews and Muslims call it by other names (see page 137).

relics discovered?

In the early 5th C some bones discovered outside the northern gate were deemed to be those of the first Martyr, and in 460 Eudocia built a church to house these relics. Eudocia herself was also buried there.

The church was destroyed in 614, and rebuilt as a small chapel later. This was enlarged by the Crusaders in the 12th C, but as it lay outside the city walls they demolished it themselves prior to Salah al-Din's siege in 1187. In the 13th and perhaps 14th C a small Christian hospice stood on the site.

In 1882 excavations revealed remains of a 5th C Byzantine church with a mosaic floor. These were identified as those of the church built by Eudocia.

French purchase from Greeks

In 1884 the French Dominicans purchased the site from its Greek Orthodox owner, and founded the Convent of St. Etienne and the École Biblique et Archéologique Française. In 1895 they commenced work on a new basilica over the Byzantine remains. It was designed in the Byzantine manner by Boutaud, a French architect, and consecrated in 1900.

The church is facing the main gates, and the mosaic floor of the Byzantine structure is preserved within. Outside in the courtyard, surrounded by a colonnade, are some tombs and cisterns from the early period.

The Visit

Heavy stone roof

The design of the new church originally called for a wooden roof, but after a fire in a similarly designed building in France it was changed to stone. The weight of this was so great that Gothic-type piers, not normally a feature of Byzantine style, were added as supports.

The edifice is massive, 26 metres high including the pediment. The interior walls are embellished with marble and other decorations. The Byzantine mosaics are covered with rugs but they can be lifted for viewing. However, as they are below floor level the dim light will not let you see much, despite the three very long windows stretching the full height of the building from above the entrance. A torch might be useful.

The École Biblique, built in the Gothic style, occupies the southern side of the colonnade. To the north of the basilica is a bell tower and the Dominican monastery.

▸ Anglican Cathedral of St. George.

Continue north on Nablus Road past the petrol station on the right and cross over the road. The US consulate is on the left. Further along is the East Jerusalem YMCA also on the left. Just before you get to the end of the road, on the right you will see the **Anglican Cathedral of St. George**.

In 1841 the German Lutherans and the Anglicans established a joint Protestant bishopric in Jerusalem. By the mid 1880s this partnership had become strained. The Anglicans complained their clergy had not received a fair share of the office of bishop, a title that was originally supposed to alternate between the two churches. In 1886 the association was terminated and the Anglicans set up their own organisation. A year later the Archbishop of Canterbury dispatched Bishop Blyth to Jerusalem as Anglican bishop. Blyth planned a new centre for his church, which was to serve as the

St. George's Cathedral, 19th C

Anglican headquarters in the Middle East.

a little bit of England

Land was acquired on the Nablus Road just southwest of the Tombs of the Kings, and construction began in 1891. The cathedral and other buildings, named St. George's Close, were designed by George Jeffery on the lines of an Oxford college. The original complex comprised the cathedral, consecrated in 1898, and the bishop's residence completed at the same time; there were also separate schools for boys and girls, and training workshops.

outstanding landmark

In the early 20th C the church was enlarged, and the high bell tower, fashioned after the tower of Magdalen College, Oxford, was added. Completed in 1912, it was named for Edward VII who had recently succeeded to the British throne. Many praised the building as the most impressive in Jerusalem, and it remains a striking landmark. George Jeffery was much applauded for his design.

Today there is a very fine hospice in the grounds where you can stay. For details see the relevant section on accommodation.

St. George's certainly provides a touch of England on foreign soil!

► Tombs of the Kings

Nablus Road now bears slightly to the right where it is joined by Salah al-Din Street, which begins just facing Herod's Gate. A few metres down Salah al-Din, on the north side are located the so-called **Tombs of the Kings**.

History

Really tomb of a queen

In the late 19th century erroneously believed to be the tombs of the Kings of Judea (see below), the tomb complex still carries this title. It is in fact the tomb of Helena, Queen of Adiabene, a kingdom in what is now NE Iraq, then nominally under Parthian control but enjoying a good measure of independence.

incestuous marriage

The story of Queen Helena is related in detail by Josephus. He tells of how King Monobazus fell in love with his sister Helena and made her his wife. When a son was born he was named Izates. At that time there were many Jewish merchants living in Adiabene, and one, a certain Ananias, introduced the Jewish faith to Helena and Izates. Eventually, in AD 30, they both converted to Judaism.

When Monobazus died around AD 35, his eldest son, also named Monobazus, became king; but he stepped down to accommodate

Helena's wish that Izates should rule.

famine relief

Once Helena had made sure that the throne was safe and the government in good order, she went to live in Jerusalem where she spent nearly all the rest of her life. This would have been around AD 44.

"Now her coming was of great advantage to the people of Jerusalem; for whereas a famine did oppress them at that time, and many people died for want of what was necessary to procure food. Queen Helena sent some of her servants to Alexandria with money to buy a great quantity of corn, and others to Cyprus to bring a cargo of dried figs; and as soon as they were come back, and had brought those provisions, which was done very quickly, she distributed food to those that were in want of it, and left a most excellent memorial behind her... When her son Izates was informed of this famine he sent a great sum of money to the principal men of Jerusalem."
Josephus, Antiquities, XX:2:5

(This famine is probably the one mentioned in Acts 11:28.)

Helena is supposed to have built a fine palace which was destroyed with the Roman rasing in AD 70. She also built this tomb complex to the north of the city.

Jerusalem sepulchre

Izates died at the age of 55, around the year 60, and stricken with grief Helena returned to her country and died soon afterwards. The new king, also a Monobazus, had both their remains sent to Jerusalem where they were buried *"at the pyramids which Helena had erected; they were three in number, and distant no more than three furlongs from the city of Jerusalem."* (Antiq.XX:4:3).

Adiabene continued to assist the Jews, and during the first revolt Josephus records a particular instance where *"the Jews lost only twenty-two, of whom the most valiant were the kinsmen of Monobazus, king of Adiabene..."* (Josephus Wars II:14:2).

Jewish legend

There is a Jewish tradition that this was the tomb of Ben Kalba Savua, a wealthy first century Jew and, according to the Talmud, the father-in-law of the famous sage, Rabbi Akivah. During the first revolt and Roman siege of the city he provided food for the Jews there. In 1835 the site was visited by Rabbi Chayim Hurwitz who wrote, *"This is indeed a wondrous cave [of Kalba Savua] ... I thank Almighty God for granting me the privilege of visiting this holy place..."* (Chayim Hurwitz, Love of Jerusalem, 1844). After the excavation of the tomb and the subsequent removal of a sarcophagus to Paris (see below), a Hebrew newspaper of the day wrote, *"Before our eyes they are removing the bones of the great men of Israel from the graves in which they have lain for more than 2000 years.... our eyes have seen this sight in a cave thought to be the tomb of...Kalba Savua of blessed memory."* (HaMagid, 1863).

a case of mistaken identity

The first archaeological dig on the site was conducted by the

French archaeologist, De Saulcy, in 1863. He unearthed two stone sarcophagi, later removed to the Louvre, and believed them to be of the Kings of Judah, a deduction that later proved erroneous. And that's how the place acquired its name!

Aramaic revelation

One of the sarcophagi had a two line inscription. The first line read *malkata tsaddan*, and the second, *malkat-a tsada*. Both lines are Aramaic, and both mean the same, Queen Tsada, but the first is written in Syriac characters, the other in Hebrew. Tsada is Helena's Aramaic name, Helena being Greek.

conditional gift to the French

It is interesting to note that some Jews were so determined to have the site declared to be as De Saulcy had first thought, the Tombs of the Kings of Judah, that in 1878 a wealthy French Jew bought the site and gave it to the French government in a deed of gift. The last part of clause three of this deed stipulated, *"To ensure permanent preservation of this plaque, on which shall be inscribed in French, Hebrew and Arabic the name of the place: 'The Tombs of the Kings of Judah'"*. This plaque remains today!

The Visit

Wide steps

The mausoleum is indeed an impressive edifice. You enter from Salah al-Din Street into a courtyard and then down a nine metre wide flight of rock hewn steps. On the right, and to the centre are channels which directed rainwater into two cisterns at the bottom. This water may have been used for ritual purification. At the bottom is a vaulted entrance dome some eight metres high which leads into an interior court almost 27 metres square where the remains of two pillars were found. The flat architrave is decorated with a wreath and the frieze is ornamented with leaves and a central rosette. The three pyramids mentioned by Josephus were above the facade, but these have not endured.

rolling stone

To the rear of the facade is an ante-room and at the southern end an opening leads to steps descending to the burial chamber. This opening was sealed by a rolling stone, the grooves of which can still be seen.

At the bottom of the steps is a largish square hall with burial chambers leading off. In these chambers, at differing levels, are niches in which the bodies were placed. As there are so many of these, it is assumed that the tomb was originally designed as a family tomb for many generations.

You may visit the Tombs of the Kings from 07.30 to 17.00. There is an admission fee, and a flashlight is useful.

▸ The American Colony

Return to Nablus Road, and continue north. Passing Abu Ubaida Street, you arrive at the cul-de-sac, Louis Vincent Street. This is part of **the American Colony**, which at the beginning of the 20th C possessed a far more rural aspect than it does today. On the left is the

American Colony Hotel, one of the best hotels in Jerusalem. The hotel, a favourite haunt of foreign journalists, is about all that survives of the original district. A very fine example of Ottoman building, much of the ambience of the earlier age still lingers.

good restaurant

Built as the summer home of Rabbah Effendi, a member of the important Husseini family, it was constructed in 1897. Although I can't always afford to stay here, I do indulge myself at the restaurant, especially the summer barbecues, whenever possible.

The American Colony was founded by a group of fundamentalist Christians from the US and Sweden headed by Anna Spafford. Although it once embraced a large community, it is now really just known for the famous hotel. A home for orphan babies built by the Spafford family in the Muslim Quarter of the Old City still operates. Incidentally, although Swiss managed, the hotel is still owned by the Spafford family.

lucky sheikh

Continuing north on Nablus Road, which now starts to descend towards the beginning of **Wadi Kidron** (called here Wadi Joz), you pass a mosque. You'll recognise it from its low minaret. This is the **tomb of Amir Hussan al-Din al-Jarrah**. Sheikh Jarrah, as he is more often called, served under Salah-al-Din and was much venerated by local people who credited him with bringing good

---

St. John's Ophthalmic Hospital

THE Ophthalmic Hospital of the Knights of St. John was established in 1882, by the modern British equivalent of the medieval Order. During a visit to Jerusalem by the Duke of Kent, a Knight of the Order, he decided that such a hospital was needed and it would be the best way in which his Order could serve the city at that time. Until its establishment there was no specialist eye hospital in all of Palestine.

It's first location was facing Mount Zion, on the road to Bethlehem where the Mount Zion Hotel now stands (above the Hinnom Valley). The then governor of Jerusalem, Rauf Pasha, contributed some of the money that helped to procure the site.

The hospital became renowned throughout the country and indeed throughout the entire Middle East, and leading eye surgeons devoted some of their time to serving the institution.

The success of this hospital stimulated the Jews to open ophthalmic departments in their own hospitals, partly to dispense with the need for Jews to enter a "Christian" facility (though this one had no missionary ambitions). It thus ended up serving, almost exclusively, the Arab population.

After the 1948 war, and the subsequent division of the city, the hospital moved to its present Sheikh Jarrah location.

St. John's Ophthalmic Hospital remains the only hospital of its type in the entire Holy Land, and is still an important medical institution for the Palestinians who are treated, if necessary, free of charge.

fortune. Although this building dates from AH 1313 (1895/6), a Dervish monastery stood here earlier and was identified by the explorer E. Robinson in 1835.

The name Sheikh Jarrah has been applied to the fashionable quarter located on the hill NE of the tomb. The quarter is the location of many consulates and homes of wealthy Palestinians. **St. John's Ophthalmic Hospital** is also situated there. St. John's, which caters mainly to the Palestinians, free of charge, was established in 1882 (in a different location) by the modern British order of the Knights of St. John (see box page 188).

► **Tomb of Simon the Just**

Tomb in the valley

Almost at the bottom of the hill a road leads off to the right in a slightly backwards direction. Less than 50 metres along it forks. Take the left one, Othman Ibn Afan Street, although you will search in vain for a name sign. A very short way along, a track-cum-road turns off to the north and enters the beginning of Wadi Kidron or Wadi Joz. This is Abu Bakr al-Sadik St. and a sign nailed to a post points to the **Tomb of Simon the Just** which is at the end of the curving road in the wadi.

pious priest

Simon the Just, or Shimon ha-Tsaddiq in Hebrew, was the High Priest of Jerusalem in the 4th C BC: *"When Onias the high priest was dead, his son Simon became his successor. He was called Simon the Just, because of both his piety towards God, and his kind disposition to those of his own nation."* (Josephus, Antiquities, XII:2:5). Simon is referred to in rabbinical literature, and is best known for his saying, *"Upon three things the world is based: upon the Law, upon divine service and upon charity."* (Ethics of the Fathers (Heb. *Pirkei Avot*) 1:2).

19th century visitors

Sources reveal that Jews have venerated this cave as Simon's tomb for at least 350 years, and probably longer. It is also associated with the celebration rites of the Jewish holiday of Lag ba'Omer, 33 days after Passover, when the three-year-old sons of Orthodox Jews receive their first haircut. W. M. Thompson writing in his 1859 book, "The Land and the Book" wrote:

"I once entered on the thirty third day after Passover (Lag Ba'Omer) a day consecrated to the honour of Simon. Many Jews were there with their children. Like all other sects in the East, they make vows in reference to shaving off hair from their own and their children's head in honour of some saint or shrine... The surrounding fields and olive orchards were crowded with gaily dressed and merry Hebrews."

Thompson was obviously unfamiliar with the long-standing Jewish custom! There were many other similar reports during the 19th C and if you happen to be in Jerusalem on this day and go to the tomb, you will find the practice very little changed.

bought by Jews

In 1876 a group of devout Jews purchased the cave, and it is now a small synagogue and place of pilgrimage. Jewish rules for such places must be observed by visitors. On most days, especially the Sabbath and Holy Days, people from the nearby ultra Orthodox suburbs come here to pray.

really a Roman tomb

Unfortunately for the fur-hatted and long-coated worshippers who trek in the blazing sun to this site to pray, the cave is not what they believe it to be! It was researched by the archaeologist Clermont-Ganneau in 1871. He discovered a Roman inscription on a wall of the antechamber with the name Julia Sabinus, who may have been the wife of Julius Sabinus, an officer in the Roman Tenth Legion, the legion which garrisoned Jerusalem. It is generally accepted among scholars that this is her tomb!

plenty more to see

From here return to the American Colony, and those with the time and inclination can continue with me to the most Orthodox Jewish neighbourhood in Jerusalem (or perhaps anywhere?) and then take a stroll along the Street of the Prophets where there are 19th century buildings of architectural note. To do this follow Walk No. 2, below.

Walk No. 2 – Mea She'arim, Shivtei Yisrael and Prophets Streets

---

MAIN FEATURES: **Mea She'arim Qtr. – Italian Hospital – St. Paul's Church – Houses and buildings on Prophets and Ethiopia Streets – German Hospital – English Hospital (Anglican School).** TIME: **2-3 hours**

If you are continuing directly after Walk No.1, instead of retracing your steps down Nablus Road take the right fork into St. George St., continuing along and across the main highway into Shivtei Yisrael Street (Judges of Israel Street). There is a petrol station on the north corner, and a church opposite.

▸ Mea She'arim Quarter

Continue roughly south on Shivtei Yisrael Street. To your right is the Mea She'arim quarter which can be entered via Mea She'arim Street, the last street on the right (west) before the traffic lights. This quarter is home to the most ultra orthodox of Jews, some so extreme in their views that they do not recognise the modern State of Israel because it is not a theocracy. Here in a world unlike any other in Jerusalem, more reminiscent of the 19th century ghettos of Eastern Europe, a whole community lives, trying to avoid the march of time around them.

reaping a hundredfold

Mea She'arim was one of the earliest Jewish quarters to be established in the extra-mural city and its construction commenced in 1874. Its builders were, in the main, Jews from Lithuania and

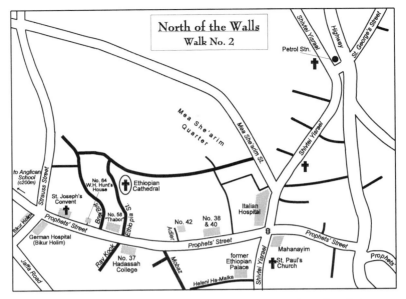

Poland who previously lived in the Old City. They founded a settlement society called Mea She'arim: *"Now Isaac sowed in that land, and reaped in the same year a hundredfold [Heb. Mea She'arim]. And the Lord blessed him."* (Gen.26:12).

less desirable neighbourhood

The society was not rich, and most of its members lived on donations from abroad. Land in the Jaffa Road area where most of the Jewish development was occurring was outside their budget and so chose an area north of the walls. This was purchased from the Arab villagers of Lifta, a village to the west of the city.

well protected

The design was planned by Conrad Schick, the noted 19th C Jerusalem architect (whose name you will become familiar with on this walk). It was intended to be a square surrounded by oblong blocks of houses which acted as a perimeter wall. The neighbourhood was entered through six iron gates which were closed at night time, or any other time the inhabitants might choose. These gates stood until about 1915 when they were removed.

only the Orthodox

Mea She'arim was governed by a committee who promulgated a series of regulations. These related to hygiene and religious matters. For example, residents were forbidden to sell their property to anyone not considered a "good" Jew (i.e. a religious one). No so-called "new ideas" were permitted and all residents had to adhere to the strict rabbinical interpretation of Jewish Law.

extremist tendencies

While the district did not start out as being more conservative than some of the other new Jewish areas (most of the Jews of Jerusalem at that time were observant), by the late 1880s the trend to more extreme conservatism developed. This continued into the 20th C, especially with the influx of non-religious Jewish Zionists and the adoption by many of new ideas in religious practice. In 1935 this trend caused a split within the community of Mea She'arim. An ultra-extremist group was formed, calling itself the Neturei Karta (Aramaic for Guardians of the City). This group was anti-Zionist. Later, when the State of Israel came into being they opposed it, stating that only the advent of the Messiah could bring this about, and then it would be governed by the Torah (Law). Around the quarter one can see many anti-Zionist slogans daubed on the walls.

holding back the clock

Today Mea She'arim is, perhaps, the most conservative Jewish area in the world. A stroll along the main thoroughfare and side alleys is like taking a journey in a time capsule to the days of the East European ghettos. The style of male attire, fur hats included, hails directly from 19th century Poland; there is nothing "Jewish" in its origin. The women all wear head coverings for modesty in keeping with the Law – either scarves, or wigs which are generally so smartly coiffed that they defeat the purpose! Stockings and long sleeves are a must whatever the weather. Children are everywhere – "be fruitful and multiply" is taken literally here.

a fascinating glimpse

Though there are no particular sites of interest in Mea She'arim, the area can be fascinating, and you may well find it gives you a rewarding insight into a distinctive way of life. The people are for the most part friendly, provided you respect their privacy and dress in a modest way. Women should not leave their arms or shoulders exposed and men should avoid wearing shorts. Be prudent when taking photographs, and on the Jewish Sabbath don't take any at all!

Return to Shivtei Yisrael St. and continue the short distance towards the crossroads.

▸ Italian Hospital (Ministry of Education)

Remarkable building

The huge castle-like building on the west (left) is now occupied by the Israeli Ministry of Education. It was once the **Italian Hospital** and ranks among the most striking of buildings in Jerusalem.

Work on the hospital started in 1912 but it took till 1920 to complete. It was built by the Italian architect Antonio Barluzzi, who also designed the church at Bethany, in the Renaissance style. It comprised three wings each having three storeys. The main entrance was through the central wing and above it a square tower was constructed. This was copied from the tower of the Palazzo Vecchio in Florence. Originally the structure was decorated with blazons, insignia of different Italian towns and religious symbols. Most of these have now been removed. Nearly all of the hospital staff were Italians.

During the Second World War it was taken over by the British authorities and used as a military hospital and headquarters for the RAF. During the 1948 war it was an Israeli forward position. Later it was returned to the Italians and continued to function as a hospital. In the early 1960s it was sold to the Israeli government.

It can be visited with permission.

cross the street

Shivtei Yisrael Street now crosses over the Street of the Prophets, Rehov Haneviim in Hebrew, and continues towards the NW corner of the Old City. Three buildings in the continuation are worth seeing.

▸ "Mahanayim" (now part of Ministry of Education)

Across the road and on the SE corner of the crossroads, with its main frontage in Shivtei Yisrael St. is the leafy mansion built by Johannes Frutiger, a Swiss Banker, and named Mahanayim, or Two Camps, from a verse in Genesis 32:2.

This was one of the finest residences in Jerusalem, designed by Conrad Schick (a busy man!), with over 40 rooms on three floors. The grounds were extensive and incorporated Frutiger's own stables and carriages.

Jacob Johannes Frutiger, a Swiss banker, originally came to Jerusalem to manage the Krichona Missionary Bank, founded by another Swiss, Christian Friedrich Spittler. The bank was instrumental in financing the development of various places in the "new" city. Later, Frutiger set up his own bank, The Frutiger & Co Bank, which was the Jerusalem agent of the Ottoman Bank.

The Frutiger Bank participated in the construction of some new Jewish neighbourhoods, which included Mahane Yehuda.

banks collapse

In 1892 another bank, the Bergheim Bank, set up in 1851, collapsed, and this caused depositors to withdraw money from the Frutiger Bank. This in turn led to the failure of the institution in 1896, and Frutiger was forced to sell his lovely house.

varied ownership

It was purchased by the Evelina de Rothschild School which was at that time situated around the corner in the Street of the Prophets. Later, for a short time, it was used as the residence of the British High Commissioner. In 1951 it was taken over by the Israeli government, and since then has been used by the Ministry of Education. While still impressive, its use as an ordinary government office has reduced much of the original charm.

▸ St. Paul's Church

Next door (south) is **St. Paul's Church**. Two British missionary societies were at work in 19th C Jerusalem: one, the London Society for Promoting Christianity amongst the Jews, was, as the name implies, devoted to proselytising the Jewish population. The other, the Church Missionary Society, or CMS, was more active among the Arab population, especially those from the Eastern Churches. This society erected St. Paul's in 1874. The very street was, until the establishment of the State of Israel, called St. Paul's Street. The language of worship was Arabic. The building is no longer used as a congregational church, although parts are used for services by evangelical groups.

palace of Ethiopian Empress

Almost facing St. Paul's is a narrow street, Queen Helena Street, or Heleni Ha-Malka in Hebrew. Just up this street, on the right, is the **Israel Broadcasting building**. This magnificent structure was formerly the Jerusalem palace of the Ethiopian Empress Taitu, wife of the Emperor Menelik II. She had this constructed in 1903, and it was certainly a residence fit for a queen, though as an institutional building today this is not readily discernible. Her name, in Amharic, and coat of arms is inscribed over the entrance lintel. During the Mandate, the building was leased to the British Administration and used by the Palestine Broadcasting Service, the predecessors of the current occupants. It is not normally open to visitors, but you can ask!

Return now to the junction of The Street of the Prophets and Shivtei Yisrael Street.

▸ Street of the Prophets

During the last 35 years of the 19th C, the Street of the Prophets, although not yet known by that name, was an important component in the developing extra-mural city. It became one of the major roads that led from the Old City to the new Jewish suburbs. Beginning just facing the Damascus Gate, it eventually joins the Jaffa Road near the Mahane Yehuda market.

lined with olive trees

The survey map of C. W. Wilson of 1864 shows a road along the general lines of the present one and this, judging by the abundance of olive trees along its length, must have been very rural. The only building marked is a sanatorium located on the site where the Anglican School is today (see below).

The earliest description of the area is given by the British artist William Hunt, who later built his house along the street. He recorded in the early 1860s that it was *"a bleak and deserted hill from which there was a spectacular view of the Old City, its walls, the Haram al-Sharif and the Holy Sepulchre"*. Today this view is only available from the eastern end of the street.

change of name

Unlike the Jaffa Road to the south and the Mea She'arim Quarter to the north, this area was developed mainly by Christians, and was to contain some very fine buildings, most constructed in the late 19th and early 20th C. During this period it was called the Street of the Consuls, as the US, Ethiopian, Polish, Spanish, British, Austrian and Italian consulates were situated along, or near it. It acquired its present name from Sir Ronald Storrs, the first British governor of Jerusalem, who gave it that title because of a tomb which Muslims believed to be the burial place of the Prophets, which was situated in the courtyard of the Nabi Ukasha shrine, an early Mameluke edifice that existed there at that time.

another Empress's house

From the corner where you now stand, proceed west along the street past the Italian Hospital; on the same side are **numbers 38 and 40**. Readily identifiable from the mosaics on the facades, the houses

195

here were originally intended as a residence for Empress Zaudita of Ethiopia. The empress ordered the construction on the advice of a noblewoman who, after visiting the city, urged her to build herself a residence there. The resultant structure never actually became her home. It has over 90 rooms and parts were used as the Ethiopian Consulate and other parts rented out, as much of the building is today. Though this relatively new building is now decaying, the facade is still resplendent with mosaics. These include the royal lion and motto which is inscribed in Ge'ez and translates "The Lion of Judah has triumphed".

in place of a tent
West of these buildings, on the corner of Adler Street is **No. 42**, now a technical school. It was in this area that, in 1898, a huge tented camp was erected for the Kaiser Wilhelm II during his visit to Jerusalem. Afterwards the Sultan made a gift of the land to the Germans. The first building here was the German Probst House, the residence of the German Protestant Provost. This two storey house was built in 1910 in typical old German style, and on the wall that fronts Adler Street is an inscription from Psalm 122:6 *"Wünschet Jerusalem Glück"* (Pray for the Peace of Jerusalem). When the British Mandate was established the house became the residence of the governor of the city, Sir Ronald Storrs.

Later the building was turned into a school; initially one for Arab youths then, after the establishment of the State of Israel, the present technical one.

early Hadassah Hospital
Some 40 metres further, on the opposite (south) side of the street is number 37, the **Hadassah College**. Originally the Rothschild Hospital, the forerunner of which was established in the Jewish Quarter of the Old City in 1835, it moved to this location in 1888 and was the first Jewish hospital outside the city walls. In 1918 it was taken over by the American Women's Zionist organisation, Hadassah, and became one of the best equipped hospitals in the region. In 1939 the hospital moved to new premises on Mount Scopus where it still functions.

Crossing back to the north side, the first street along is a narrow lane, **Ethiopia Street**. Make a brief detour along it to see the Ethiopian buildings described in the box on the next page.

▸ "Thabor" (Swedish Theological Institute)

On the corner, and continuing for some distance along the Street of the Prophets is a high stone wall. This is **number 58** and is the house that the architect Conrad Schick designed and built for himself. The house was named "**Thabor**" after Psalm 89:12: *"The north and south Thou hast created them; Tabor and Hermon shout for joy at thy name."* This name and the date of building, 1882, are inscribed over the entrance.

worth trying to get in
Thabor is an exceptionally lovely building; it was and still is one of the finest residences in the entire city. Planned around an inner patio and garden, it is quite enchanting. The entrance gate and

Ethiopian Buildings in the New City

UNLIKE many other black African nations, the Ethiopians have been Christian since the 4th century. Their royal house traces its ancestry back to the union of Solomon and the Queen of Sheba, an ancient kingdom in Yemen which also ruled over ancient Ethiopia.

Though present in the Old City since the 7th C, the Ethiopian community did not fare well. Short of funds and political clout, many of their "rights" in the holy places were severely reduced or lost over the centuries (see section on Church of the Holy Sepulchre).

This notwithstanding, towards the end of the 19th C, though small in number they were able to make their presence felt in the Jerusalem then springing up beyond the walls. Thanks to the finance provided by the emperors Johannes IV (r.1879-1889) and Menelik II who ruled until 1913, numerous elegant buildings were constructed, up until the 1920s.

In 1880, the head of the community in the city, Mamher Walde Sema'et, purchased land in a site the Ethiopians would call *Dabre Gannet*, Mount of Paradise. This lay just north of the Street of the Prophets, along what is now Ethiopia Street. An Ottoman *firman* dated 1882 authorised the construction of a circular church 22 metres in breadth and height. Completed in 1893, it was dedicated to the Virgin with the name *Kidana Maharat*, the **Convent of Mercy**. The design is typically Ethiopian with the *makdas*, sanctuary, a separate entity in the middle of the church. There are doors on three sides and a window on the fourth. They carry inscriptions in Amharic, Arabic, French, and Italian. The top of the church is crowned with a black dome and an Ethiopian cross, and over the northwestern and southwestern entrances is a carved lion, the Lion of Judah, one of the Ethiopian emperor's titles. In the compound surrounding the church are the convent's residential quarters, other offices and a bell tower.

The church's main gate, from 1897, also has carved lions and an inscription in Ge'ez, the language of the Ethiopian Church (as opposed to Amharic, the Ethiopian vernacular), which translates "Victory to the Lion of Judah, Menelik II, King of Kings of Ethiopia, 1889".

Other Ethiopian buildings were soon erected in the vicinity, the most notable being just south of the church and titled the **House of Emperor Menelik II** – though he never actually stayed there. On the facade you can see a lion, the insignia of the Ethiopian royal house, and an inscription stating that the building was constructed by the emperor.

The Ethiopian building occupying **Nos. 38 and 40** along the Street of the Prophets and the former **Palace of Empress Taitu**, located on Heleni Ha-Malka Street, are described in Walk 2 of this chapter. Of the numerous other Ethiopian buildings in the vicinity, most have since been taken over by others, either completely or on a rental basis.

balcony above it are built in an old style, and the second balcony is recessed with a circular window, adding an oriental touch.

Today it houses the **Swedish Theological Institute** and interested visitors are not usually turned away. Ring the bell by the entrance.

home of British artist

A very short distance past Thabor is **number 64.** This was the home of William Holman Hunt, the British artist who lived from 1827 to 1910. Hunt spent quite some time in Jerusalem, and some of his best work was created here. He first arrived in the city for a short sojourn in 1854. He returned about 15 years later and bought this piece of land where he constructed the house.

► Convent of St. Joseph

The **Convent of St. Joseph** is the next building, although it is well hidden behind a high stone wall. Built between the years 1887 and 1893 this three storey, once impressive, building belongs to the French sisters of the Order of St. Joseph. In the courtyard is a statue of the Order's founder, St. Emillie de Violar.

faded splendour

Built in French Renaissance style, this was indeed a splendid building – now rather shabby. A sweeping stairway leads to the main entrance which is preceded by a balcony. The entrance door with attached pillars on each side has the Order's emblem engraved above. The arched windows are constructed from sculptured stones.

Only a handful of sisters live here now, and part of the building serves as the **Lycée Français de Jerusalem.**

Again, a visit might be possible, at least into the courtyard. Ring the bell near the metal door to the left of the entrance gate.

► The German Hospital (Bikur Holim)

Across the road, on the corners of the Street of the Prophets and Strauss Street is the German Hospital, now **Bikur Holim Hospital,** the main part of which faces it in Strauss Street. The hospital was built in the 1890s, and was meant to replace an existing German hospital which had stood in the Old City since 1850. It was much used by Arabs, and all who needed attention were treated practically free of charge. Designed by Schick, it has a clearly 19th century German air about it. Above the entrance is a verse from Exodus 15:26 inscribed in German and Arabic, *"I am the Lord who healeth thee".* The Hebrew name of the hospital is now also inscribed. At the top of the building is a chapel and a bell tower.

► The English Hospital (Anglican School)
Missionary stronghold

The last building of interest along this street is almost at the western end. Cross over Strauss Street and proceed c250 metres, till you come to the **Anglican School** on the right hand side. This building, set back from the road and approached through a large court was once the English Hospital. The land was acquired in the 1860s by the London Society for Promoting Christianity among the Jews, who first built a sanatorium nearby. This was one of the first buildings recorded in the area, and was marked on the earliest map (see above). The Central Hotel, an Orthodox Jewish establishment, now occupies the site of the sanatorium.

grammar school education

The hospital functioned from 1896, and because of the high standard of treatment Jews continued to attend until well into the 20th C, when the Jewish hospital of Sha'arei Zedek was established further west on the Jaffa Road. Later it was used by the Mandate authorities as a police hostel, and then by the Israeli military. Eventually it was returned to its owners, the Anglican Church, and is now a typical English Grammar school, educating the children of diplomats and expatriates.

The actual building forms a semicircle around the pine and carob tree filled courtyard. The main entrance is through the archway ahead, and the surrounding parts, now either classrooms or staff dwellings, were formerly the clinics.

end of the road

The Street of the Prophets ends at Kikar Herut (Freedom Square) and the junction of Jaffa Road. Continuing a few hundred metres west on Jaffa Road you'll come to the **Makhane Yehuda market** and the sites described in the last part of Chapter 16, West of the Walls.

16. West of the Walls

INTRODUCTION

As explained elsewhere in this book, Jerusalem is broadly divided between areas of mainly Jewish population, generally called "west Jerusalem" and Arab districts, "east Jerusalem", which came under Israeli control in 1967. As a result of the government's desire since then to cement the two halves of Jerusalem into a majority Jewish city, east Jerusalem is no longer exclusively Arab but now includes several Israeli (Jewish) quarters. The population of the western part remains almost 100 per cent Israeli.

West, or Jewish, Jerusalem comprises the greater part of the city within its present municipal boundaries. However, much of this is new and so holds little interest for the traveller – especially as there is so much else to see! In this chapter I will therefore confine myself to those areas and sites that I feel merit a visit. These are mainly just west of the Old City walls.

> ▸ **Walk No. 1 – West of the Hinnom Valley**

START: **Corner of Hebron Road (Old City end)**; MAIN FEATURES: **Abu Tor – Railway Station – Khan – St. Andrew's Church – Mishkenot Ha'Sha'ananim – Yemin Moshe – Montefiore's Windmill – Biblical Research Institute – Palace Building (Binyan Palas)**; TIME: **Approx. 2 hours.**

The vicinity west of the Hinnom Valley, with its spectacular views of Mount Zion and the Old City ramparts, makes a fine walk. A good place to start is at the top of the road that leads from the Jaffa Gate, across the Hinnom Valley and then up towards the Hebron Road. In the past, this entire road was thus named, (the Arabic name for the Jaffa Gate being Bab al-Halil, the Hebron Gate), but the municipality has re-named this section Rehov Hativat Ezioni, after a battalion of the Israeli army.

exceptional views

At the crossroads turn east (left) into Ha-Mefaked Street. A few metres along is a small park with a fine view across the valley to Mount Zion. Further along, another vantage point affords an even better panorama to the NE. This part of Jerusalem is known as

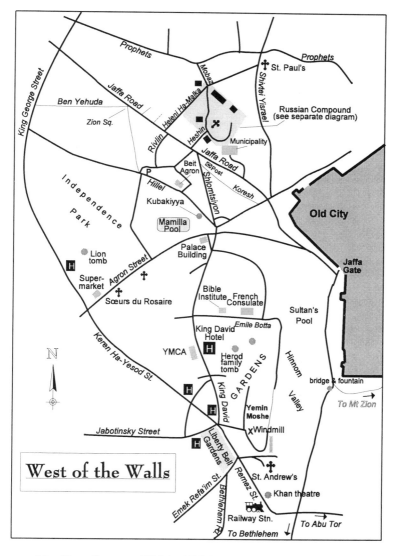

West of the Walls

Abu Tor, after one of Salah al-Din's commanders, noted for riding into battle on a bull.

Abu Tor was originally an Arab neighbourhood of Jerusalem built c1875, though a village of the same name lower down the valley existed long before. After the division of the city in 1948 the western part of Abu Tor was left in Israeli hands and thus, like the nearby and former Arab neighbourhood of Ba'aqa, was settled by Jews. If you want to follow the road round, it descends via many twists and turns into the Kidron Valley near its confluence with the Tyropoeon and Hinnom.

▶ Railway Station and the Khan

Return to the road junction and cross over the main road and continue west along David Remez Street. After c50 metres you come to the **Jerusalem Railway Station** on the left (see box, page 202 for a history of the railway).

theatrical khan

Facing the station is a very attractive complex of buildings known as **the Khan,** now a theatre and night club. These buildings once housed Mameluke and Ottoman khans and provided accommodation for travellers when the city gates were shut for the night. During the 19th C, the property was given over to silk production and silk worms were bred there. Later it was used as a storehouse. After 1967 the complex was restored and converted to its present use.

Union flag

Past this, up a flight of steps, is a building that is actually in the rear of the grounds of St. Andrew's Church (see below), flying the Union flag. This is the **British Consulate** in West Jerusalem.

Many countries have two consulates in the city, a hangover from the 1948-1967 period. As no major country recognises *de jure* Israeli sovereignty over the entire city (or indeed over any part of the city, see History), this double consulate affair persists, although as far as the British are concerned, the very modern building in the east is the main one. The original building is early Ottoman, with an arch supporting the square structure. The red-roofed building is clearly of a later construction.

▶ St. Andrew's Church

Scottish flag

Continue to the corner, turn sharp right and walk up the short inclining road to **St. Andrew's Church,** belonging to the Church of Scotland. Built in 1927 its terrace affords a grand view over the Hinnom Valley towards the Old City and Mount Zion.

Incorporating both eastern and western components in its design, the church, with its tall bell tower from which flutters the distinctive white-on-blue cross of St. Andrew, stands splendidly isolated eighty metres above the valley bed.

fallen Scots

The church was built as a memorial to the Scottish soldiers who were killed during General Allenby's Palestine campaigns in 1917-18. Part of the church floor incorporates a memorial to Robert the Bruce, the famous King of the Scots who died at the end of the 14th C. Services are held regularly in the church, whose congregation is made up of local Christian Arabs and ex-patriates. Attached is the **Scottish Hospice,** which offers medium-priced accommodation, with or without meals.

On the rock scarp in front of the church are some 8th C BC **rock-cut tombs.** Much archaeological work has been carried out here. Remains of a Byzantine church have also been unearthed.

liberty for some

Descending the way you came, the road ahead is David Street, and

The Jaffa-Jerusalem Railway

TRANSPORT from the coast to Jerusalem was always difficult in times past, taking at least a day and a half. Until the 1860s passage was usually on donkeys, camels or horses, travelling in caravans for safety. The route was controlled by local chieftains who exacted "levies"; the most notable of these was the Sheikh of Abu Ghosh, a village that commanded the approaches to the city. The levies were nothing more than protection money – by paying them the traveller was safeguarded from robbers.

In the 1860s a more secure carriageway was built and this enabled diligences and the like to carry travellers in more comfort.

However, from the mid century onwards proposals were mooted for constructing a railway. Around 1865 a German engineer published plans for a line that would link Jerusalem with Jaffa, and another that would extend down to Jericho; but as railways were very few in the Ottoman domains, nothing was seriously done.

In 1876 Abdul Hamid II became sultan and his more modern attitude resulted in a number of railways being built throughout Turkey proper.

In 1880 Yosef Navon, a Jewish Ottoman subject – and grandfather of the Israeli politician and former president Yitzhak Navon – revived the idea and by 1888 had managed to obtain a concession to lay a track from Jaffa to Jerusalem, with an option to extend it to Damascus. Unable to raise the necessary capital for the project, Navon was compelled to sell the concession to a newly formed French company, Société de Chemin de Fer de Jaffa, a Jerusalem operation which was able to procure the required funds.

Work began in the summer of 1889 and was completed three years later. The line was opened with all pomp and ceremony, with important officials from Constantinople present. For his work on the project Navon was awarded the Ottoman title of *bey*.

The steam-hauled journey took three and a half hours over a narrow gauge track, running through the picturesque valleys of the Jerusalem hills, and one train a day ran each way. It still takes over two hours and the frequency has only been increased to two!

In 1922 the Mandatory government acquired the railway line from its French owners and the original narrow gauge track was changed to standard gauge.

The two storey station has not changed very much since it was built, although the surroundings certainly have.

on both sides are parks. The one on the left is the **Liberty Bell Park**, named after the replica of the Philadelphia bell in the centre, a gift from that US state.

> ### Mishkenot Ha'Sha'ananim

First homes

The very pleasant and attractive greenery on the right is **Bloomfield Park** and is the bequest of a wealthy Canadian Jew. To the east of this, across the park, is the very smart, now restored, residential area of **Yemin Moshe**, to the immediate south of which is the likewise restored **Mishkenot Ha'Sha'ananim**, the first Jewish district to be built outside the Old City walls. A large **windmill** (see below) stands at the top of the area.

peaceful habitations

The name Mishkenot Ha'Sha'ananim, is derived from the verse in Isaiah 32:18, *"My people shall abide in peaceful habitation, and secure dwellings, and quiet resting places"*.

Although other building projects outside the city walls predate these houses, they formed the first attempt to build an actual neighbourhood beyond the city confines.

History

After having made a number of visits to Jerusalem prior to 1850, Sir Moses Montefiore was conscious of the miserable condition many of his co-religionists dwelt in within the city walls. He was determined to provide not only a healthier environment for them, but also a more secure livelihood.

Louisiana legacy

In 1855 during his fourth visit to the city, he managed to buy some land west of the part of the Hinnom Valley called the Sultan's Pool. Most of the money came from the bequest of a rich New Orleans Jew, one Judah Touro, which Sir Moses administered.

defensive design

Montefiore engaged the British architect William Smith to design the buildings, and construction began in 1857. By 1860 some of the houses were ready, and Jews from the Old City moved into them. The almost fortress-like homes were designed to provide security against bandits, as safety conditions outside the walls were still bad. The walls were some one metre thick and the windows and doors faced east – towards the city walls. The openings were even bolstered by iron bars, especially imported from Britain for the purpose.

relative luxury

Each house comprised of two rooms, kitchen, storeroom and a small plot of land in front. This was vastly different from the prevailing conditions in the overcrowded Jewish Quarter of the Old City. The restored buildings now house a restaurant, a music centre and more.

▶Yemin Moshe (Memorial to Moses)

In the early 1890s the heirs of Sir Moses decided to build another residential area just to the north of Mishkenot Sha'ananim. This was called **Yemin Moshe** as a memorial to the benefactor.

exclusive neighbourhood

Both Mishkenot Sha'ananim and Yemin Moshe were badly damaged in the 1948 war and, as they were situated on the cease fire line after the cessation of hostilities, the area remained largely empty until 1967. They have since been extensively renovated, and although the original construction was intended to house Jews of lesser means, they now rank among the most expensive of properties in Jerusalem.

In spite of the "newness" of the revamped area, Yemin Moshe is very attractive and a wander among the narrow and stepped streets can be quite rewarding.

► Montefiore's Windmill

A miller's tale

The windmill that stands at the top of Yemin Moshe is known as **Montefiore's Windmill** and was built at the same time as Mishkenot Sha'ananim to provide a source of income for some of the residents, as well as providing flour at a cheaper price than could be obtained from Arab millers, who at that time held a monopoly. As Jews were unused to operating a flour mill, Montefiore brought over millers from England (Canterbury) to teach the trade. Later, with the advent of steam-driven mills, the windmill became outmoded and fell into disuse. It has now been restored and is open to visitors.

first class travel

Inside the windmill, displayed behind glass, is a model of the diligence that Sir Moses would use to journey from Jaffa to the city. The original, which was also once displayed, was destroyed by fire.

church property

The Greek and Russian Orthodox churches own important land in West Jerusalem. As this cannot be sequestrated in the same way as Palestinian land can, title to these areas is still in their hands.

Further north in the park and east of the **King David Hotel**, one of Jerusalem's most famous and expensive hostelries (see section on accommodation), is the **Herod Family Tomb**, the property of the Greek Orthodox Church.

Herod the Great does not lie here

The reasons for applying the name of the Herod family to this tomb complex are very vague to say the least, and are based mainly on unclear references by Josephus in his "Wars". No concrete evidence linking the place to the Herod family has been discovered. In any case, the historian makes it clear that Herod the Great was buried at his fortress palace of Herodion, SE of Bethlehem. The tomb is thought to date from between 50 BC and AD 50, which would cover the correct time span.

possibly looted

Entered in 1891, anything and everything that may have once been there had long gone, apart from two sarcophagi decorated with carvings. These are now in the Greek Orthodox Patriarchate Museum (see page 84).

Unfortunately the tomb is no longer open to the general public, so you'll have to be content with the forecourt. The entrance, once sealed by a rolling stone, is in the SW corner of the court, and inside a descending passage leads to four chambers.

West of the tomb is a large renovated building, now a **cultural centre**. This stands on the site of the Byzantine church of St. George of Nikephoria. Nothing much of the church remains now, although it was clearly marked on maps of the 1930s.

► Biblical Research Institute

Following the path north, you soon come to Emile Botha Street. Turn west, left. Along this late 19th C street are the **French Consulate** and the **Biblical Research Institute**, a Vatican establishment. Both of these are fine buildings, displaying an elegance of a bygone era. The Institute was built in 1927, and houses an extensive library and exhibition of archaeological artefacts from all over Palestine. **The Institute, actually a Jesuit monastery, is open to the public Monday, Wednesday and Friday from 09.00 to 12 noon.**

Past the Institute turn right into King David Street (after the filling station). Continue down the hill to the intersection. Cross over and turn left into Agron Street.

▸ The Palace Building (Binyan Palas)

A few metres up, on the far corner of Ben Shimon Street, is the **Palace Building** now the Israel Ministry of Commerce and Industry. Although a comparatively modern building, its history is a microcosm of the development of 20th C Jerusalem.

former hotel

This very fine four storey building of unusual design was constructed in the late 1920s, using both Arab and Jewish labour. It was formerly the Arab owned Palace Hotel, standing on land that was then the property of the *Waqf*, the Muslim Religious Endowment. In 1936 it became the HQ of the Peel Commission, the body that first recommended the partition of Palestine. After 1948 it was taken over by the Israeli government.

Over the entrance facade is an inscription in Arabic detailing its erection in 1929. The interior is very striking. Two spiral staircases, one each side, reach up to a surrounding gallery on each floor, with the various rooms leading off. The whole is supported by smooth pillars. You may find it worth a visit, and if you leave your passport at the guard's desk you will be allowed in.

Our next walk continues from this point, up Agron Street.

▸ Walk No. 2 – The Centre of West Jerusalem

START: **Bottom of Agron Street;** MAIN FEATURES: **Independence Park – Mamilla Pool – Mamilla Cemetery – Nahlat Shiva – Russian Compound;** TIME: **1-1.5 hours**

Home for lepers

In the mid 19th C the area around Agron Street was quite uninhabited and thus was chosen as the site of Jerusalem's first Leprosarium built by the Germans in the late 1860s. Now gone, remnants of the hospital lie within the **Dominican Convent** further up the street.

time for a break

Across the road is the **Mamilla Cemetery** and the **Mamilla Pool**, both now incorporated into **Independence Park**, a favourite expanse of greenery in the heart of the city. During my sojourn in the city I would often come here to enjoy the relative quiet. If it is noontime you might decide to have a picnic lunch here, and suitable foods can be bought at the supermarket at the top of Agron Street. There is also a public convenience in the east of the park, and it is kept very clean!

► Mamilla Pool

A path leads from Agron Street into the cemetery and towards the pool, c50 metres away. Probably hewn in the Herodian era this reservoir measures almost 100 metres long and 65 metres wide. When full it could hold nearly 40,000 cubic metres of water. A channel once linked it with the Old City and its waters were fed into the Birkat al-Batrak, or Pool of the Patriarch (see page 63).

From Mameluke times until very recently the pool was an important source of the city's water supply and was used right through the British Mandate period. During the 1948 war its water was essential to the besieged western city. It is now redundant.

► Mamilla Cemetery

There has been a Muslim cemetery here from at least the 13th C, and probably a Christian one before. It is named after a Saint Mamilla, and in the 12th C a church dedicated to this saint stood here. Little is known of this person but he may have been one of the Christians who, according to tradition, were massacred here by the Jews and Sasanians in 614. In the western part of the park a cave known as the **Lion's Tomb** is supposed to be the mass burial place. Jewish tradition has it that the cave is the tomb of Jews massacred by the Greeks long before.

resting place for the learned

At one time Mamilla was the largest Muslim cemetery around Jerusalem, but only a few of the grave stones now remain. According to the 15th C Arab historian, Mujir al-Din, many Muslim men of scholarship and jurisprudence were interred here.

Just west of the pool is a Crusader tomb building reused by Muslims later. However a more interesting one lies in a copse about 75 metres NE of the pool.

fine ex-Crusader tomb

This is **the Kubakiyya**, the tomb of Emir Aidughdi al-Kubaki, once a Mameluke governor of Safad (in northern Israel). Undoubtedly originally Crusader, it was rebuilt to suit the needs of the Muslim gentleman who is buried there. The fact that it was a Crusader tomb reinforces the thought that the area was once a Christian burial site, perhaps reaching back to the Byzantine era.

The rectangular edifice is surmounted by a drum on which rests the dome. Above the windows and entrance are ornamented arches with some of the decoration appearing to be re-used Crusader work. Atop the entrance is an inscription with the date, 1289, and name of the Emir. The sepulchre inside is more reminiscent of a Crusader sarcophagus than a Muslim tomb.

► Nahlat Shiva

From the cemetery you can now exit into Hillel Street, a busy thoroughfare that runs almost parallel to Jaffa Road. Cross the road and walk west, turning right immediately past the car park. Follow the road round and turn left into a narrow street, Rivlin Street.

old world charm

This area, known as **Nahlat Shiva,** is the third Jewish area to be settled outside the Old City walls. The land was acquired in 1869 by seven people (*shiva* means seven), and divided amongst them. Only having enough money to build one house, they allocated this by lottery and it was won by a Joseph Rivlin, who is remembered by the central street name. Between 1872 and the outbreak of the First World War the area developed very quickly and boasted nearly 1000 residents. There were many courtyards and produce gardens. Even with these gone, Nahlat Shiva retains a certain quaintness and charm, encouraged by the restaurants, bars and cafés that abound.

Rivlin St. leads into Jaffa Road, the main artery of West Jerusalem. Turn right, and after crossing the road turn left into Heshin Street, a short rising street, towards the pale green domes of the Russian cathedral ahead. You have now entered the **Russian Compound,** or Migrash Ha'Russim in Hebrew, one of the largest building undertakings in Jerusalem during the second part of the 19th C.

▸ The Russian Compound

History

The increase of Russian pilgrims visiting Jerusalem in the 19th C necessitated the building of extra facilities for them. Until then they had tended to stay in the Greek Orthodox establishments.

sultan's gift to the tsar

During the early 1850s the Russian Palestine Society purchased land on an elevated area some 400 metres from the NW corner of the Old City. Until then the Ottoman authorities, for security reasons, had not allowed any constructions within half a kilometre of the city walls. This changed in 1853 when the sultan presented the tsar with a further tract of land complementing that already purchased by the Russians. With this gift a *firman* was granted, permitting them to build a compound upon the land.

A Russian traveller and writer, visiting in the early 1860s, likened the compound, with its high walls, to a small town, with church hospices, a hospital, consulate and large water reservoirs. He described the buildings as being of huge slabs of Jerusalem stone, with flat roofs.

the first bells of Jerusalem

The centrepiece of the compound was the Church of the Holy Trinity, a shining white building topped by an array of green cupolas. It was the first church in Jerusalem to have bells, which were cast and brought from Russia. The church was consecrated in 1872 in the presence of Prince Nikolai and a large retinue.

nicknamed "Bevingrad"

The walls long gone, during the British Mandate most of the buildings were rented out to the government. As a constant target for Jewish terrorists the compound was heavily fortified, and during the final years of the Mandate earned the nickname "Bevingrad" after the much despised British foreign minister. In the mid 1950s the

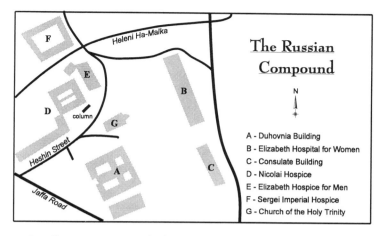

The Russian Compound

N

A - Duhovnia Building
B - Elizabeth Hospital for Women
C - Consulate Building
D - Nicolai Hospice
E - Elizabeth Hospice for Men
F - Sergei Imperial Hospice
G - Church of the Holy Trinity

Israeli government acquired nearly all the buildings from the Soviet government with the exception of the church and the southern part of the Duhovnia Mission Building.

▸ The Visit

The buildings are as follows (the letters correspond to those on the above plan).

A. The Duhovnia Mission Building. This, the largest of the buildings, was constructed in 1863. Besides being the location of the Russian religious delegation, it also had a hospice for VIPs and a library that at one time housed over 17,000 volumes. Until recently the northern wing was the seat of the Israel Supreme Court. The southern wing remains the property of the Russian Church and is the offices and residence of the Russian Orthodox Patriarch.

B. The Elizabeth Hospice for Women. During the Mandate this was used as a prison, and a number of Jewish guerillas convicted of murder were hanged here. It is now a museum, the **Hall of Heroism**, Hechal Ha'Gevurah.

C. Russian Consulate. This small building was originally a bathhouse, later converted to the office and residence of the Russian consul.

D. Nikolai Hospice. This begins at the lower end of Heshin Street where it houses the **Jerusalem Magistrates' Court**. It is also the main **police station** of the city.

E. Elizabeth Hospice for Men. This was designed with rows of rooms to hold two men each; as such it was ideal for its present function as a **prison!**

F. Sergei Imperial Hospice. Named for Prince Sergei Romanov, President of the Provoslavic Palestine Association and son of Tsar Alexander II. Built between 1886 and 1889, it now houses the **Israel Ministry of Agriculture** and incorporates a small **agricultural museum** and the offices and shop of the **Israel Nature Society**.

G. The Church of the Holy Trinity.

At the very centre of the compound and dominating the area is this gleaming church, still in active use. Built of white stone, the green domes, some topped with Provoslavic crosses, give it the characteristic Russian look. On each side of the gabled facade are octagonal bell towers that house the bells mentioned above.

The design is typically Provoslavic: a basilica in the form of a cross, the transept being in the centre. The dome and the walls have paintings portraying the life of Jesus.

pillar for Herod's Temple

Behind the church, and lying on the ground, is a monolithic **pillar** uncovered during the church's construction. It is some 12 metres long and has an average width of 1.8 metres. Dating from Herodian times, its size is similar to pillars used by Herod for the Royal Portico of the temple, as recorded by Josephus. It was probably quarried nearby, and it seems it split while being transported and was abandoned.

▸ Other sites in West Jerusalem

There are a number of other places in West Jerusalem, some ancient and some new, which you might like to see should time allow. As these are quite distant from one another I will deal with them on a one by one basis.

▸ The Knesset Building

The Knesset is the Israel Parliament. Its permanent building was constructed in the early 1960s with funds donated by James de Rothschild and his family. **Buses 24, 9 and 99 will convey you there**. The elevated, rectangular building with its flat roof is easily recognisable. **On Sundays and Thursdays there are guided tours in English. These start at 11.00 and 14.30.** You will require your passport. Of course no great history or tradition is associated with this new legislature, but of interest inside are beautiful wall tapestries and mosaic floors designed by Marc Chagall.

Facing the entrance gate is a large seven branch bronze candelabra, **menora** in Hebrew, decorated with scenes from Jewish history. It was a gift of the British Government.

▸ Monastery of the Cross

Situated in a valley south of the Knesset building, this ancient monastery stands out against its modern surroundings.

History

Valley of the Cross

According to an ancient tradition it was from this valley that the tree on which Jesus was crucified came. It is not clear who built the original monastery but it would have been in the latter part of the 5th C. This was destroyed by the Sasanian Persians in 614 and later rebuilt. The Fatimid Caliph, Hakim, pillaged the monastery in 1009, but by the mid 11th C it had been restored by the Georgians who were then in possession.

nobles' sanctuary

Later, Georgians of note lived here, including one of their national poets, Shota Rustaveli. In the 17th C due to financial difficulties the Georgians sold the property to the Greek Orthodox Church who remain the owners today. In the latter part of the 19th C the building became a theological seminary and additional rooms and offices were built to accommodate them. Recently the building has been completely refurbished.

It is open to the public Monday to Friday 09.00-16.00, Saturday till 14.00. There is an entry fee. **Buses 24 and 99** pass by so you can get to it from the Knesset.

The Visit

The monastery is surrounded by high stone, fortress-like walls, as being outside the city walls it was open to attack by marauders. Close to other buildings today, it was isolated until comparatively recently. Entry is via a low opening into a courtyard. To the right are the monks' rooms and to the left is the refectory.

lovely ancient building

The church is a basilica with a central nave and six square pillars. Part of the floor is covered with mosaics that date back to the original construction. On the walls are frescoes that relate the tradition about the Holy Tree. At the end of the church, behind the altar, is an opening that leads to the spot where the tree grew.

The Monastery of the Cross is one of the most attractive sites in the western city. You can get an exceptionally good view of it from the Israel Museum (see page 256). At night the walls are floodlit, making it even more enchanting. See it!

▸ Makhane Yehuda Market

About 3km along the Jaffa Road from the Jaffa Gate is **Makhane Yehuda,** Jewish Jerusalem's main market. This colourful market place is best visited on Friday mornings when it is thronged with shoppers gathering supplies for the oncoming Sabbath.

tasty produce

The main market street is a covered area, but shops and stalls can be seen in the surrounding streets. When I lived in Jerusalem I would often come here to buy the freshest, and cheapest, of produce, and the freshness really shows on the well laid out stalls. I especially liked the stalls selling parsley, mint, coriander and other herbs used in profusion in this part of the world – some salads (e.g. *tabouleh*) call for cupfuls of both parsley and mint.

pick your own

It is normal practice here for the customers to select their own fruit and vegetables. You'll also find here the usual conglomeration of merchandise that tends to line market streets – shops offering cheap plastic and glass housewares, spices and nuts, bulk pasta, rice and dried pulses; and of course meat, fish and poultry shops and stalls, all strictly kosher (in accordance with Jewish dietary laws) – they display certificates to that effect. Many of the stallholders are Jews from oriental backgrounds, while a good proportion of the customers are the ultra-orthodox. Sampling is a practice taken for granted, particularly from the mouthwatering displays at the olive and pickle shops. However, queueing is not such a normal practice and if you wait patiently to be served, you may never be!

If you have the time, an interesting diversion from the usual sightseeing.

Just east of the market, in the direction of the Old City, are a couple of buildings you should see while in the vicinity.

▸ Sundial

At number 92 Jaffa Road, on the north side, is a building with a large sundial at the top of the facade. Built around 1906 the building was once the tallest in Jerusalem with 5 storeys. The sundial was added in 1918 by a Rabbi Moshe Shapira, who lived in Mea She'arim. There are two clocks. One (left) displaying the time once used by Muslims for prayers, and the other standard time.

The building was damaged by an earthquake in 1927, and by a fire in the 1940s. In 1980 the facade was renovated. You can read all about it on the information plaque.

▸ Former British Consulate

Further east along Jaffa Road on the south side is the Makhane Yehuda Police Station, number 83. Erected in the early 19th C by the Ottomans as a guardpost along the highway to Jaffa, it became the residence of the British Consul around 1865, and served as such until the British occupation in 1918. The pair of lions at the entrance are the work of a well known 19th C Jerusalem sculptor, Simkha Shlomo Diskin.

As you no doubt can see, this is one of the oldest of the "new" areas and dates from about 1875 onwards. Unfortunately many of the fine stone buildings have not been well maintained and, like many downtown areas in other cities, those who live here tend to comprise the poorer sections of the community.

17. Bethlehem

INTRODUCTION

While the town of Bethlehem is a most interesting and agreeable place to visit, it by no means lives up to our childhood image! Bearing no resemblance to the serene, snow-covered illustrations on Christmas cards, Bethlehem today is a busy Palestinian market town, where for most winters snow is a rarity – especially in the month of December!

traditional life

A few hours spent in Bethlehem will not only allow you to see the historical sites, but will enable you to witness the contrast between Jerusalem, with its massive modern Israeli development, and a Palestinian town with a proportion of its population still largely traditional.

ever closer to Jerusalem

Situated about 8 km south of Jerusalem's Old City walls, modern growth has extended Jerusalem's boundaries, now placing the two ancient cities no more than a kilometre or so from one another.

As with all the towns on the West Bank, Bethlehem is no longer under Israeli control as it was between 1967 and 1995. However, on the peripheries Israeli checkpoints monitor all traffic in and out. But this does not affect visitors and, like everywhere in the Palestinian areas, you will receive a warm and customary Arab welcome.

HISTORY

Had it not been for the fact that the Gospels name Bethlehem as the birthplace of Jesus, this small Judean town might never have made it onto the tourist map. For even though the story of Ruth was enacted near here and it was also the birthplace of David, who comes here for those reasons?

house of bread or meat?

More than one Canaanite settlement carried the name Bethlehem (another still exists in Galilee), and the origin of its name is arguable. In the Tel Amarna Letters of the 14th C BC, a city in the vicinity of Urusalim called Bet Ninib is mentioned. Ninib was a god also known as Lahamu, god of food or grain. However as this mention is not too clear many writers choose not to go beyond the apparent translation of the Hebrew name Beit Lehem, House of Bread. The Arabic name, Bayt Lahm means House of Meat, though this name could be a corruption of the Hebrew. In the Old Testament the town is referred to as Beit Lehem, Beit Lehem-Ephratah or just Ephratah, which translates as "fruitful". All three names possibly reflect the natural fecundity of the town's environs and, with the abundance of cultivated land to the east and south, this remains true today.

early Old Testament

The first mention of the town in the Bible is as the place where Rachel was buried: *"So Rachel died and was buried on the way to Ephrath (that is Bethlehem)"* (Genesis 35:19). Later, Bethlehem became the centre of the tribe of Judah.

The story of Ruth and Boaz as related in the book of Ruth was enacted in and around Bethlehem, and David the second king of Israel, was one of their descendants. In the latter part of the reign of Israel's first king, Saul, the town was occupied by the Philistines, but retaken later by David who had a particular liking for water from a certain well there (II Samuel 23:15).

Bethlehem remained a city of Israel throughout the Davidic and Solomonic periods, and after the division of the kingdom became part of Judea when it was fortified by David's grandson, Rehoboam, the first King of Judah.

Nativity of Jesus

On the basis of Micah's 8th C prophecy, *"But as for you, Bethlehem Ephrathah, too little to be among the clans of Judah, from you One will go forth for Me to be ruler in Israel..."* (Micah 5:2), early Christians identified Bethlehem as the birthplace of Jesus.

The accounts of the birth of Jesus in Matthew and Luke differ in several respects, but are united in giving Bethlehem as the location. In the gospel of John his birthplace is given as Bethlehem solely on the basis of the above Old Testament prophecy (John 7:40-42).

Luke's version helps us to identify the year, as he says the birth occurred at the time of the Augustan census undertaken while Quirinius was governor of Syria (of which Judea was then a part). This would date the event around 4 BC. This is confirmed by Matthew, who in 2:19 of his gospel records Herod's death and, in 2:22, records the succession of Archelaus to the throne, events that took place in the same year.

Justin identifies manger

Following the destruction of Jerusalem in AD 70, Jews, including those who had embraced Christianity, were forbidden to live in the area, and it was not until the 2nd C AD that an actual location was recognised.

The "precise" site of Jesus' birth was identified in the mid 2nd C by Justin Martyr who placed the manger in a subterranean cave. By the end of the century this cave was being venerated as such and has been ever since.

In 325 at the behest of his mother Helena, the emperor Constantine built the first great basilica over the cave. The Bordeaux pilgrim who visited in 333 described this cave as "once being a manger".

This basilica was destroyed by the Samaritans during their revolt against the Byzantines in 529, but rebuilt by Justinian in the same century, and his construction, with some alterations, is essentially what survives today.

Bible translated into Latin here

In the 5th C Jerome settled in the town and, as well as founding two monasteries, translated the Bible into Latin, a translation that was eventually to become the Vulgate, the authorised Latin Bible.

In 634 Bethlehem was taken by the Arabs, and in 638 the caliph 'Umar came to the church to pray.

crowning of Crusader kings

A severe earthquake in 748 badly destroyed the town, but gradually it was rebuilt. In 1099 the town was taken by the Crusaders, who were welcomed by the mainly Christian population, just prior to the onslaught on Jerusalem. The first two kings of the Crusader Kingdom of Jerusalem, Baldwin I and II were crowned in the basilica.

theft of Bethlehem star

Like the Church of the Holy Sepulchre in Jerusalem, the Church of the Nativity has seen many squabbles over jurisdiction by the various Christian denominations who have "rights" there. The most serious was in 1847 when the silver star which supposedly marked the exact spot of the birth was stolen. This caused an international crisis over control of the holy Christian sites, and was a contributing factor in the outbreak of the Crimean War.

In later years Bethlehem was a quiet, mainly Arab Christian town within the Ottoman Empire, a place of pilgrimage for those hardy enough to endure the rigours of the journey and the hostelries where they were quartered.

under British rule

Unlike other towns in Palestine, Bethlehem remained rather passive during the British Mandate period. The presence of a Christian majority and the lack of Jewish settlement freed the town of some of the extremes provoked by the Arab/Jewish struggles of that time.

modern Bethlehem

In 1947 there were c8,000 inhabitants, three quarters of them Christian. This demography changed sharply after the 1948 war, when numerous Palestinian villages in the Jerusalem vicinity were overrun by the Israelis, causing many refugees to flee to the relative safety of Arab Bethlehem. Refugee camps were set up on the perimeters of the town and one, Dheishe, became one of the largest on the West Bank.

annexed to Jordan

After the war Bethlehem, in common with all the territory west of the Jordan not occupied by Israel, was annexed to the Kingdom of Jordan and placed in the *muhafazat* (governorate) of Jerusalem. Cut off from the Mediterranean, and with tourist access only via Amman, Bethlehem – like Arab Jerusalem – suffered a decrease in tourism, till then an important part of the local economy.

In the Six Day War of 1967 Bethlehem was quickly overrun by the Israeli army, and by then its population had grown appreciably, reaching over 30,000 by the 1970s with the Muslims now forming the majority.

Israeli military occupation

Initially Israeli occupation brought some economic benefits to the town, especially as regards easier tourist accessibility. But the fact that the town was in occupied territory and governed by a military regime that would brook no opposition, far outstripped these gains for the bulk of the local population.

The refugee camps that lay on the outskirts of the town were populated entirely by families whose fathers were dispossessed as a result of the 1948 war. They became hotbeds of resistance to the occupying forces who were seen as trying to further deprive them. So persistent was the resistance that it proved a very difficult problem for the Israeli military to handle, and considerable force and ill-treatment was used to try to keep order, methods which were never really successful.

un-Christmas-like Christmas

During the years of Israeli occupation the whole character of the town changed, with the central square, Manger Square, in front of the Church of the Nativity, resembling an armed camp rather than the frontage to one of Christendom's holiest shrines. At Christmas time this was even more pronounced as everyone entering the area, locals and visitors alike, were subjected to rigorous security searches. I can recall on one occasion being refused entry until I had deposited the smallest of penknives with the police!

prosperity for some

In spite of this, certain elements of the town did prosper during those years. The Israelis were keen to foster tourism which also profited their own economy. The beneficiaries were mainly drawn from among the Christian community, who were less radical than the Muslims and owned most of the tourist related businesses. But the majority of the town's citizens, and those who lived in the refugee camps (now really just dilapidated suburbs), remained poor, as any stroll around the inner streets and alleys will confirm.

emigrating Christians

Tourism was not enough to stimulate general economic confidence and this, coupled with Israeli heavy-handedness and, later, the effects of the long-running *intifada* (uprising), caused many Christian Palestinians to leave the country to join families who had gone before them. Many fear that if this decline is not halted there will be but a handful of Christians remaining in what should be the quintessential Christian city.

Bethlehem University opens

In 1973 a university was opened. Though sponsored by the Vatican it is for the benefit of all and provides instruction in both Arabic and English. Enrolling almost 2,000 students, and with a teaching faculty of over one hundred, it is an important place of learning for local Palestinians, many of whom come from very impoverished backgrounds. However, the university has had to contend with the tensions and struggles that are indigenous to an occupied land. These have often spilled out into open confrontation with the Israeli military, resulting in punitive measures being taken against the institution, such as forced closure for months on end.

help from outside

Thanks to its biblical connections, Bethlehem has benefitted from the generosity of many Christian institutions the world over in the form of medical establishments, schools, orphanages and more. All these cater to the needs of Muslims as well as Christians, and in many cases serve the population of the entire West Bank.

moderate mayor

Although the town went through some very rough times after 1967, Bethlehem has been somewhat less militant than other West Bank localities. The mayor, Elias Freij, a Christian, has been a moderating influence, and while never at one with the occupiers was never in favour of violent resistance. He has served as mayor since pre 1967 and continues in that office today. (Mr Freij is also Minister of Tourism in the Palestinian Authority).

uprising and Gulf War

Bethlehem and the surroundings played a significant role in the Palestinian *intifada,* and during that time the town was often off limits even to tourists.

During the Gulf War, Bethlehem (along with the rest of the West Bank and Gaza) was placed under an almost constant curfew, and this writer who lived there throughout that period was witness to the distress and privation this caused.

where next?

The future for the city, as with the rest of Palestine, lies with what final arrangement will be made with Israel, but without a close linkage to Arab Jerusalem further difficulties will arise. History does not record a time when the two places were not under the same sovereignty, and the establishment of an international border between them would be detrimental to Bethlehem's inhabitants, tourists and pilgrims alike.

PHYSICAL AND SOCIAL GEOGRAPHY

Bethlehem is situated on a limestone ridge above two valleys, one to the north and one to the south. To the east the ridge falls away towards Beit Sahur and into the Judean desert, and to the west inclines into Beit Jalla and the Judean hills. Both these localities are mainly Christian and together with Bethlehem itself can be said to form "Greater Bethlehem", as they constitute a continuous built up area. South, on the road to Hebron, is the UNRWA refugee camp of Dheishe which is in reality part of the town.

no room to spread

Much land around the area has been sequestered by the Israeli government for the expansion of Jewish Jerusalem and the building of Jewish settlements. In spite of the Autonomy agreements, at the time of writing this process continues, severely limiting Bethlehem's opportunities for future growth, necessary in a society whose birth rate is particularly high.

old town

Bethlehem's old town is typically oriental, with narrow streets and

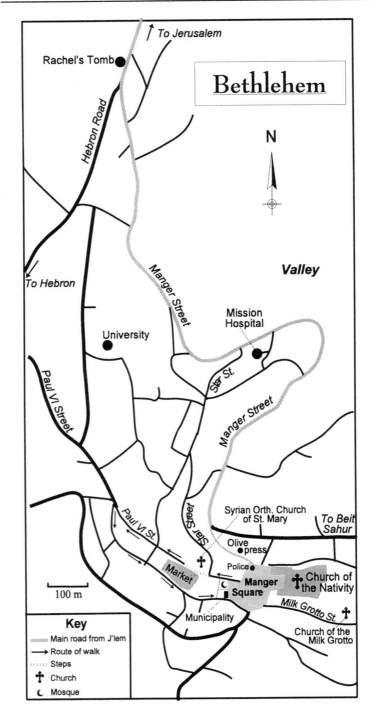

Bethlehem

N

To Jerusalem

Rachel's Tomb

Hebron Road

To Hebron

Manger Street

Valley

University

Mission Hospital

Star St.

Paul VI Street

Manger Street

Paul VI St.

Star Street

Syrian Orth. Church of St. Mary

To Beit Sahur

Olive press

Police

Market

Manger Square

Church of the Nativity

100 m

Milk Grotto St.

Municipality

Church of the Milk Grotto

Key

Main road from J'lem

Route of walk

Steps

Church

Mosque

alleys, many vaulted. Much of this area is now commercial, but poorer dwellings are intermingled with the workshops.

Christian denominations
The Christians comprise, in the main, Roman Catholics (Latins), Syrian Orthodox – who came mostly after the First World War from Anatolia in the wake of Turkish massacres of Christians – and Eastern (Greek) Orthodox, the largest Christian denomination in (Arab) Palestine.

ECONOMY

Rural atmosphere
Bethlehem can be described as a market town with villagers from the surrounding areas coming in daily to sell their produce. You can partake of the atmosphere in the vibrant and colourful market (see below).

The region has some light industry, mainly the manufacturing of items for sale to pilgrims and tourists. These include mother-of-pearl trinkets and jewellery and carved olive wood ornaments such as camels, crosses and manger sets. There is also production of pharmaceuticals, clothing and stone-cutting for building purposes.

HOW TO GET THERE

Regular buses ply the route from the East Jerusalem bus station near the Damascus Gate, and Palestinian service taxis run from the taxi station opposite that gate.

If you have time and the weather's not too hot, it's a fine walk from the Jaffa Gate to Bethlehem. The distance of about 8 km takes about an hour and a half, and you'll get some very fine views. I love this walk, and can recommend it. You can always hop on a bus or service taxi if you feel tired along the way.

Whichever way you travel start as early as you can, as transport is usually less frequent towards late afternoon and certainly in the evening.

carry identity
It is especially important to carry your passport when visiting Palestinian towns. This is mainly to show at the Israeli checkpoints rather than to satisfy the Palestinian authorities.

THE VISIT

Along the way
Just outside Jerusalem, on the left side of the road, and before you enter the built up area of Bethlehem, is the **Monastery of Mar Elias**. Originally built with a fortress-like appearance because of its isolation, the lines have long since softened, although its defensive character is still evident.

This is the burial site of a 5th C Patriarch of Jerusalem, Mar (Saint) Elias. Elias was a monk from Egypt, and many miracles of healing are attributed to him. The first building on this site dates from the 6th C, and after being destroyed by an earthquake it was rebuilt in the 13th C. It is a Greek Orthodox institution.

▸ Rachel's Tomb

Shrine for all

Continue south towards Bethlehem, and just after c1.5 km you come to an Israeli Army checkpoint. Past this, and on the right is a walled structure known as Qubbat Rahil, Dome of Rachel, in Arabic, and Kever Rakhel, **Tomb of Rachel**, in Hebrew. The building is easily recognised by its cupola, and on most days crowds of black-coated orthodox Jewish men and shawled Jewish women wait to pray at the Matriarch's cenotaph within.

married two sisters

Genesis, chapters 29 and 30, relate in detail the story of how Jacob met Rachel and, after being tricked into marrying her elder sister, eventually made her his second wife. Of Jacob's many children from his wives and concubines, his two favourites were Rachel's sons, Joseph and Benjamin. It was in giving birth to the latter that the Matriarch died:

> *"Then they journeyed from Bethel; and when there was still some distance to go to Ephrath, Rachel began to give birth and she suffered severe labour. ...So Rachel died and was buried on the way to Ephrath (that is Bethlehem). And Jacob set up a pillar over her grave; that is the pillar of Rachel..."*
> Genesis 35:17-20.

Of course the above-quoted narrative does not infer that Rachel was buried so close to Bethlehem; "on the way" could mean many other places on the route from Bethel, which was north of Jerusalem. Nevertheless tradition, both Jewish and Muslim, fixes this as the site.

pilgrims visit

In ancient times this spot was marked by a mound of stones (the pillar?), and was visited by many pilgrims. The Jewish traveller from Moorish Spain, Benjamin of Tudela, visiting in c1163 mentioned a pile of stones covered by a domed structure. This was probably the main part of the present building.

acquired by Jews

Although always venerated by Jews, it was not until the 19th C that the site became an important venue for pilgrims. In 1841 the Jewish philanthropist, Sir Moses Montefiore, purchased the site. The actual shrine or cenotaph, in an internal room, was then kept locked and only opened for visits by Jews mainly on Sabbath eves (Fridays).

Between 1948 and 1967, being in Jordanian territory, Jews were unable to visit. Since 1967 it has become a major Jewish place of pilgrimage, especially for women who see in Rachel the ideal wife and mother.

The actual building is mainly a Muslim structure, and Muslim graves practically surround it. The shrine is nowadays almost exclusively for Jewish use. Since 1967 the site has been turned into a virtual synagogue.

Rachel's Tomb is open between 08.00-18.00 hours, except Fridays when it closes at 13.00; closed Saturdays and Jewish holidays.

twisting road

Continuing south past Rachel's Tomb for c200 metres, you reach a fork in the road. The main road continues to Hebron, whilst the road to the left enters Bethlehem proper. This road, Manger Street, winds along the top of the ridge on which the town stands. Every now and then, when there is a gap between the buildings on the left, you can snatch fine views down into the valley below. The road snakes along the ridge and, while often seeming never ending, it is in fact only 1.2 kilometres until you reach the main square, **Manger Square** and the **Church of the Nativity**.

Palestinian flag

Manger Square (no prizes for guessing why it's called that!), while not the physical centre of the town, is certainly the civic and touristic one. The huge basilica occupies the entire eastern side of the plaza. On the northern side is the town's main police station, where from 1967 till just before Christmas 1995 the Israeli flag was flown. Now it is the Palestinian flag that flies there. The main part of the town is to the west, and south.

▸ Church of the Nativity

As described in the history of Bethlehem, although the area had been venerated earlier as the site of Jesus' birth, it was Justin Martyr who identified the "actual spot" in the mid 2nd C. This was inside a cave, and must have looked very different from the traditional Western concept of a barn.

History

Built over cave

Although as old as the Church of the Holy Sepulchre in Jerusalem, the Church of the Nativity has not figured as prominently in history or archaeological research. Originally constructed in 325 by the emperor Constantine, it was the first basilica to be erected over the nativity cave; the present basilica was erected over the remnants of this.

the first church

The first church, preceded on the west by a courtyard porticoed on all sides, was c26 metres square. It was divided into a central nave, nine metres wide with two aisles on each side, delineated by rows of columns. The floor was covered in mosaics. To the east and at a lower level was an octagon which was built above the birth cave. This was approached by a flight of steps.

This basilica was rased in 529, and little of it remains today.

Justinian's church

The basilica built by Justinian in the 6th C had a slightly different design to Constantine's, and although altered over the centuries remains in essence what we see today.

The western courtyard of Constantine's building was made into a narthex, the nave broadened and the aisles made narrower. Some of the columns and capitals that survived the destruction were reused.

resting place of kings

After the Crusader conquest of Jerusalem the first two kings of the

Church of the Nativity

Crusader Kingdom of Jerusalem, Baldwin I and II were crowned in the basilica.

In 1844 an earthquake seriously damaged the church, and restoration had to be undertaken.

The Visit

The church is situated on the west side of Manger Square, and the impression is of a fortress-like building. The paved courtyard, dating from the 1930s, lies over the atrium of Constantine's construction. The building to the right is an Armenian monastery, and normally closed to visitors.

mind your head

As you approach the church, the massive nature of the construction becomes even more evident, and you may begin to wonder where the majestic entrance is in the expanse of solid wall! When it finally comes into view it proves to be but a tiny, single doorway a mere 1.2 metres high which compels all but small children to bend low in order to enter. Some like to believe that the door was designed thus so that all who enter do so with humility; but however gratifying this may seem to the devout, the actual reason lies elsewhere, as I shall now explain.

thwarting the invaders

The original Justinian design incorporated three normal height entrances and a huge lintel. Fragments of these can still be seen if you look hard enough. One door is close to the wall of the monastery, while another is nearly masked by the abutment north of the entrance. Threats of invasion, and Muslim fanaticism in particular, gradually made protection of the building an overriding consideration and the church gradually took on its fortress-like appearance; walls were strengthened and the doors all but disappeared, so that by the late Mameluke period only this low and narrow entrance was left. Whether it was made so low to prevent horse-mounted raiders from entering or just to prevent the place being rushed is not clear, but whatever the reason it certainly enhanced the protection of the holy place.

vast and ancient

Once through the low door you find yourself in a very dimly lit vaulted ante-chamber, part of the 6th C church narthex. From here we can ingress the actual basilica through a wooden door, beautifully carved by Armenian craftsmen, around 1227. Devoid of seating or any other furniture, the first impression is of vastness, perhaps emptiness, certainly of age – despite the many restorations over the centuries.

mosaic decoration

The wide central nave is flanked by two aisles on each side, delineated by rows of eleven red limestone columns with Corinthian type capitals. Though some of these columns may be from Constantine's 4th C construction, most are Justinian. Some are decorated with mosaics dating from the Crusader restoration and depicting various saints, the Virgin and Child and other biblical figures. Similar decorations can also be seen on the walls, especially the northern one, where one series illustrates the genealogy of Jesus. Another shows the cities where the early Ecumenical Councils were held.

a peep through the floor

The plain paved flooring is punctuated in a few places with wooden openings through which you can glimpse quite large sections of the mosaic flooring that covered Justinian's basilica. The segments in the nave are the best preserved, but the dim light may not reveal all. In the southernmost aisle is a stone font dating from the Justinian rebuilding.

A raised area (choir) at the end of the nave stands directly above the grotto of the nativity. This elevation dates from the Crusader restoration. The main altar at the eastern end belongs to the Greek Orthodox as does the one on the south, the **Altar of the Circumcision**. The other two, the **Altar of the Virgin** to the north and the **Altar of the Three Kings** to the NE, are the property of the Armenians. Legend has it that the latter covers the spot where the eastern kings, the Three Wise Men, dismounted.

fancy frills

From the north and south sides of the high altar, flights of red limestone steps, dating from the Justinian rebuilding, lead down to the **Grotto of the Nativity**. The bronze doors at the entrance are also of Justinian origin. The cave in which the birth is venerated is irregular in shape, low and has walls partly covered in marble. In the traditional Orthodox manner, it is decorated with icons and lamps, and like the basilica itself radiates a powerful aroma of incense made more intense by the subterranean and enclosed location. In the apse on the eastern side is the silver star that is supposed to designate the exact position of the natal event.

Catholic site

Having no rights in this grotto, the Latins have their own. Steps on the southern side of the grotto lead to their **Grotto and Altar of the Manger** identified, according to Latin tradition, by Queen Helena. Return to the main church.

▸ Church of St. Catherine

Death on a wheel

From the north side of the basilica, doors lead into the cloisters of the Church of St. Catherine, the main Latin church in Bethlehem. Built in 1880 with money from the Emperor of Austria, it stands on the site of a former, smaller church dedicated to her. A Christian martyr, Catherine of Alexandria, met her tortuous death on a wheel (hence Catherine wheel). A rendition of the saint tied to the wheel can be seen near the entrance.

St. Catherine's church is a "living" church and on Sundays it is full of local worshippers, many of whom are young people. It is in this church that the Christmas mass is celebrated by the Latin Patriarch.

slaughter of the Innocents

From inside the church steps lead down to various grottos which are now inaccessible from the Church of the Nativity. One, the **Grotto of the Holy Innocents**, is said to be where some of the children were slaughtered by Herod (Matthew 2:16). Another is dedicated to Joseph, the husband of Mary while another is supposed to be the tomb of Jerome (Hieronymus) who translated the Bible into Latin. Various other grottos are associated with other saints.

Return to Manger Square by passing through the western cloisters of St. Catherine's. These very atmospheric cloisters were rebuilt in the late 1940s using columns and capitals of a Crusader building that stood on the site. The monastery of St. Jerome may have stood here, and consequently the designers thought it fitting to place a statue of the saint here.

▸ Chapel of the Milk Grotto

Lactic lava

At the SE corner of the square a narrow street runs to the east, along the southern walls of the Church of the Nativity. About a quarter of a kilometre along, on the right is the **Chapel of the Milk Grotto**, situated in the Franciscan Convent.

In here there is a cave formed from chalky white rock. According to legend – and by now you will know how important these are in this part of the world – the baby Jesus, with his family spent the night (or nights) here. While feeding her infant son, a drop of Mary's milk spilt on the ground. As a result it is believed by some, that eating the white and chalky rock from which the cave is formed will enhance a woman's milk supply, an essential commodity in a society

where the bearing of children is a woman's annual task.
You can visit daily from 08.00-11.30 and 14.00-17.00.

> **▸Town Walk – A stroll around the town centre**

Back on Manger Square the inquisitive can now visit some of the
real Bethlehem, and an easy circular walk can be made giving you
a glimpse of the old town and everyday life. Allow about an hour to
an hour and a half for this.

lofty belfry
Walk up the street at the NW corner, just past the **Mosque of
Omar**, a modernish prayer house. This is Star Street. About 100
metres along the road bears to the right while ascending steps lead
straight ahead. On the right is the **Church of St. Mary**, of
comparative recent construction. It has the highest bell tower in the
entire area, and is a landmark for miles around.

ancient Aramaic bible
The church belongs to the Syrian Orthodox Christians, many of
whom fled to Bethlehem from the Turkish pogroms of 1915 and
later. Usually there is a guardian present who will be pleased to show
you around, although being newish there is not too much to see. The
best of what there is is a very ancient Bible written in Aramaic
(Syriac), the prayer, and once vernacular, language of these people.

▸ Bethlehem Market

Colourful people – and produce
Walk up the steps and almost at the top, you can turn left into
Bethlehem's market place or souk. Here is a vibrant corner of the
town, with many smallholders, especially women, journeying daily
from the villages around Bethlehem to sell their produce.

Most squat on the ground with mounds of their home-grown
produce heaped around them. Depending on the season, to name but
a few, there will be vast barrels of black and green grapes, pyramids
of oranges, lemons and clementines, cabbages and cauliflowers,
huge, misshapen but taste-full tomatoes and, of course, heaps of the
Arabs' beloved broad beans (*ful*). The variety attests to the fertile
soil of the area – despite the easily garnered impression of a
landscape sprouting nothing but stones.

Palestinian embroidery
The women are generally clad in traditional dress, some brightly
coloured but most in long black robes brightened with hand-stitched
traditional Palestinian embroidery.

There is a section of the market for second hand clothes, and these
are also piled in mounds while women sort through searching for a
wanted item. Almost everything, no matter how old, can be made use
of by somebody.

photograph with care
Be cautious when taking pictures of traditional Muslim women as

From Olive to Oil

EACH autumn the pungent aroma of olive oil wafts from Bethlehem's olive press, situated in a large shop near the top of Manger Street, just a stone's throw from the Church of the Nativity. The olive press, deserted for most of the year, becomes a bustling hive for a few weeks from late September until early November. Villagers from all around Bethlehem come here to have their crops pressed.

Palestinian women in village dress surround the building. They sit on bursting sacks of olives as they await their turn at the press. Amid empty plastic and tin containers, children scramble around to pass the time; in nearby coffee houses men in flowing robes and headdresses discuss this year's crop and the price it will bring.

Since biblical times this thick, green liquid has been a precious commodity. Always essential to the lives of the native population, the distinctive régional dishes take their unique flavor and aroma from pure cold-pressed olive oil.

Lighting and medicine were among its ancient uses, and, after being perfumed, it was used to anoint kings and nobles. Hezekiah kept oil in his treasure house along with his gold and silver (II Kings 20:13); the biblical lore surrounding it survives: the oil is synonymous with joy and gladness (Is. 61:3) and failure of the harvest is considered a calamity (Hab. 3:17-18).

Harvest time is late September through October and requires the labour of the whole family – and Palestinian families are usually large! Often more than a dozen people work in a grove each day.

Pressing time always creates excitement, breaking the daily routine of the land labourers. Clattering machinery, babbling voices, and the heady aroma of raw, pounded olives fill the air.

The olives are weighed before being poured into a vat. Here they are crushed by two large revolving millstones, which create an almost deafening noise. The stones of the Bethlehem press are 55 years old – they still do their job loud and strong! The pulp falls through into a lower vat, where it is shoveled or scooped up by the armful by men wearing aprons splattered with the pulverised black and green olives. The walls are also stained with the mash, and the floors are slippery from the oil.

The pulp is next spread on fibre mats with a hole in the middle. These are threaded one on top of the other onto a steel spindle about two metres high. When the spindle is full of mats, the whole is put under a powerful hydraulically operated press, which squeezes out all the juices. In a modern press, this liquid – a mixture of water and oil – drains through a series of pipes into a centrifugal machine which separates the oil from the water. Finally, a steady stream of pure, virgin oil pours into the last stainless-steel vat.

The atmosphere around this last vat is always charged with expectancy. Serious, tense faces watch as their year-long labour flows through a funnel into the containers they have brought to be filled. The farmer's yield is calculated according to the type of olive, at twenty to thirty percent of the gross weight. Five to ten percent of the yield goes as payment to the press owner.

Man and wife carry away the treasured harvest, strapped to a donkey or in the back of a van, continuing the age-old cycle. Soon the work of the olive press will come to an end and its closed shutters will be bypassed unnoticed for another year.

they often find this offensive. Try to use a long focus lens so that you will be some distance from your subject.

Leave the market the way you entered. Continue up the steps and along the narrow winding street or alley which, in spite of bearing the impressive name of Pope John Paul VI, is little more than a typical Middle Eastern souk. To the left and right little side alleys lead off and many of these are vaulted.

poverty on the sidelines

A brief detour down some of these will reveal, unfortunately, the true state of many of Bethlehem's citizens who live in virtual poverty. You may, for example, see a woman cooking for her family over an open stove in a courtyard, or washing her hair in a bucket on a table. As picturesque or exotic as this may look, it is not done from choice but from necessity, there being no place for proper facilities in the room or rooms her family occupies.

modern and traditional

Some of the old shops, with their vaulted ceilings, have now the air of the present day about them with bright lights and gaudy displays. Others are still traditional, both in appearance and type of merchandise: coffee grinders, olive merchants, kebab and felafel sellers and the like, exuding their tempting aromas as you walk past. Yet others are simple workshops where traditional and manual skills are employed. The entrances to their cubbyhole shops are dark in contrast to the bright sunlit street, but if you look inside you will see blacksmiths working at their anvils, tailors hunched over ancient sewing machines, or cobblers holding nails in their mouths as they hammer a new sole onto a battered shoe.

southern valley

Eventually John Paul VI street broadens out, before continuing NW into a more modern part of the town. My route, however returns to Manger Square by the road to the southeast, Farahiyeh Street, which parallels Pope John Paul VI Street. Farahiyeh St. runs along the edge of the southern ridge, and to your east you get, every now and again, views down into the valley below. You now realise that old Bethlehem stands between two valleys. Notice how many of Bethlehem's homes are built in the valleys and up the steep side streets that reach them. Continue down the street, through the vault by the entrance to the market from this east side, till you reach Manger Square. Just before you enter the square is the Municipality building where there is a **tourist information office**.

NEAR BETHLEHEM

Beit Sahur has always been a Christian settlement, and remains largely so today. Unlike the Bethlehem Christians, those of Beit Sahur actively opposed the Israeli occupation, and at one point their refusal to pay taxes to the military government provoked a very harsh response.

Beit Jalla is a modern settlement of mainly more well-to-do families. Many of Bethlehem's wealthy live there. The opulent residences confirm this! At the western extremity of the town is the **Cremisan Monastery** belonging to the Selesian Fathers. It is one of the two wine producing monasteries in the area, the other being at Latrun on the Jerusalem-Tel Aviv highway. You can usually visit the Cremisan cellars, and the monastery has a shop where you can buy its produce. Worth a visit if you have time to spare, but if you're even an amateur connoisseur, don't expect anything too exciting on the palate.

▸ Shepherds Fields – Kanisat al-Ru'at and Khirbet Siyar al-Ghanim

From below Manger Square the road continues east some 1.5 km to the large village of Beit Sahur. Tradition places the fields from which Ruth gleaned in this neighbourhood, as well as the fields where *"shepherds were abiding...keeping watch over their flocks by night."* (Luke 2:8) and those who visit Beit Sahur do so, in the main, to visit these fields. Whatever the truth of this story, Christian pilgrims have been coming here since at least the 4th C when the place is mentioned by Egeria. Bishop Arculf, mid 8th C, was amongst many other early travellers.

choose which one!

The problem is that there are two such sites, one Greek Orthodox, and one belonging to the Franciscans which is recognised by Catholics and Protestants. They are about half a kilometre apart. The directions to both are clearly signed.

The Orthodox location, known as **Kanisat al-Ru'at**, the **Grotto of the Shepherds**, is the most interesting. Here you'll find the ruins of a church thought to have been built by Queen Helena in the 4th C.

The church was destroyed in the early 7th C. Soon after it was rebuilt as a monastery and this was in use until the Crusader era. What were left of the ruins have now been carefully conserved, although there is not much to see apart from the crypt, which you enter down a flight of steps. The church was a triple apsed building with a barrel vaulted roof, and a careful look will reveal some traces of ancient (original?) frescoes and mosaics.

The ruin was still used for the occasional service until the 1950s when a modern construction replaced it.

Kanisat al-Ru'at can be visited from 08.00 to 11.30, and from 14.00 to 17.00.

field of the Franciscans

The Franciscan site is about half a kilometre away and is known as **Khirbet Siyar al-Ghanim**. Here were found the ruins of a 5th or 6th C monastery which the Franciscan excavators identified as the Shepherds Field.

Like the ruins above there is not a great deal that has survived, so don't expect to see much. Near the ruins a new church of unusual design has been constructed. Built to resemble a tent it houses a sculpture of an angel, presumably the one that "visited".

Visiting hours here as at the Orthodox site.

There are no sites pertaining to the story of Ruth, Naomi and Boaz which was enacted around Beit Sahur.

18. Bethany

INTRODUCTION

Home of Lazarus, Martha and Mary

Bethany was the town where Jesus was anointed with perfumed oil in the home of Simon the Leper (Mark 14:3). Jesus also returned here after his triumphal entry into Jerusalem (Mark 11:11). But the village's main claim to fame is that it was the home of Lazarus and his sisters, Martha and Mary. It was Lazarus who Jesus raised from the dead, according to John's Gospel (11:38-44). And it is to see the tomb where this event is supposed to have taken place that visitors come to Bethany.

bordering on the desert

The village lies at the eastern extremity of Jerusalem and is now part of the Jerusalem municipal area. Called al-'Azariyya (which means Lazarus) in Arabic, the village hugs the SE slope of the Mount of Olives, just a short distance from barren desert. Until about 100 years ago the route there lay over the mount.

Al-'Azariyya is today a largely urban community. Until the end of the 19th C its inhabitants were mainly poor farmers who eked out a living with olive, fig and pomegranate orchards planted on terraced steps, scraped out of the rocky slopes. E. Robinson who visited around 1835 estimated that no more than twenty very poor families lived there, though other travellers doubled this number.

improved status

In the early 1880s a new carriage road was built linking Jerusalem to the River Jordan and Jericho. This enabled easier access for Christian pilgrims to the holy places at the river and also helped to give al-Azariyya, till then largely neglected, more importance.

Today Bethany, though no longer very poor, has the typical living standards of a Palestinian village. The few finer homes that may be seen in no way reflect the norm. With a population of about 4000, the main occupations are small workshops and the usual construction work offered by the Israelis to the Palestinians.

The Israelis have recently constructed a new Jerusalem-Jericho road which begins north of Mount Scopus and misses Bethany altogether. Thus the village has lost much of its through traffic.

HISTORY

There is certainly no hard evidence to be found in Bethany of the New Testament events described above, and the tomb could have belonged to others. Undoubtedly a village stood in the area from early times and this is likely to have been that of Ananiah in the territory of Benjamin as recorded in Nehemiah 11:32. The NT name Bethany is a corruption of this: Beit Ananiah = Bethany.

longstanding tradition

It seems that the first church to be built here was in the 4th C, and this was just a small building. In 333 the Bordeaux Pilgrim referred to a crypt, and around 390 Jerome mentions a visit to the Tomb of Lazarus as well as the house of Mary and Martha. According to the nun Egeria, who came to Palestine especially to study liturgical practices, some sort of liturgy was said here during the seventh week of Lent.

Between then and the late 7th C a more substantial building was constructed and this was visited by the travelling Bishop Arculf from Germany around that time.

varied fortunes

In Crusader times a Benedictine convent was constructed in Bethany, then one of the wealthiest in the Latin kingdom. At the same time, the Byzantine church was rebuilt over the Tomb of Lazarus. With the departure of the Crusaders from the land the building fell into ruins.

In the 16th C a mosque, the Mosque of al-'Azar was erected in the courtyard of the church facing the entrance to Lazarus' (who is also venerated by Muslims) tomb. Although some Christians were still permitted to visit the tomb, the church lay in ruins until 1952 when the Franciscans built a new church to the east.

Not to be outdone, in 1966 the Greek Orthodox erected a church of their own nearby.

How to Get There

The Arab bus, number 43, from the Damascus Gate bus station is the quickest way. A better way for walkers is over the Mount of Olives. Follow the route to Bethphage as detailed on page 152 and from this monastery there is a signed path to Bethany. Along most of the journey you will be rewarded with the grandest of views, wonderful in springtime! Walk there and take the bus back.

THE VISIT

The few sites to visit are located along an ascending road that doubles back west from a sharp right-hand bend along the Jericho Road.

▸ Church of St. Lazarus

The first, and most prominent, building is the Franciscan **Church of St. Lazarus**. This is a new structure dating from 1954 and designed by the architect A. Barluzzi who also designed (among others) the Church of the Flagellation along the Via Dolorosa.

Standing on the site of the Byzantine church, its silver dome, circular drum and rectangular bell tower make it very visible among the other buildings of the village. A few remnants of the ancient building have been incorporated into the modern cruciform design. On the facade is a mosaic depicting the three personages associated with the area, Lazarus, Mary and Martha. There are altars at both ends and these are embellished with carvings that depict the NT story.

► Tomb of Lazarus

Ascending the road a little further, you come to the present entrance to the **Tomb of Lazarus**, passing on the way the 16th C **Mosque of al-'Azar**, which stands on the atrium of the Byzantine structure. The entrance to the tomb was once in this atrium, but after the mosque was erected it was moved to its present location.

A flight of rough stone steps descends into the interior, reaching an ante-chamber. You will have to stoop in order to enter the actual burial chamber. The original, now sealed, entrance can be noticed on the east (right) wall of the ante-chamber.

Further still up the hill is a Greek Orthodox church, but this holds no particular interest.

19. Ein Karem

INTRODUCTION

Situated in a deep valley a few kilometres SW of Jerusalem the delightful, formerly Arab village of Ein Karem has now been incorporated into Jerusalem's municipal boundaries. The village's claim to fame is that it is generally perceived to be the "city of Judea" referred to in Luke 1:39 as being the home of Elizabeth and Zacharias, parents of John the Baptist, and the place where the precursor was born.

spring of the vineyard

The location's name is derived from the spring or *ein*, the water of which was once used to irrigate the plentiful vineyards, the *karem*, of the village. Some identify the place with the Beth-Hacarem mentioned in the book of Jeremiah, although this name now graces a leafy Jewish suburb closer towards the city.

That Ein Karem was once an Arab village is architecturally unmistakeable. Its former inhabitants all fled in 1948 in the wake of Israeli atrocities in the nearby village of Deir Yassin. The departure of these Palestinians proved fortuitous for the fledgling Israeli government, as ready-made homes were made available for the influx of Jewish immigrants, and it was mainly those from the Maghreb that were settled in Ein Karem.

sought after homes

These solid stone houses stand firm today, a credit to the sturdy construction methods of a bygone era. Many are now sought after by Israelis seeking something different and more tasteful from the standard flimsy pressed block (albeit stone-faced) buildings that cover much of the land today. Wander around the narrow lanes and get a closer look at many of these fine residences. Above the entrances you might find an Arabic inscription or decoration. Notice also the arched windows and often original wrought iron grilles.

artists' village

Ein Karem's picturesque character has attracted a number of artists to dwell in its midst, and their studios and ateliers can be found dotted here and there in the village.

Ein Karem, 19th C

HOW TO GET THERE

Ein Karem can be reached from Jerusalem's central bus station on the number 17 bus. This travels along Herzl Avenue past **Mount Herzl**, whose cemetery is the resting place for many of Israel's leaders, and past **Yad Va'Shem**, the Museum of the Holocaust (both open to visitors). As there is a splendid view on the descent into the village, I recommend you alight from the bus just where it turns right past Mount Herzl and before it starts the descent into the village. You can then admire the view, and continue into the village on foot, a very easy downhill walk of about one kilometre. Cars should follow the same route.

THE VISIT

Besides the lovely village itself, two churches provide the main focus of interest for the visitor.

▸ Church of John the Baptist

In the village centre turn north, right, up Ha'Sha'ar Alley, and 50 metres ahead are the gates to the **Church of John the Baptist**.

History

The first church to be built here was in the 4th C, but this was destroyed in the late 5th or early 6th C. The church-monastery was rebuilt by the Crusaders at the beginning of the 12th C. After the Arab reconquest it was turned into a caravanserai.

In 1485 the site was given to the Franciscans, and in 1675 Spanish monks began to settle there. They rebuilt most of it, and what we see today is basically that refurbished structure. Around 1850 the monastery was enlarged to its present state.

The Visit

Step into the large courtyard, and on the west wall you will see renditions of Luke 1:68-74, Zacharias' hymn of praise, in a variety of languages. They are painted on ceramic tiles made by the monks of the Benedictine abbey at Abu Gosh, a village west of Jerusalem.

The church building is approached up stairs into a porch. There, through an opening in the floor you can see part of the mosaic floor from the original Byzantine structure.

painting of the visitation

The basilica is divided into three aisles by six huge piers. The centre aisle terminates in an apse with the altar dedicated to the precursor. To the south, right, is the Chapel of the Visitation with an altar consecrated to Elizabeth, John's mother. There are also statues of Zacharias, his father, St. Francis of Assisi and, in the centre, one of Mary, mother of Jesus. Above the altar is a painting depicting the visitation (Luke 1:39ff).

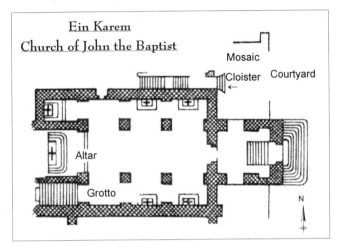

John's birthplace

To the north, left, steps lead down to the **Grotto of St. John**. This is a natural cave, and according to tradition the place of John's birth. The lintel above is inscribed in Latin with the lines *"Blessed be the Lord God of Israel, for he has visited us and accomplished redemption for His people."* (Luke 1:68). Above the altar there is a painting of Elizabeth presenting John at the Temple, and the story of his naming (Luke 1:59-63).

Back in the church on the north wall west of the grotto is an unnamed Byzantine tomb.

The Church of St. John the Baptist may be visited daily from 08.00 to 12 noon, and from 15.00 to 17.00.

Mary drank here

Return to the main street and continue across into the street almost opposite, Ha-Ma'ayan Street, the Street of the Spring. At the end, c100 metres, on the left is a fountain named variously **Mary's Fountain** or the **Fountain of the Virgin**. Above is a small mosque with a hexagonal minaret, dating from Mameluke times. According to tradition Mary stopped and drank from the spring. Do not do likewise as the liquid is no longer clean!

▶ Church and Convent of the Visitation

Turn west, left, and a rising and curving path brings you to the modern **Church and Convent of the Visitation**. To the left of the path is the Russian Orthodox **Convent of the Sisters of the Rosary**, closed to visitors. At the end of the path, a flight of steep wide steps leads to the iron gate of the Convent of the Visitation.

more ceramic tiles

This Franciscan church was built in 1955, and is best known for its translations of the Magnificat, Mary's song of thanksgiving (Luke 1:46-55). These are displayed on ceramic plaques and there are renderings in over 45 languages. The church, designed by the Italian architect Barluzzi, incorporates a square bell tower and a chapel below the main church. On the outer wall a mosaic portrays Mary astride a donkey on her journey here from Nazareth.

Inside the chapel, built on the supposed site of Zacharias' house, are paintings of the occurrences in the lives of John's family.

The church itself has a very modern air about it and the paintings around depict events recorded in the Gospels.

You can visit this convent every day from 09.00-12 noon, and from 15.00-17.00.

▶ St. John in the Wilderness

Some 5 km west of Ein Karem is the **Monastery of St. John in the Wilderness**. It's not very easy to reach unless you have a car, but you can get a bus from West Jerusalem's central bus station as far as Even Sapir and continue from there on foot. If you are with a vehicle continue west through Ein Karem until you come to a road junction. A signpost points left to Hadassah Hospital and the village of Even Sapir. Continue towards this village, and just before the entrance you'll see a sign pointing along a dirt road on your right to the monastery, about 2 kms away.

welcoming monks

The monastery was erected by the Franciscans in the mid 19th C in the area where Luke 1:80 tells us, *"The child (John) continued to grow, and become strong in spirit, and he lived in the desert until the day of public appearance to Israel"*. In the grounds is a spring called by Muslims **Ein al-Habis**, the Spring of the Hermit. There is also a cave where we are told John actually dwelt. Few people come out here and you will be shown around gladly.

20. Monastery of Mar Saba

INTRODUCTION

The exotic blue-domed Monastery of Mar Saba, poised in a stupendous location overhanging Wadi al-Nar, or Wadi Kidron, is one of the most breathtaking sights in Palestinian territory – or indeed anywhere. In spite of its isolation – or perhaps because of it – it should be included in every traveller's itinerary.

Situated in the Judean Desert just 16 kilometres east of Bethlehem, Mar Saba's physical proximity to the urban centre belies its actual isolation.

place of refuge

For thousands of years the Judean wilderness has been a refuge for the oppressed as well as a haven for ascetics seeking a contemplative way of life. Expressing his thoughts about the place where he hid from Saul's anger, David wrote the words to Psalm 55 quoted above. The prophet Elijah fled there from the wrath of Queen Jezebel, taking refuge in its many caves, where we are told he was fed by ravens. And the gospel of Matthew tells us that the same desert saw Jesus fast for forty days and nights.

Egyptian example

Desert monasticism, started by St. Anthony in Egypt, soon spread to Palestine and it is no wonder then that many early Christians seeking a monastic way of life, chose the same (biblical) location as the characters mentioned above. In Byzantine times many monasteries were established in the remotest parts of this wilderness. Although most have now either disappeared or are in ruins, two still function in spite of a dwindling population: St. George of Koziba in Wadi Kelt, between Jerusalem and Jericho, and Mar Saba, the more isolated of the two.

HOW TO GET THERE

You will require a vehicle to get to the monastery. There is no public transport.

Leaving Bethlehem to the east and proceeding through Beit Sahur, the road to Mar Saba passes by the **Monastery of St. Theodosius** or Deir Ibn 'Ubaid and the village of **'Ubaidiyya**. The directions are signed.

famous abbot

The Monastery of St. Theodosius was founded in the early 6th C by the saint after whom it is named. Its main claim to fame is that its one time abbot was Modestus, the restorer of so many of Jerusalem's churches and shrines after the destruction wrought by Chosroes II in 614. At the beginning of the 9th C some 70 monks resided there, but Bedouin attacks resulted in the deaths of many. It was mentioned in Crusader times as still being inhabited, but by the 17th C had been abandoned. Taken over by local people, the buildings were used as storehouses, stables and the like. The site was returned to the Greek Orthodox Church at the end of the 19th C who, after excavating the area, rebuilt it.

alternative route back

Just past the monastery a road to the left leads down and across the Kidron stream, eventually reaching Jerusalem near Bethany. You might want to return that way.

After you pass through 'Ubaidiyya, a typical Palestinian village, you encounter the desert proper, with nearly all traces of greenery gone.

view across the wilderness

About 4 kilometres further on the road makes a sharp right turn and begins a short but very steep descent around hairpin bends. Be very careful here as there is no crash barrier! From the crest, where there is a widish shoulder, you can park and take in the fine view across the desert to the monastery. You will be able to see the twin towers which precede it. It is now a straight run to Mar Saba, and all you are likely to pass on the way are yellowish sheep trying to feed on the dry desert scrub.

The narrow winding road which reaches the monastery was, until some 20 years ago, little more than a desert track. Now surfaced, the strip of black asphalt stands out starkly against the sandy wilderness. The road ends at Mar Saba – indeed the ravine prevents it continuing elsewhere! Only when you finally arrive do you get the full impact of the enchanting character of the complex.

the desert will (sometimes) blossom

In summer the heat is blistering and noontime temperatures can reach 40+ degrees Celsius! As elsewhere in this region, spring is a lovely time to come here as the desert is then frequently clad in a grassy coating, with a profusion of wild flowers, especially after a rainy winter. Autumn is also an acceptable season. By then the ground will have been scorched brown by the burning sun and this wilderness aspect has its own, more dramatic, attraction. Whatever the time of year, try to arrange to be there in late afternoon, when the views are enhanced by the ruddy glows of a desert sunset.

HISTORY

Together with St. Catherine's in Sinai, Mar Saba ranks as the oldest functioning monastery in the Christian world. Like St. Catherine's, it has maintained an uninterrupted existence, defying the history of the region.

the Valley of Fire

Mar Saba sits perched over a deep ravine, part of Wadi Kidron (here called Wadi al-Nar in Arabic, the Valley of Fire), cut by the stream as it winds its way from Jerusalem down to the Dead Sea, a descent of over 1200 metres. Muslims, Jews and Christians identify the Kidron Valley with the Valley of Jehoshaphat where Joel 4:1-2 says the final judgment of the nations will occur. While many place this site further back along the valley, below the Mount of Olives (see page 178), the monks of Mar Saba believe that this deep ravine is the valley alluded to.

Mar, or Saint, Saba (Sabas) was one of the most well known monks of Byzantine Palestine and provided a model for the form of monasticism known as laura. He is honoured by both the Orthodox and Latin churches.

early desires

Born in Cappadocia in 439, he expressed a desire for a monastic way of life at an early age. When he was 18 he travelled to Jerusalem and pursued this vocation under the direction of Euthymius, a leading exponent of monasticism at that time. Euthymius encouraged the semi-hermitical life of the laura. He sent the young Sabas to Deir al-Mukalik where he was under the instruction of Theoctistus. (This monastery, now just a ruin, bears the name Khan al-Ahmar and is situated in the Israeli industrial area of Mishor Adumim, a settlement on occupied Palestinian land off the Jerusalem-Jericho road.)

cavern dwelling

In 483 Sabas left this monastery and became an anchorite living in a cave on the sides of Wadi al-Nar which, as the crow flies, was not very far away across the desert. Soon other anchorite monks joined him in the wadi and by 490 the community numbered at least 150 monks, and became a laura with Sabas as supervisor. The first building was erected in 491 and enlarged in the early 6th C.

archimandrite

In 492 the Patriarch of Jerusalem, Sallustius, made Saba the superior of all anchorites of the lauras of Palestine, and he became an important theologian, particularly noted for his condemnation of Monophysism. Sabas founded three other lauras, six monasteries, and four hospices before his death on December 5th, 532. He was interred at the monastery where his embalmed body is venerated to this day.

lion tamer

One of the many legends attached to Sabas is of a lion who attacked and tried to eat him, only to be tamed and kept as a pet!

In 614 the monastery was sacked by Chosroes II, but soon recovered. For centuries it was the most important monastery in the land, visited by many noted theologians and boasting a large library of theological works.

In Crusader times it is recorded that over 300 monks resided there. In the 14th C the Venetians removed the relics of Sabas to Italy.

seized by Arabs

One of the first western visitors of modern times was R. Curzon who described it in his *Visits to Monasteries of the Levant*, London 1850. He writes how, as he approached the monastery on horseback down the al-Nar ravine, he was captured by Bedouin before being taken to the monastery.

Russian renovation

In the 1830s and again in the 1840s the complex was damaged by earthquakes. Between 1870 and 1880 the monastery was restored by the Russians. By the early 20th C the population had dwindled to about 50 monks, visited only by a hardy few.

In 1965 the Pope decided to return Sabas' relics to the monastery, and this was effected with great celebration by the Orthodox church. First brought to the Church of the Holy Sepulchre in Jerusalem, they were then accompanied by a procession of priests, monks and hundreds of faithful, to the Mar Saba monastery where they can be seen today.

THE VISIT

Mar Saba is open daily from 08.00 to 17.00. Women are not allowed inside, but they should not be put off from coming here as it is the monastery's exterior, coupled with the extraordinary physical location, which makes this excursion into an experience.

Park your car just in front of the northern (left) tower. Make sure you leave it in gear! Before visiting the actual monastery take some time to explore the area and admire the magnificent views.

tough hike

The best panorama of Mar Saba is obtained from the east side of the ravine, opposite. To get there is a long, rough, and hot hike, but if you like to hike it's worth the effort. Make sure you have at least a litre (preferably more) of water per person with you. It requires walking to the north end of the ravine, crossing over, then hiking back. Although there is a good path on the west side, there is none on the east and the hike will involve a lot of scrambling.

foul water

Most of you will content yourselves with the views obtained from the western side, and these are quite spectacular. The stream below is sadly very polluted, but a fresh water spring still gushes down there and it is above this that St. Saba's original cave abode lies.

azure cupolas

The monastery complex with its fortress like walls, so necessary for defence in former years, comprises an assortment of buildings, towers and the two distinctive blue domes which add a welcome splash of colour to the sandy desert tones.

The twin towers at the entrance are known as the **Towers of Women**, but really only the south one (right) should carry that title – it was used to accommodate women, segregating them from the monks in the monastery. Called **St. Simeon's Tower**, it was built in 1612. The northern tower formed part of the defensive system.

Skirt round this northern tower and walk along the path atop the ravine to obtain fine vistas of the complex. Similar views can be obtained from beyond the southern tower.

English speaking welcome

Entry is via the low gate in the west wall. Pull the bell and after a while a monk will open it and welcome you in. At my last visit this was a young novice from Cyprus who spoke excellent English and who proceeded to act as my guide.

mummified body

From inside the door a stepped passage leads down to the main courtyard, and the main church with its large china-blue dome. Here your guide will show you the embalmed relics of St. Saba. The five aisle church has a single apse. Although parts of it are undoubtedly ancient, most is quite modern as it was rebuilt in the late 19th C. The bell tower, also with a blue dome, is named for the Annunciation.

stacks of skulls

On the NW side of the courtyard a church dedicated to St. Nicholas stands by the cave where Sabas had his original church. Inside and behind a grille are stacked hundreds of skulls, belonging to monks killed by the Persians in 614 and in subsequent attacks. The main doors of the iconostasis date from the late 15th C.

The rest of the complex is taken up, mostly, by the monks' cells and offices, and small workshops where some icons and rosaries are made, mainly as gifts for distinguished visitors.

no mod-cons

The monastery has no electricity or telephone, and the monks have refused all offers to connect them to these.

As already mentioned, you can return to Jerusalem via the road that crosses the Kidron stream and the village of Abu Dis, but be warned – this road is in poor condition.

240

PART III

INFORMATION FOR TRAVELLERS

21. General Information

WHEN TO GO

Almost any time, with the exception of December through February. These months can be cold and wet, and although there are many sunny and mild days you would be taking a chance. The days are also too short for much sightseeing. From April onwards the climate is warm and dry, and ideal for touring. The summer months are also quite a good choice, providing you rest between noon and 3pm, the hottest part of the day. In July, August and September the temperature can climb to over 30 degrees C. However, humidity is pleasantly low and summer evenings are cool and refreshing.

GETTING THERE

♦ **By air**

If you are only travelling to Israel and the Palestinian areas then you will arrive by air. El-Al, Israel's national airline, is an international airline, and it flies from most countries. BA operates a daily service from Heathrow, as do most other airlines from their respective countries. However, these scheduled flights are expensive, and you can do much better, at least from the UK, by taking a charter. These fly mainly out of Gatwick (and Luton in the summer), Manchester, and some other regional airports. Depending on the time of year return flights cost from £190-230. There are a few travel agencies which specialise in these, and the best one is Blue Line Travel Ltd., 17 Hendon Lane, London N3 1RT, tel: 0181 346 5955, fax: 0181 346 2576.

The international airport is Ben Gurion International Airport, situated about 48 kilometres west of Jerusalem. You can get to and from there by either bus or taxi. Note that the Jerusalem central bus station is on the western fringe of the city so you will require either another bus or a taxi to take you from there to your hotel.

♦ **By sea**

A car and passenger ferry links the port of Piraeus (Athens) with the port of Haifa in northern Israel. It stops at Cyprus on the way and you can also get on/off there.

♦ By land

You can reach Jerusalem from Jordan via the King Hussein Bridge. A bus from Amman will take you to the Jordanian border, and once across take a Palestinian (shared) taxi to the city, about 40 km away. This route can be tiresome but will suit those who have been visiting Jordan first. You can also cross from Aqaba in Jordan to Eilat in Israel and travel north to Jerusalem by bus, a journey of several hours. There are also two land border crossings between Egypt and Israel: one at Rafah and the other at Taba on the Red Sea. There are no border crossings from Lebanon and Syria into Israel.

ENTRY FORMALITIES

A valid passport is required. Most nationalities don't require an entry visa. In case of doubt a travel agent should be able to advise you. A three-month tourist visa is stamped in your passport on entry. As some Arab countries will refuse you entry if there is an Israeli stamp on your passport, you can ask the Israeli passport officer not to stamp your actual passport, only your entry card. If you have any intention of visiting Syria, Lebanon or the Gulf States it would be wise to request this. It is quite usual and will not offend.

ARRIVAL IN JERUSALEM

You arrive in the city either from the east or west. If the former, you are most likely coming from across the river from Jordan, and (if you are not with a group) you will end up at the taxi station by the Damascus Gate. Arriving from the west, either from somewhere else in Israel or directly from Ben-Gurion Airport, you will alight at the main central bus station on the western extremity of the city.

best to book

If you have not made hotel reservations in advance I recommend you at least phone a few from the bus station so that you don't run around unnecessarily. To be able to use a public telephone you need a special card. You can purchase these at the airport (or any post office if you have come from another town). Budget travellers should look opposite the Damascus or just inside the Jaffa Gate, where some of the lowest priced hotels and hostels are located. Refer to section 7 – Accommodation, below, for names and addresses of accommodation in all categories. From the central bus station, buses 6 and 20 go to the Jaffa Gate, number 27 goes to the Damascus Gate. Or you can of course take a taxi.

Jerusalem is fairly easy to get around, although the buses do tend to get crowded. Distances are not very great.

---

2. CURRENCY AND COSTS

♦ Money in use

The local currency is the (New) Israel Shekel and is abbreviated NIS or IS. It is divided into 100 *agorot* (sing. *agora*). There are coins of one, five and ten shekels, and notes of ten, twenty, fifty and one hundred. The shekel is also used in the Palestinian areas. Israel's economy is inflationary, and prices are always on an upward trend.

The Israel shekel is tied firmly to the US dollar, and many prices are only quoted in that currency. Even on a day-to-day basis many large or imported items such as homes, cars, household appliances etc are priced in dollars. You should note that all hotels, except perhaps the very cheapest hostels, post their prices in USD. Car hire is also quoted in dollars. Your bill is settled in dollars either by credit card, travellers' cheque or (not recommended) cash. For that reason take travellers' cheques in USD. Many hotels will not accept travellers' cheques for payment in any other currency, as working out the equivalent is too difficult. You will also find some cash handy as this can be exchanged more readily than TCs.

♦ Changing money

This can be done at any bank. If you have a credit card, either Visa or MasterCard, you can draw local currency from the automatic teller machines outside many banks. You can also do this at the bank's foreign exchange counter. All banks change TCs issued in the major currencies. Big hotels also change TCs and/or càsh but the rate will not be as good as banks. You can cash a Eurocheque at banks; shops rarely accept them.

East Jerusalem, the Old City and Bethlehem have authorised money changers. They handle mainly cash with a rate sometimes better than a bank. A few may accept TCs but don't count on this. In any case, for these the rate will be less preferential. These establishments can come in very handy on Friday afternoons, Saturdays and Jewish holidays, when all banks are closed.

♦ Credit Cards

Most shops in the western city accept the major credit cards, Visa, MasterCard and AMEX. Shops in the Old City may display credit card logos but then be reluctant to actually accept them without charging a premium. If you intend to bargain – and bargain you must – it must be either cash or TCs. The better restaurants also accept plastic, but check first with the smaller ones. Hotels generally take cards, but if you are staying at a lower priced one check beforehand.

Always keep your copy slips in case you discover something on your statement that should not be there!

♦ Hotel budgeting

Israel is an expensive country; substantially more expensive than many other Mediterranean countries, especially those nearby. Like everything else, what you spend depends on your personal tastes and wherewithal. As a rule of thumb your visit to Jerusalem will cost more than a visit to Paris, all things considered. As with most destinations, accommodation will be your biggest outlay; prices vary from season to season, and from the Palestinian to the Israeli sides of the city. In general, category for category, Palestinian owned hotels will be a little cheaper, though not in every case. For a list of hotels in the various categories, see Section 7 below.

sorting the seasons

Seasons are very important when it comes to price, and these also vary between Palestinian and Jewish hotels. A rough guide is as follows:

Palestinian hotels: High season runs from one week before Easter to mid June, and again from October to mid November plus the week of Christmas. "Regular" season, a term used by some establishments, includes the summer months of July, August and September. During this time prices will be somewhat lower than the HS. (Some hotels do not offer this season, and instead include part of it in their HS and part in their LS rates.) Low season is generally from mid November to the end of February, but excluding the week of Christmas. In all cases the hotel sets its own dates, so you will have to check.

Israeli hotels: Their high season periods include the Jewish holidays of Passover (in spring) and the New Year festivities (September or early October). Therefore April through to October is high season. A few deem June and July as a "mid" season. Winter is low season. I'm sorry if this sounds complicated but that's how it is.

the bottom line

Guide prices for accommodation are as follows: Hostels with dormitory style accommodation – USD 5-10. With the exception of some budget priced hotels which cost between USD 60-75 for a double room with breakfast, expect to pay from USD 85 to over 150 for acceptable lodgings, far more if you are accustomed to the best.

In addition to hotels there are a number of Christian pilgrim hospices. The prices of these vary considerably.

Some travel agencies can book you a hotel at a price lower than you would get yourself. Blue Line (see above) can certainly arrange this for you, but it will be a hotel in the Western part of the city.

♦ Food and drink budgeting

In general eating and drinking is quite expensive. You can eat better for less in London than in Jerusalem. Prices are slightly lower in the Palestinian parts of the city. If you can exist on fast foods and the like, be prepared to spend about USD 12 to 16 per person per day for two such meals. If you enjoy a good dinner in a restaurant it will cost you anything from USD 25 to 40 a head at an East Jerusalem restaurant and from USD 35 to whatever you want to spend at a fancy West Jerusalem place. You will also need to budget an amount for cold drinks etc, especially during the warmer times of the year. Allow USD 5 per person.

♦ Transportation costs

As you will be able to see almost everything by walking, needing only a few bus rides, this will be no more than a few dollars per person. If you rent a car for three days (see below) this will cost you between USD 90 and 120.

♦ Entrance fees, etc

As my guide relates, there are numerous places where an entrance fee is charged. Allow USD 20-30 per person for the trip, more if you intend to visit many museums.

3. WHAT TO TAKE

♦ Clothing etc.

From spring onwards, take lightweight clothing. Nowadays shorts are acceptable, though not on the Haram al-Sharif. Women will also have to cover their arms there; shawls are loaned at the entrance gates. Even in the height of summer Jerusalem can be quite cool in the evenings, so a sweater or light jacket is essential. A good and comfortable pair of walking shoes is a must. Do take a hat (or buy one there); you'll find walking around under a hot sun far more pleasant if your head is covered. Jerusalem, like the whole region, is an informal place and you will not have to dress up, even in the best hotels or restaurants.

Although all your personal hygiene goods are readily available they will cost much more.

♦ Photography

Jerusalem is a wonderful place for photography! The sights, architecture and especially the people all combine to make it a photographer's dream. Because of the bright light 100 ASA film is adequate. If you generally like to carry much equipment, remember that in a hot climate this can be tiresome. From my own experience, the less you carry the more you are inclined to use it. One zoom lens of about 35 to 85mm should do for most situations. A polarising filter for darkening the blue sky and for use as an ND filter is useful.

Keep your camera out of the sun as much as possible. Likewise your film should be kept as cool as possible. Only carry what you think you'll require for the day. Bring enough film for your needs. It will cost you more there. If you have to buy film locally, and you are particular, buy it from a shop, and not a peddlar. Check the expiry date!

Never photograph in religious Jewish areas on Saturday. This applies particularly to the Western Wall and all of the Jewish Quarter. Some religious Jews and most traditional Muslim women do not like to be photographed at any time, and may warn you off.

♦ Travel Insurance

Take out proper travel insurance! Most companies put the area in the Europe price band. If yours does not then apply to TIA, Suite 2, Percy Mews, 775b High Rd, North Finchley, London, N12 8JY. Tel: 0181 446 5414, Fax: 0181 446 5417.

♦ Useful items

My indispensables are a small travel iron and an electric "dipper" element for boiling water in a cup, plus tea and instant coffee. If you take these items don't forget the cup and a teaspoon! If you are staying in a lowish priced hotel a screwdriver tester can come in handy to check actual supply!

Don't forget a **pocket compass**. The guide is written with the use of this in mind!

4. HEALTH

You do not require any special inoculations, but it is sensible to have up-to-date tetanus protection. In case of emergency the hospitals in Jerusalem are excellent. For non-serious ailments pharmacies are happy to recommend a suitable remedy.

Everyday first aid items such as aspirin or paracetamol, wound plaster and antiseptic ointment are all obtainable in any local pharmacy. Don't forget any medications you usually take.

stomach upsets

Unfortunately, those of us who live in a generally sanitised society have lost a lot of natural immunity to even mild stomach infections. The change of diet etc and different ways of preparing food can easily bring on stomach upsets, especially in hot climates. Thankfully they don't usually last more than a couple of days.

abstinence the best remedy

I have found the best way to deal with the problem is to abstain from food totally for a day or two. Drink plenty of fizzy sweet drinks; the sugar will sustain you. After the runs have stopped continue for another day or so eating "safe" food such as yoghurt, plain rice and hard-boiled eggs. Avoid fresh salad and fruit. Medication doesn't usually help – such infections last 2-3 days with or without any. If you have never taken diarrhoea blockers such as Imodium or Lomotil, consult your doctor before buying them. With some people they cause very severe stomach cramps, worse than the symptoms!

dehydration

In the hot summer months it is very important to drink a lot. Never walk around without drinking; there are plenty of kiosks, or you can carry a bottle of water. Drink as a matter of course; not only when you feel thirsty. The first signs of dehydration are tiredness, headache and a sick feeling. A good swig of even lukewarm water will alleviate all these like magic.

5. THINGS TO KNOW

♦ Time

Oct-April GMT+2, April-Oct GMT+3.

♦ Day of rest

The Jewish sabbath is Saturday, and this starts from sundown on Friday and ends at sundown on Saturday. No buses run in the Jewish parts of the city. Shops are not open at all in the western city, although a few cafés and restaurants are. East Jerusalem, including the Old City (with the exception of the Jewish Quarter), is open as usual.

The Muslim day of rest is Friday, but you will see little sign of resting! Although the Old City shops are closed in the early morning they open after morning prayers, and Friday is a busy shopping day.

Some Christian owned shops close on Sunday while others do not. However in Bethlehem most do close.

♦ Opening hours

Banks: Sun-Tues-Thur: 08.30-12.30 and 16.00-18.00
Mon, Wed: 08.30-12.00
Fridays 08.30-12.00.

Shops: In general these are open from 09.00 to 19.00, though some smaller shops observe a siesta and close from 14.00-16.00. Shops in the Palestinian areas do not keep strict hours and may stay open later.

248

♦ Telephone communications

You can make international calls from most hotels, but the price will be high. The alternative is to go the International Telephone Centre behind the main Post Office in Jaffa Rd. Public telephones for local calls use special tokens or cards, sold at all post offices.

From outside the country, the international code is 972 plus 2 for the Jerusalem area.

♦ Electricity

Power is 220V. The local socket is a non standard three pin affair. Two pin plugs with thin pins (the type normally found on electric razors etc) usually fit these.

♦ Public holidays

Jewish Holidays: As the Jewish (and Muslim) calendars are lunar, holidays do not fall on the same Gregorian date every year. However, as the Jewish calendar does incorporate a leap year, these holidays are always in the same season. The main ones are:

Passover: Late March or April
Pentecost: Late May or early June (7 weeks after Passover)
New Year; Late September or early October
Yom Kippur: 10 days after the New Year
Tabernacles: 5 days after Yom Kippur.

Muslim Holidays: The main Muslim holidays are Eid al-Fitr, which lasts three days at the end of the fasting month of Ramadan, and Eid al-Adha which falls about two months later. The Muslim calendar does not have a leap year so the dates of these holidays moves back against our calendar by 11 days every year. In 1998 the first of these is on January 30th, and the second on April 7th.

6. CAR HIRE

Most of the big international agencies are represented. There are also some local ones which will give you a slightly better deal. You will need either your national driving licence or an international one. You will be asked to sign an open credit card slip, which will be completed when the car is returned. In order to get a decent rate you will have to rent for three days minimum. Most cars are airconditioned, and you'll appreciate this during the hot months. Many of the rental agencies are situated on King David Street (see map of West Jerusalem). A few are as follows:

Avis – 22, King David St., tel 02 249001
Eldan – 24, King David St., tel 02 252151 (this is a local firm offering reasonable prices)
Eurodollar – 8, King David St., tel 02 235467
Europcar – 8, King David St., tel 02 248464
Sa-Gal – 14, King David St., tel 02 248003
Holy City, Road No. 1, nr American Consulate, tel: 02 820224

♦ **Driving**

Driving is on the right. Seat belts are compulsory. City speed limit is 50 km/hr, and outside 80. When visiting such places as Mar Saba, drive carefully as the roads are very narrow; and when passing through Palestinian villages watch out for the many children.

---
7. ACCOMMODATION

Jerusalem has many hotels, but getting a bed can still be difficult. Numerous groups visit the city and pre-book many of the medium priced hostelries. Easter is the most difficult time for finding a room as it is can also coincide with the Jewish Passover. During this period, East Jerusalem hotels are packed with Christian pilgrims while those in the western city attract Jewish visitors. If you intend to be in the city at this time, it is essential to book well in advance. My advice is months in advance, making sure you have paid a deposit and have obtained written confirmation of a room. Although Easter is a particularly interesting time to be in Jerusalem, you will find rooms easier to get just before or just after.

Hotels must post the room price in the room, usually on the door. It's worth checking it to ensure you have not been overcharged.

east or west?

As both Arabs and Jews come from the same hospitable culture, whichever part of the city you choose to stay, a very warm and traditional Middle Eastern welcome awaits you.

Most Palestinian hotels will place you closer to the Old City and other main sites of interest, but some of the lower priced ones are not up to European standards. Most Israeii hotels are modern and have full amenities. They also adhere to the very strict Jewish dietary restrictions (i.e. they are kosher).

HOTELS – EAST JERUSALEM

The following is a partial list of hotels in the eastern part of the city. When calling from within Jerusalem, omit the prefix (02). When calling from abroad, omit the zero and just dial the '2' after the country code.

♦ **Lower priced**

New Imperial. Near Jaffa Gate. Tel: 02 272000, fax: 02 271530.
Lawrence Hotel. 18 Salah al-Din St. Tel: 02 894208, fax: 02 271285.
Metropole Hotel. 6, Salah al-Din St. Tel: 02 282507 fax: 02 285134.
Mount of Olives. Tel: 02 284877, fax: 02 894427 (rather out of the way).
New Regent. 20, Azzahra St. Tel: 02 284540, fax: 02 894023.
Rivoli Hotel. 3, Salah al-Din St. Tel: 02 284871, fax: 02 274879.

All these hotels are quite basic. You should be able to get a double room for USD 75 or less.

♦ **Medium priced**

Alcazar Hotel. 6, Almutanabi St. Tel: 02 28111, fax: 02 287360.
Azzahra Hotel. 13, Azzahra St. Tel: 02 282447, fax: 02 734066.
Capitol Hotel. 17, Salah al-Din St. Tel: 02 282561, fax: 02 894352.
Mount Scopus Hotel. Sheikh Jarrah. Tel: 02 828891, fax: 02 828825 (out of

the way).

Palace Hotel. Mount of Olives. Tel: 02 271126, fax: 02 271649.
Pilgrims' Inn. Al Rashid St. Tel: 02 284882, fax: 02 894658.

At these establishments a double room will cost between USD 70 and 120.

♦ Top end

National Palace. 4, Azzahra St. Tel: 02 273273, fax: 02 282139.
Pilgrims' Palace (very well located). Sultan Suleiman St. Tel: 02 272416, fax: 02 894658.
St. George Hotel. Salah al-Din St. Tel: 02 277232, fax: 02 282575.
Seven Arches Hotel. Mount of Olives. Tel: 02 277555, fax: 02 271319. This hotel, once a Sheraton, is by far the best situated of all Jerusalem's hotels, offering a fantastic panorama over the city. Its drawback is the distance from the city, though they do run a shuttle service. Because of this the price is a bargain. No longer offering all the luxury of the international chain, it is still very elegant and a good deal if you don't mind the travelling.

A double room at the above hotels will go for up to USD 150.

The American Colony. Tel: 02 279777, fax: 02279779. East Jerusalem's best hotel, and for many the best in the city. Expect to pay between USD 210-250.

HOTELS – WEST JERUSALEM

♦ Lower priced

Menora Hotel. 24, King David St. Tel: 02 253311, fax: 02 242860.
Zion Hotel. 10, Dorot Rishonim. Tel: 02 259511, fax: 02 257585.
These are among the cheapest and will cost up to USD70.

♦ Medium priced

Ariel Hotel. 31, Hebron Rd. Tel: 02 719222, fax: 02 734066.
Jerusalem Tower. 23, Hillel St. Tel: 02 209209, fax: 02 252167 (at the top of a high rise building in the centre of town).
Park Plaza. 2, Wolfson St. Tel: 02 6528221, fax: 02 6528423.
Tirat Bat-Sheva. 42, King George St. Tel: 02 232121, fax: 02 240697.
These hotels will cost up to USD 140.

♦ Top end

King's Hotel. 60, King George St. Tel: 02 201201, fax: 02 201211.
Lev Yerushalayim. 18, King George St. Tel: 02 300333, fax: 02 232432.
Windmill Hotel. 3, Mendele St. Tel: 02 663111, fax: 02 610964.
Mount Zion. 17, Hebron Rd. Tel: 02 724222, fax: 02 731425. (Very well situated with a wonderful view.)
Renaissance Jerusalem. 6, Wolfson St. Tel: 02 6528111, fax: 02 6511824.

These establishments charge between USD 160-200, the last two being the most expensive.

♦ Five star range

Then there are the luxury hotels at USD 200 and above: Those listed below are the most centrally located.

King Solomon Hotel. 32, King David St. Tel: 02 695555, fax: 02 241774.

Larrome. 3, Jabotinsky St. Tel: 02 756666, fax: 02 756777.
Paradise Jerusalem. 4, Wolfson St. Tel: 02 6558888, fax: 02 6512266.
Sheraton Jerusalem Plaza. King George St. Tel: 02 298666, fax: 02 231667.
King David Hotel. King David Street. The most expensive of them all – where foreign heads of state sleep the night. The prices here reach over USD 400.

CHRISTIAN HOSPICES

Christ Church. Tel: 02 6277727/29, fax: 02 6277730. Just inside the Jaffa Gate. Comfortable rooms.
St. Andrew's Church. Tel: 02 6737235, fax 02 6731711. Likewise provides comfortable accommodation.
Notre Dame Centre. Tel: 02 6279111, fax: 6271995. Facing the New Gate, this establishment also boasts a high standard restaurant.
Rosary Sisters Guest House. Agron St. Tel: 02 258529, fax: 02 235581. This convent is a particularly pleasant place to stay and offers very reasonable prices. Because of this it is very popular so you will have to book months ahead.
Sisters of Sion Convent. Situated on the Via Dolorosa (see map of Muslim Quarter).
Maronite Convent. Behind Christ Church near the Jaffa Gate. (See map of Armenian Quarter).
St. George's Cathedral Guest House. Tel: 02 6282146, fax: 02 6282253. This is supposed to be an excellent place to stay. (See map North of the Walls, Walk No.1).
There are also two **YMCAs**, one in West Jerusalem facing the King David Hotel, and the other in East Jerusalem, along Nablus Road. The former is the higher priced, costing upwards of USD100.

HOSTEL ACCOMMODATION

There are a number of hostels catering to young travellers situated on the Street of the Prophets facing the Damascus Gate (see map).
Both the hospices at **Christ Church** and **St. Andrew's** also offer dormitory accommodation (see above). The best hostel, so I have been told, is the **Lutheran Hostel**, tel: 02 6285105, fax: 02 6285107. It is on St. Mark's Street inside the Old City (see map of Armenian Quarter). This is a very secure place, but does have a curfew. It's most suitable for females.
Armenian Catholic Hostel: 41 Via Dolorosa St., tel: 02 284262.
There are a number of private hostels in the western city also, such as **the King George Hostel** at 15 King George Street and **Beit Shmuel** at number 13 on the same street. There is an official YHA hostel on the corner of Agron St. and King George Street (see map of West Jerusalem), the **Bernstein Youth Hostel**, tel: 02 6245875.

PRIVATE HOMES

Finally you can elect to stay with an Israeli family on a bed and breakfast basis. This can be arranged through an agency called **Bed and Breakfast Jerusalem**, tel: 02 6511270, fax: 02 6511272. You will get a very good breakfast but it will not include bacon with the eggs! The cost is from USD 37 for a double room and USD 32 for a single. You might find that some of the places on offer are far from the main city. Check first!

A tip or two

As for my recommendations. If you have an adequate budget then stay at the American Colony. You may never stay in a more delightful hotel. The buffet breakfast is one of the finest I have had and the restaurant serves what is arguably the best food in town. The Pilgrims' Palace is also a good choice, but make sure you get one of the better rooms. For a more realistic price, the Rosary Sisters Guest House is hard to beat, but as stated you will have to book a long time beforehand.

8. FOOD AND DRINK

As you have already been warned in the section on budgeting, you can expect to pay good money for a meal in Jerusalem, especially at some of the fancy-but-not-so-good restaurants. Some of these sport elaborate names and prices to match, but with mediocre food. That being said there are plenty where you can eat very well indeed.

where's the salt beef?

In East Jerusalem you will find, as you would expect, the wonderful Arab food now so popular in Europe. What may surprise you is that this is also what you will largely find in West Jerusalem. If you thought that the food of the Jewish state was the typical food ascribed to Jews in Europe and America, you will search almost in vain for it! I cannot tell you where to get salt beef, latkes (potato pancakes), chopped herring or any of the other delicacies beloved by the Jews in Britain and the US. No, so far as food is concerned, the Israelis choose Arab! Humous, grilled lamb, couscous, stuffed aubergine, spit roasted meat, and everything else you'll find in Arab countries. With so many Jews immigrating to Israel from Arab lands where they shared a common cuisine for centuries, their food soon became the staple of the local diet.

Big Mac has arrived

However, you'll find fast food joints serving the standard fare, but you'll pay more for it than at home. There is one recently opened **McDonald's** restaurant in the city at 4, Shamai Street (in the western city), off King George Street. Here a "Big Mac" and a medium portion of fries costs around IS 18, about USD 8.50. **Pizza Hut** also have a local franchise, situated in a shopping mall in Malkha, a west Jerusalem suburb. A medium not-too-fancy pizza goes for about IS 41, about USD 16.50. There are also a number of local hamburger houses in and around King George Street where the prices are a bit lower than Mac's.

local street eats

In spite of the advent of McCulture, the local fast foods still reign supreme and these will cost you considerably less, though you may have to eat standing up! Felafel is sold almost everywhere. For those who are not familiar with this ME delicacy, it consists of fried patties of spiced chickpeas stuffed into a round pitta bread and topped with salad and various spicy sauces. There are some places where you pay, get a pitta and then fill it up yourself with as much of everything as you want. You can even refill – provided you use the same piece of pitta bread!

turkey done up like lamb

Another substantial street delight is *shwarma*. This is made from a huge piece of meat constantly rotating on a gas fired grill. As each layer becomes cooked the carver slices off the pieces, and these, like the felafel, are stuffed into a pitta bread and topped in the same way. The meat is turkey, although a piece of lamb fat is place on top of the grill to baste the meat and supposedly bestow a lamb flavour. (The dish should be made entirely of lamb, but you will be hard pressed to find the real thing in Jerusalem as lamb is very expensive here.) Places serving this food can be found in West Jerusalem at the lower end of King George Street near the Jaffa Road and around the Mahane Yehuda Market further west on Jaffa Road.

You will also find similar places in East Jerusalem and the Old City but some will not be open in the evening.

best humous in town

For a sit down lunch try a local humous (a chickpea purée) which will be far superior to the western supermarket variety you may have tried. The best in all the city is served at **Abu Shukri's** along al-Wad Street in the Old City. It's just past the Via Dolorosa on the left side. An unpretentious place, this small eatery is often very full. They only serve humous and the dishes that go with it: felafel, ful (Egyptian brown beans), and salad.

The humous is dreamy and the felafel is the richest and crispiest you will ever taste. Ask for the humous to be served with a topping of pine nuts lightly browned in olive oil – out of this world! It will add an extra special touch to what is already special. The renowned excellence of Abu Shukri is reflected in the prices, and you will pay more than in other similar eateries – but it's worth it. A lunch with the additions mentioned above plus a drink will set you back about USD 8 each; no fortune. This place is so well known that other restaurants in the western city have tried to usurp the name, but this is the real thing. (Forgive my enthusiasm, but as I write this from my home in England my mouth waters!)

Abu Shukri's is a daytime eatery – closed in the evening. Don't leave Jerusalem without eating there.

♦ Eating out – East

For those who enjoy a good evening meal in a restaurant, East Jerusalem sports a number of these. Among those specialising in grills and Middle Eastern food are the **National Palace Hotel** (see list of hotels) and the **Philadelphia Restaurant** (tel: 02 6289770) not far away. **Maswadeh** is another popular restaurant in the same vicinity serving excellent grilled meats and chicken. Your repast at these places will cost USD 25 upwards per person.

Towards the end of Salah al-Din Street there is the **Golden Chicken** which serves spit broiled chickens and is reasonably priced.

The Notre Dame Centre facing the New Gate boasts a spacious restaurant, serving European and local food. An à la carte meal will cost from USD 40 a head.

The best of all in East Jerusalem (and probably the most expensive) is the **American Colony Hotel**. They often have "speciality" nights featuring a particular cuisine. In the summer there are barbecues around the swimming pool. These are very good eat-as-much-as-you-like affairs for an inclusive price.

◆ Eating out – West

West Jerusalem has many more restaurants, and as this part of the city is more lively at night, some may find it more congenial.

where to find kebab and shashlik

Restaurants termed "oriental" refer to those with Middle Eastern and North African kitchens. There are a number of reasonably priced oriental eateries along Agrippas Street, which runs south of Jaffa Road behind the Mahane Yehuda Market. These specialise in char-grilled meats, especially the pungent fat-tailed lamb of the ME. Some serve the food of the Maghreb such as couscous. Expect to pay here between USD 25 and 40 a head. In the centre of the western city, **Shemesh**, on Ben Yehuda Street, is a popular local restaurant.

Likewise in the area of Nahlat Shiva (see page 208) there are quite a few places to eat – some with al fresco dining. In particular there is one with an Argentinean flavour, **Pampas**, which is very popular. Although some of these tend to charge more than their worth, the atmosphere of the area is lively and trendy. If you're looking for a disco or night club, try around here.

a taste of Morocco

If you like Moroccan food in a plush Moroccan atmosphere, there is **El Marrakesh** located at 4, King David Street just up from the corner with Agron Street (see map page 200). Prices here are inflated but the food is authentic and the ambience good. Another such restaurant is the **El Morocco** which can be found at the Jerusalem Centre No.1 near the central bus station. Expect to pay upwards of USD 45 at these places.

coffee break

A touch of Middle Europe can be found in West Jerusalem in the many cafes, some with streetside seating areas. Ben Yehuda Street, a walking mall which leads off Jaffa Road (see map), has a fair number of these. They serve coffee, pastries, ice cream and the like. If you are on a tight budget check the prices first!

And there is an authentic **Ben and Jerry's** ice-cream parlour at the top of Hillel Street just off King George Street.

As mentioned elsewhere in this book a picnic lunch is also a good option, and not just for those who have to watch their expenditure. If you buy a few pitta breads all sorts of fillings can be stuffed inside. Local cream cheese is ideal for this, especially if a few slices of (peeled!) cucumber goes in as well. A good pocket knife will be essential for such a snack! You will find an excellent selection of local yoghurts and other dairy produce on the supermarket shelves. Try some of the many different olives. Most places will sell you as much or as little as you want. Always peel or thoroughly wash vegetables and fruit!

◆ Drink

Alcoholic beverages: All the usual canned beers can be found. There are two local brews, Maccabi and Goldstar, which are fine. Imported wines and spirits are expensive. Local wines are not, and except for the very cheapest, those produced in Israel are quite acceptable. In stores in East Jerusalem and Bethlehem you will also find wines produced at the Cremisan Monastery in Beit Jalla. I can't particularly recommend these. You may also see wines from the Latrun (Trappist) Monastery which, while not the best, are drinkable.

Tea and coffee: Like everywhere in the ME, tea is the main daily drink. Drunk in glasses, it is always served black, often with lemon or mint. Coffee is the Muslim Arab social drink, replacing the stimulating effects of (prohibited) alcohol. Consumed à la Turkish, it is strong and sweet and is flavoured with cardamon pods during preparation. In West Jerusalem coffee will be served as you are used to in the West.

Soft drinks: Many brands of soft drinks, both international and local are available. Fresh juice is also popular, especially citrus and carrot. The local water is perfectly drinkable, but bottled spring water, often imported and costly, is generally served in restaurants. If you consider this expense unnecessary, insist on iced tap water!

9. MUSEUMS

There are a great number of museums in Jerusalem, the three most important being the Israel Museum, the Rockefeller Museum and Yad Vashem, the Holocaust Memorial Museum. I don't intend to guide you around these places, preferring to leave that to the excellent books to be found at the entrances, but a brief explanatory introduction is in order on the above three.

▸ ISRAEL MUSEUM

Visiting hours: Sunday, Monday, Wednesday, Thursday 10.00-17.00; Tuesday 16.00-22.00; Friday and eve of Jewish holidays 10.00-14.00. There is an entrance fee, and guided tours in English are conducted.

The museum, established in the mid 1960s, is situated on a ridge not far from the Knesset building on Rehov Ruppin. It is a modern complex of buildings mostly interconnecting. Although mainly devoted to items of Jewish and local interest, there are also exhibits from around the world. The most famous section is the **"Shrine of the Book"**, a separate building which houses sections of the Dead Sea Scrolls, including the renowned Isaiah Scroll.

▸ ROCKEFELLER MUSEUM

Visiting hours: In spite of this being in Arab east Jerusalem, the hours are the same is for the Israel Museum above.

Once the Palestine Department of Antiquities Museum, since 1967 it has been under the jurisdiction of the Israel Museum. It is located almost facing the NE corner of the Old City walls on Suleiman Street. J. D. Rockefeller provided much of the funding for the establishment − hence it's popular name. The Jerusalem stone construction of the museum possesses a very characteristic style. It houses some of the artefacts found during major excavations undertaken in Palestine from the first half of the 20th C.

From a purely archaeological aspect it is more interesting than the Israel Museum.

▸ YAD VASHEM

This is a memorial and remembrance to the six million Jews who perished in the Holocaust of the Second World War. It is situated in the very west of the city, and can be reached by bus from the Central Bus Station.

The main section is the Hall of Rememberance with a mosaic floor recalling the names of concentration camps. Very graphic photographs of the atrocities make a visit here into a harrowing and thought-provoking experience.

For the enthusiast

Some of the city's other interesting museums have been mentioned in the touring text, but if you can't get enough of them, you may want to try either or both of the following:

Museum of Natural History, Mohilever Street, W Jerusalem. **Open:** Sun-Fri 10.00-13.00; Mon, Wed 16.00-18.00; Sat 10.30-13.00. Closed during August. Admission fee, but no charge on Saturdays. Buses 4 and 18.

Mayer Institute for Islamic Art, 2 Ha'Palmach Street, Rehavia, W Jerusalem. **Open:** Sun-Thu 10.00-13.00 and 15.30-18.00. Sat & eve of holidays 10.30-13.00. Closed Fridays. Tickets for Saturdays must be bought in advance. Bus No.15.

22. Language

LOCAL LANGUAGES

Arabic and modern Hebrew are the official local languages, but almost everyone speaks a fair to excellent English – which they all love to practice – so you won't be lost without any skills in either of these tongues. In addition, French is spoken widely, especially among the Jewish population of North African origin. Road signs and street names are generally posted in English as well as in the official languages.

Both Arabic and Hebrew are written from right to left and, while related, having many similar words and grammatical forms, an understanding of one doesn't necessarily mean an understanding of the other. Each has its own script.

Though not essential because of the linguistic skills of most citizens, knowledge of a few words, especially everyday greetings, in the local languages might come in useful, as well as being friendly.

Pronunciation

A word on pronunciation. Some sounds may be difficult to produce as we do not have them in English. In the vocabulary they are given as follows.

Arabic	Hebrew	
gh	r	this is like the French "r", but more guttural.
kh	kh	similar to ch in Scottish "loch". The Arabic sound is more aspirated, the Hebrew more guttural.
'a	'a	a glottal stop similar to how butter may be pronounced by those who drop the t's, bu`er, but farther back in the throat.
H		this is a very aspirated 'h'. When making it you should feel a slight grating in your throat.

VOCABULARY

Greetings

An initial greeting and one that is frequently used is *salaam alaikum* (Arabic) and the similar *shalom aleikhem* (Hebrew) meaning "peace be to you". The reply is made by reversing the order of words, *alaikum salaam* (A) and *aleikhem shalom* (H) – "to you [also] be peace".

Other common greetings are:

	Arabic	**Hebrew**
hello	*marhaba* or *ahlan wa sahlan* or just *ahlan*	*shalom*
hello as reply	*marhabtein* or *ahlan beek (beeki* f)	*shalom lekha* *shalom lakh* (f)
how are you?	*kayf haalak?* *kayf haalik?* (f)	*ma shlomkha?* *ma shlomekh?* (f)
fine, excellent	*kwayyis (kwayyisa* f)	*metzuyan*
thanks be to God (often the reply to "how are you?")	*ilHamdu lillaah*	*toda le'el*
God willing (an answer to everything!)	*inshallah*	*be'ezrat ha'shem*
goodbye	*ma'a salaama*	*shalom*
good morning	*sabah ilkheer*	*boker tov*
good morning (reply)	*sabah innur* ("morning of light")	*boker or* ("morning of light")
good evening	*masa ilkheer*	*erev tov*

Common words and phrases

yes	*na'am* or *aiwa*	*ken*
no	*la*	*lo*
thank you	*shukran*	*toda*
for nothing *or* you're welcome	*afwan*	*al lo davar* or *bevakasha*
please (request)	*min fadlak (fadlik* f)	*bevakasha*
I'm sorry, excuse me	*ana 'assif ('aaifa* f)	*slikha*
what is your name?	*shu ismak? (ismik* f)	*ma shimkha?* *ma shmech?* (f)
my name is...	*ismi...*	*shmi...*
where are you from?	*min wain inta?* *(inti* f)	*m'ayin ata (at* f)
I am from...	*ana min...*	*ani mi....*
do you speak English?	*bititkalim (btitkalimi* f) *inglisi?*	*ata medaber (at medaberet ...?* f) *anglit?*
I speak...	*ana bititkalim...*	*ani medaber (medaberet* f)
how much (does it cost?)	*bikaam* or *adaish*	*kama ze oleh?*
expensive	*ghaali*	*yakar*
cheap	*rakhees*	*zol* or *bezol*
very	*'awi*	*me'od*
something	*Haaga*	*mashehu*
something cheaper	*Haaga 'arkhas*	*mashehu zol yoter*
may I?, is it possible?	*mumkin?*	*efshar?* or *ha'im efshar?*
impossible, you can't	*mish mumkin*	*ee efshar*
how many?	*kam?*	*kama?*
how many kms?	*kam kilometer?*	*kama kilometrim?*
is there (any)?	*fi...?*	*yesh?*
there is not (any)	*ma fish...*	*ayn*
open	*maftuuh*	*patuakh*
closed	*musakkar*	*sagur*

what is this?	shu hadha?	ma zeh?
big	kabeer	gadol
small	sagheer	katan

Getting around

aeroplane	al-tayara	matos, aviron
airport	al-mataar	sdeh te'ufa
bank	bank	bank
bus station	mahattat al-bas	takhanat autobusim
bus	bas	bus
car	sayyara	mekhonit, auto
church	kaneesa	knessiah
gate	bab	sha'ar
hospital	mustashfa	beit kholim
left (direction)	shimaal	smaal
mosque	jami	misgad
petrol (gas)	benzeen	delek
pharmacy	saydaliyya	beit mirkakhat
police	shurta	mishtara
post office	maktab bareed	beit ha'doar
railway station	mahattat al-qitaar	takhanat rakevet
right	yameen	yamin
ruins (historical)	khirbet	khurvot
site (historical)	ataar	atar
square	midaan	kikar
straight on	duughri	yashar
street	shari'a, tariq	rekhov
synagogue	beit kaneesa	beit knesset
tourist office	maktab al-siyaha	misrad tayarut
train	qitaar	rakevet

At the hotel

breakfast	fitar	aruhat boker
clean	nardif	naki
dirty	wishikh	melukhlakh
full	malyaan	maleh
hot water	mayya sukhna	mayim khamim
hotel	otel, funduq	beit malon
night	leela	lilah
room	ghurfa	kheder
shower	doosh	miklakhat, doosh
soap	sabun	sabon
the bill	al-hissab	ha'kheshbon
towel	futa, manshafa	magevet

Food and drink

apple	*tuffaaH*	*tapooakh*
apricot	*mishmish*	*mishmish*
banana	*mooz, banana*	*banana*
bread	*khubz, aish*	*lekhem*
butter	*zibda*	*khemah*
carrot	*gazar*	*gezer*
cheese	*gibneh*	*gvinah*
coffee	*'ahwa*	*café*
egg	*beid*	*beitzah*
fish	*samak*	*dag*
fruit	*fawakeh*	*peirot*
juice	*'asir*	*mitz*
meat	*lahma*	*bassar*
milk	*halab, laban*	*khalav*
mineral water	*mayya ma'daniyeh*	*mayim ma'adanim*
orange juice	*'asir burtu'aan*	*mitz tapuzim*
orange	*burtu'aan*	*tapuz*
restaurant	*mat'am*	*missada*
tea	*shay*	*teh*
vegetables	*khudra*	*yerakot*
water	*mayya*	*mayim*
yoghurt	*laban*	*yogurt, leben*

Time

day	*yom*	*yom*
hour	*sa'a*	*sha'ah*
today	*alyom*	*ha'yom*
tomorrow	*bukra*	*makhar*
week	*usbu'a*	*shvu'a*
year	*sana*	*shana*
What time is it?	*assa'a kam?*	*ma ha'sha'ah?*
It is 3 o'clock	*assa'a talata*	*ha'sha'ah shalosh*

Days of the week:

In Arabic the days from Sunday through Thursday are simply called "the first" through to "the fifth". The Hebrew adds the word "day", *yom*, e.g. *yom rishon* = the first day = Sunday. Saturday is the Sabbath in both languages, even though Friday is the Muslim day of rest.

	Arabic	**Hebrew**
Sunday	*ilhadd*	*yom rishon*
Monday	*iltneen*	*yom shaynee*
Tuesday	*ittalaat*	*yom shlishee*
Wednesday	*ilarba'*	*yom riviee*
Thursday	*ilkhamees*	*yom khamishee*
Friday	*ilgum'a*	*yom shishee*
Saturday	*isabat*	*yom shabat*

Numerals

Numbers 1-10:

Arabic: *wahad, itneen, talata, arba'a, khamsa, sitta, saba'a, tamanya, tisa'a, ashara.*

Hebrew: *akhad, shtayim, shalosh, arba, khamesh, shesh, sheva, shmoneh, tesha, esser.*

Numbers 11-20:

Arabic: *hadashar, itnaashar, talattaashar, arba'taashar, khamastaashar, sitaashar, sab'ataashar, tamantaashar, tisa'taashar, ishreen.*

Hebrew: Add the suffix *essreh* for numbers 11 to 19, e.g eleven = *akhad-essreh* etc. Twenty = *essrim.*

Some fractions:

Arabic: half *nuss;* quarter *ruba;* threequarters *talata ruba.*

Hebrew: half *khetzi;* quarter *reva;* threequarters *shalosh-reveh.*

Hebrew uses the same numerals as in the West. The Arabic numerals are written as follows:

٠ = 0	٦ = 6
١ = 1	٧ = 7
٢ = 2	٨ = 8
٣ = 3	٩ = 9
٤ = 4	١٠ =10
٥ = 5	٢٥ = 25

Glossary

The glossary explains the following —
♦ Architectural terms used.
♦ The various nations, dynasties, and groups of people referred to.
♦ Non-English words normally rendered in the original.

Abbreviations: **H** Hebrew; **A** Arabic; **L** Latin; **Fr** Medieval French; **Gr** Greek; **I** Italian; **R** Russian

Abbasids (A)	Caliphate dynasty (750-968) centred on Baghdad which succeeded the Omayyads.
Achaemenid Persians	Ancient Persian dynasty which lasted from 559-330 BC. Their empire stretched at one time as far west as Macedonia and Libya. Rulers included Cyrus II and Xerxes. It ended in 330 BC when Darius III was defeated by Alexander at Issus.
agora (Gr)	Market and public meeting place.
aisle	The part of a basilica that lies either side of the nave.
apse (L)	Curved and vaulted end of the nave in a church.
aron kodesh (H)	Cupboard in synagogue for housing the Scroll of the Law (Tora) *Lit*: holy cupboard
Ayyubids (A)	The dynasty (1176-1260) founded by Salah al-Din or his father.
bab (A)	Gate.
basilica (L, Gr)	Building, usually a church with a central nave and an aisle each side.
bimah (H)	Pulpit in a synagogue.
birka (birkat) (A)	Pool.
Byzantine (L)	That part of the Roman Empire which was ruled from Byzantium (Constantinople).
caliph (A)	Head of Islam after Muhammad. From the Arabic word *Khalifa,* meaning successor. Caliphs eventually became dynastic with no relationship to religious knowledge, and the first four were not accepted by all Muslims.
capitals (on columns)	The head of a column often decorated.
cardo maximus (L)	Main street of Roman city, usually running from north to south.
citadel (It)	Fortified part of a city, often elevated.
colonnade (L)	Area flanked by columns and roofed.
Corinthian (capital) (Gr)	Column capital decorated with acanthus leaves.
cupola (L)	Dome.
decumanus (L)	Major east/west street in a Roman city.
diwan (T)	Arched reception area at one end of courtyard in Ottoman house.

Eastern Orthodox	That part of the Byzantine rite which has as its head the Byzantine Patriarch of Antioch. Often called Greek Orthodox, they use Arabic as their prayer language.
Fatimids (A)	A Shi'ite dynasty (970-1055) of caliphs centred on Cairo.
Ghor	Arabic name for the Jordan Valley.
Greek Orthodox	General term for followers of the Byzantine rite of Christianity, but correctly only applies to the Orthodox Church of Greece.
hammam (T)	Turkish or Arab bath.
Hasmoneans	Jewish dynasty which followed the Seleucid rule in Palestine 152-37 BC.
Hospitaliers, Knights of St. John	Order of (Christian) Knights who once had responsibility for taking care of pilgrims in Jerusalem. In Crusader times they became a military order.
iwan (T)	See **diwan**.
khan (T, A)	Inn where travellers and merchants could stay and trade in a city. Also called caravanserai but the latter term is more correctly used for inns outside cities.
khirbet (A)	Ancient ruins.
lintel (Fr)	Horizontal beam (of stone) above a door.
madrassa (A)	Islamic theological school.
Mamelukes	Slave soldiers of Turkic origin who took power in 1250 in Cairo and controlled most of the region from 1260 to 1516.
mihrab (A)	Niche in wall of a mosque's prayer hall to orient worshippers towards Mecca.
minbar (A)	Pulpit in a mosque.
Mongols	Central Asian warrior people.
muhaafaza (A)	Governorate or province.
muqarna (A)	Stalactite-like stone decoration, usually above doorway.
narthex (Gr)	Entrance hall in an (early) church.
Omayyads (A)	Caliphate dynasty (661-750) founded by Mu'awiya, centred on Damascus.
omphalos (Gr)	monumental column.
Ottomans	Turkish tribe centred on Anatolia. Took Constantinople in 1453 and in early 16th C all the Middle East and parts of Europe. The Ottoman Empire lasted until 1918.
portcullis (Fr, L)	Grille that can be lowered across a castle gateway to prevent entry.
portico (L, It)	Porch, or area confined within columns.
propylaeum	Monumental entranceway to a temenos.
qala'a (qala'at) (A)	Fort or castle.
sabil (A)	Fountain.
saray (A)	Palace.

Sasanian Persians	Persian dynasty from 224-650 AD founded by Ardashir I. They constantly harassed the power of Rome and Byzantium. Destroyed by the Arabs in 650.
Shi'ite (A)	Muslims who supported the right of Ali, Muhammad's son-in-law, to succeed him. From the word *shia* which means faction, i.e. faction of Ali.
souk (A)	Market street or area.
Sunni (A)	Orthodox Muslim, i.e. not a Shi'ite.
tell (Aramaic)	Hill, usually an artificial one, made up of layers of succeeding civilisations.
tetrapylon (Gr)	Pattern of columns marking a major street junction in a Roman/Greek city.
thermae (L)	Roman baths.
Tora (H)	Jewish religious law.
wadi (A)	Seasonable water course.
wakf (A)	Muslim religious charitable foundation.

Bibliography

There are too many books on the subject to list more than a fraction. The
following are a varied selection which you should find interesting reading,
before or after your travels.

For a history of Palestine:

History of Syria, including Lebanon and Palestine, P. K. Hitti, London
1951

A History of the Arab Peoples, Albert Hourani, London 1991

Making of the Middle East 1792-1923, M.Yapp, Lon 1987

A History of the Arabs, P. K. Hitti, London 1970

The Blood of Abraham, Jimmy Carter. Sedgwick & Jackson 1985

For accounts of the events of the 20th C:

Seven Pillars of Wisdom, T. E. Lawrence, London 1926 and reprinted
by Penguin in 1976

Israel, The Establishment of a State, H. Sacher, London 1952

Britain and the Arab/Israel Conflict. HMSO 1993

The Palestine Triangle. N. Bethell. London 1979.

Search for Peace, Prince Hassan Ibn Talal, 1984

The Arab Israeli Wars, Haim Herzog, London 1982

Jerusalem. Teddy Kollek and Moshe Pearlman, London 1968

The Story of the Arab Legion, John Bagot Glubb, London 1948

Jerusalem, The Endless Crusade, Andrew Sinclair, London 1996

For histories at different eras:

*Allah's Commonwealth, a History of Islam in the Middle East AD 600-
1100*, F. E. Peters, New York 1973

The Latin Kingdom of Jerusalem, J. Prawler, London 1972

Jerusalem As Jesus Knew It, London 1978

Jerusalem in the 19th C, Y. Ben-Arieh, Jerusalem 1977

Herod the Great, Michael Grant, Weidenfeld and Nicolson 1971.

The World of Josephus, G. A. Williamson, Secker and Warburg 1964

The Land of The Bible — A Historical Geography, Yohanan Aharoni

For accounts of Palestinian life under Israeli rule:

After the Last Sky, Edward Said, London 1993

Dispossessed – The Ordeal of the Palestinians 1917-1980, D. Gilmour,
London 1980

For the general situation today:

Behind the Star – Inside Israel Today, Gerald Butt, London 1990

Sharing the Promised Land, Dilip Hiro, London 1996

For specific subjects:

Encyclopaedia Judaica

Catholic Encyclopaedia

and of course —

The Bible

Index

NOTES